Formal and Informal Social Safety Nets

Formal and Informal Social Safety Nets

Growth and Development in the Modern Economy

Mohammad Ashraf

palgrave
macmillan

First published in 2014 by
PALGRAVE MACMILLAN®
in the United States—a division of St. Martin's Press LLC,
175 Fifth Avenue, New York, NY 10010.

Where this book is distributed in the UK, Europe and the rest of the World,
this is by Palgrave Macmillan, a division of Macmillan Publishers Limited,
registered in England, company number 785998, of Houndmills,
Basingstoke, Hampshire RG21 6XS.

Palgrave Macmillan is the global academic imprint of the above
companies and has companies and representatives throughout the world.

Palgrave® and Macmillan® are registered trademarks in the United
States, the United Kingdom, Europe and other countries.

ISBN: 978–1–137–38895–7

Library of Congress Cataloging-in-Publication Data

Ashraf, Mohammad, 1962–
    Formal and informal social safety nets : growth and development in the
    modern economy / Mohammad Ashraf.
        pages cm
    Includes bibliographical references and index.
    ISBN 978–1–137–38895–7 (hardback : alk. paper)
    1. Structural adjustment (Economic policy)—Social aspects.
    2. Economic development—Technological innovations.   3. Income
    distribution.   I. Title.
    HD87.A757 2013
    361—dc23   2013049424

A catalogue record of the book is available from the British Library.

Design by Integra Software Services

First edition: June 2014

10 9 8 7 6 5 4 3 2 1

Contents

Figures

Tables

Preface

The financial crisis, which hit the United States and most of the rest of the world during 2007, and the Great Recession of 2007–2009 and their aftermath forced countries to revisit the issues related to social safety nets. Not surprisingly, whenever the topic of social safety nets surfaces, the talk of taxes and budget deficits, and the possible ill-effects these taxes and deficits may bring for the economy, follows. I address a small part of this vast and rather complicated issue in this book, that is, the effects of social safety nets on economic growth via increased innovation.

In this book I argue that just as a well-functioning, appropriately regulated monetary system and a legal tender are imperative for a modern economy, the provision of tax-financed government-provided formal social safety nets may also be a requirement of a modern economy. This is especially so if we want an economy to grow beyond a certain level. I realize that even the suggestion that tax-financed government-provided formal social safety nets can enhance economic growth tends to flare tempers among many. My hope, however, is that the readers of this book evaluate the argument presented here on its merits, and do not dismiss it just because it sounds like a "Liberal" point of view, or for that matter accept it if the readers happen to be left-leaning Liberals.

It is, indeed, sad that often even the admittance of having an understanding of the "other side's" argument is considered a weakness. This is perhaps a sign of intellectual-adolescence of our current socio-political environment. Politicians and policymakers dare not give an inkling of such an understanding for fear of losing their jobs. And, I am sorry to say, at times even academics, whose job is to question and develop a deeper understanding of issues, dare not appreciate for fear of becoming outcasts. I realize the perils of being a perennial outsider, but isn't a forced conformity equally alienating?

I also know full well that this is but a very small part of the overall human enterprise. I have limited the focus primarily to just the economy and economic growth for two reasons. One, on account of my training as an economist this is the area about which I am qualified to write. Second, as mundane as this business of economy may be, and it certainly is, one needs certain level of material resources to afford to engage in higher forms of intellectual activities. (Yes, I admit it. I have "physics envy.") While it is true that material resources are hardly a main ingredient in the recipe of great ideas, it is also true that material wealth does afford one the comfort to engage in higher intellectual pursuits that may lead to transformative ideas.

Because my intended audience is both economists and non-economists, in writing this book I have made every effort to make it jargon free. This is a delicate balance, though: too much jargon and you lose the non-specialist; too little jargon and you risk losing the specialist. At times, however, lack of jargon made it harder to get the point across. In those situations, after presenting the concepts using the economics terminology, I have tried to give explanations in plain English. Whether or not I have been successful in this endeavor I will let the reader be the judge. One thing I have not tried to do is to make this book a fun read. And I think I have achieved this objective rather successfully. Any pleasure a reader might get from reading this book is purely accidental. I take no responsibility.

I end this short preface with a sincere note of thanks to the editors at Palgrave Macmillan, Ms. Leila Campoli, Ms. Sarah Lawrence, and Ms. Susan Eberhart, for their guidance and help in preparing this manuscript. I am also grateful to Shweta Bharti at Integra for correcting my extremely flawed writing and making the manuscript readable.

CHAPTER 1

Why Do Social Safety Nets Matter?

Any crisis situation highlights the importance of safety nets. In recent history, examples of such situations abound. In August 2005 Hurricane Katrina reminded us the value of stronger levies; in February 2012 the Fukushima Daiichi nuclear disaster pointed to the loopholes in nuclear energy production; and in April 2010 the BP oil spill in the Gulf of Mexico showed how hard it was to control a disaster. Similar is the case with economic misfortunes and missteps. One example is the Great Recession of 2007–2009 and its aftermath. It has certainly made it clear that individuals do fall on hard times and that they do need assistance. Often hard times happen even if people have been responsible and saving for the proverbial rainy days.

As of late 2013, unemployment rate—the percentage of labor force that cannot find jobs—is still hovering well above 7 percent.[1] The unemployment rate peaked at 10 percent in October 2009, and stayed above 8 percent until August 2012.[2] As any basic economics textbook would tell you, national unemployment rate estimates, useful as they are, do not tell the whole story. For one thing, these estimates are averages—some areas suffer higher unemployment rates than others. This means that hardships suffered by individuals and families in areas where unemployment rates are higher are understated. Another important key factor is the length of unemployment. On the eve of the 2007–2009 Great Recession, the average length of unemployment was about 17 weeks. During November and December of 2011, it reached 40.7 weeks.[3]

The increase in the length of unemployment is extremely worrisome. Labor demand (or any input demand) is derived demand—employers hire workers for what they can produce, and not for their own sake. The longer an individual stays unemployed, the higher the skill loss and the lower the likelihood that he/she will find a job. The reason is that, on the one hand, since the worker would not have been using the skills on account of being unemployed, it is quite likely that there will be a drop in dexterity, making a given worker less desirable. On the other hand, since economy is dynamic, it will keep changing, and will thus need new and/or different jobs and new and/or different skills to perform those jobs. Since the worker has been unemployed, she/he would be falling further behind by not acquiring skills that he/she could have acquired had he/she been employed. This is one reason why one hears more about job training and retraining programs after a recession.

Recognizing the ill effects that the deficiency of desired skill levels may have on workers and the economy, the United States Department of Labor has a division specifically devoted to updating and upgrading labor skills. It is called the Employment and Training Administration.[4] The mission statement of this division is as follows:

> The mission of the Employment and Training Administration is to contribute to the more efficient functioning of the U.S. labor market by providing high quality job training, employment, labor market information, and income maintenance services primarily through state and local workforce development systems.[5]

The formation of the Employment and Training Administration had a forerunner. In 1946 as the United States was starting its recovery from World War II, President Harry Truman, on the request of John W. Snyder, director of the Office of War Mobilization and Conversion, appointed a commission to explore the state of higher education in the United States.[6] It is known as the Truman Commission. It resulted in the formation of a community college system—"intermediate technical institutes," as President Truman called them in his letter to the prospective members of the commission.[7] For the most part the responsibility of these colleges was, and still remains, to train and retrain labor force for the ever-evolving job requirements. These are among the various forms of formal social safety nets.

1.1. Overview of the Book

In his book *Development as Freedom*,[8] Amartya Sen writes:

> [N]o matter how well an economic system operates, some people can be typically on the verge of vulnerability and can actually succumb to great deprivation as a result of material changes that adversely affect their lives. Protective security is needed to provide a social safety net for preventing the affected population from being reduced to abject misery, and in some cases even starvation and death. (p.40)

That social safety nets are needed is not a partisan issue. During the 2012 Republican primary debates, Ron Paul, a libertarian[9] seeking the Republican nomination, was asked what should a hypothetical individual do if he/she did not have health insurance and got sick; should society leave the person to die?[10] Paul replied that the society should not leave such a person helpless. He reminisced that as a physician he had helped a lot of patients who could not afford to pay. He argued that "we've given up on this whole concept that we might take care of ourselves and assume responsibility for ourselves. Our neighbors, our friends, our churches would do it."[11] I mention this to point out that even the most ardent supporters and promoters of self-reliance recognize the need for some form of social safety nets. The question is: How to provide and finance social safety nets?

I argue in this book that formal social safety nets, as I define below, provided by the government and financed by taxes, are not only important but indeed vital for a modern economy. I argue that formal social safety nets not only provide the indigent the help they need while preserving their dignity, but may also help promote economic growth. Just as a modern economy cannot function without well-functioning financial and monetary systems, a modern economy needs formal institutional arrangements upon which individuals can rely in times of need.

The barter system served its purpose when a small number of goods and services were exchanged. However, a modern monetary system was needed as economies grew. The development of the system helped economies grow even further. Indeed, a well-functioning monetary system and economic growth go hand in hand. In the same way, informal safety nets, as I define below, served their purpose when the village populations were small and travel beyond a certain radius was a rarity. As populations and economies grew, economic prosperity allowed individuals to travel long distances. Travel further expanded trade and spurred economic growth. Travel to thus-far-unchartered territories was not just limited to satisfy curiosities of restless minds, although that was one factor, but it was also needed to find new sources to satisfy growing populations' needs. And so informal social safety nets, upon which one could rely closer to home, proved deficient when one moved sufficiently far away from home—far enough that help from family and friend was not readily accessible. (More on this point, shortly.) Deficiencies of informal social safety nets are becoming ever more apparent as time passes.

Before I go any further, let me define more precisely what I mean by social safety nets, and how informal social safety nets differ from the formal ones.

1.2. Social Safety Nets: Some Definitions

I define a social safety net as a source upon which one can rely in times of need, regardless of the help-seeker's ability to repay. The "ability to repay" part of definition is important. This precludes banks and other commercial lending institutions. A well-functioning banking system, while crucial for an economy, is not a safety net. Commercial banks are businesses that operate for profit. Banks do not lend to individuals who do not have any assets to put as collateral, or who do not have a reasonable expectation of repaying the loan along with the interest. A bank may not issue a personal loan unless the individual is employed and has a well-enough paying job, or has a reasonable expectation of getting a well-enough paying job, which ensures that the borrower will be able to repay the loan along with the interest. It may not provide a home equity loan if the owner of the house does not have built-up equity in the house. Note, however, that in this regard even the financial crisis that started in 2007 was not any different.[12] Banks, incorrectly, thought that house prices will keep on increasing. By virtue of price increases, a house purchased today will have built equity by tomorrow. Lax financial regulations further fueled the mania.[13] Even the financial intermediaries such as credit unions, which do not have a for-profit business model, are not charity organizations. Credit unions do need veritable assurance of loan repayment along with the interest. As a result these institutions do not, and cannot, serve as safety nets. Indeed, troubled times happen when one runs out of these options.

A social safety net may be formal or informal. Let me explain what I mean by these terms.

1.2.1. Informal versus Formal Social Safety Nets

In an informal social safety net, one relies on family, friends, neighbors, fraternity, sorority, or religious organizations associated with one's place of worship—church, synagogue, mosque, temple, and so on. One main defining feature of informal social safety nets is that they are relationship dependent. I will expand on this point shortly. First note that informal safety nets may be delineated into "casual" versus "organized."

By "casual" I mean that usually no formal records of favors extended or taken are kept. While how a particular family member, or a friend, or a neighbor has behaved in the past may very well determine how favors will be rendered in the future, formal record-keeping is usually not needed as a memory devise. The size of group membership is not large enough to require formal record-keeping. Family, friends, and neighbors are examples of casual informal social safety nets.

In the case of "organized" informal social safety nets, formal record-keeping is usually done. This may be due to legal reasons or for keeping a record of who contributed and how much, and who received help and in what amount. Examples of organized informal social safety nets include The Freemasonry,[14] The Benevolent and Protective Order of Elks of the United States (the Elks, for short),[15] Boy Scouts of America,[16] Girl Scouts,[17] Kiwanis,[18] YMCA,[19] YWCA,[20] and the Salvation Army,[21] among others. In the United States for these organizations to obtain a "not-for-profit" status, a detailed record-keeping is required. Furthermore, organized informal social safety nets may be divided into religious versus secular informal social safety nets. While organizations like the Elks or the Boy Scouts of America, and so on, have a religious component, they may not be attached to a particular denominational church, or a synagogue, or a mosque, and so forth. Organizations like the Salvation Army, on the other hand, are associated with a particular denomination.

A subset of organized informal social safety nets is organizations that provide social services and are religious in nature. They use some religion as their moral compass and are generally referred to as "faith-based organizations" (FBOs). It may be a particular religion or some inter-faith coalition. In the faith-based organizations literature, these organizations broadly fall under the following categories:[22]

1. Neighborhood congregations established around a church, synagogue, mosque, temple, and other places of worship. The distinguishing feature is that these organizations are limited in their geographic reach.
2. FBOs that have a network at the national as well as international levels. For instance, Catholic Charities USA is a nationwide organization. According to its website,[23]

> Catholic Charities USA is the national office for Catholic Charities agencies and affiliates nationwide. As a professional association and social justice movement, Catholic Charities USA supports local Catholic Charities as they provide help and create hope for over 10 million people each year regardless of religious, social, or economic backgrounds.

FBOs such as YMCA,[24] YWCA,[25] and the Salvation Army[26] are international organizations.
3. FBOs may also be "interfaith." Interfaith FBOs are an amalgamation of different religious faiths. Usually all larger metropolitan areas have interfaith FBOs in one form or another.[27]

Furthermore, FBOs may also differ with regard to the tax status. For instance, while all charity organizations have a tax exempt status, according to the Charity Navigator website, "Many religious organizations, like the Salvation Army, are exempt under Internal Revenue Code from filing the Form 990." According to the Internal Revenue Service website, Form 990 allows the general public to get information about the organization.[28]

Curiously, the White House Office of Faith-Based and Community Initiative and the Office of Management and Budget (OMB) were asked to define what constituted an FBO by the US Government Accountability Office (GOA) so that the performance of such an organization could be judged.[29] Both the organizations refused to provide a precise definition of an FBO. According to the GOA's report:

> [T]he White House Office of Faith-Based and Community Initiative, OMB is not planning to establish a definition for faith-based organizations. As they stated in their agency comments (June 2006), they are concerned about the practical and legal difficulties inherent in developing a uniform definition for what constitutes an [a] faith-based organization. In September 2008, OMB reported that they do not plan to develop such a definition. They note that the data is intended as a tool for providing a fuller understanding of the organizations that receive competitive federal grants and not as a definitive measure [of] the Initiative's success. In FY10 [Fiscal Year 2010], after repeated requests for a status update, OMB did not provide us with any information.

Another distinction between casual and organized informal social safety nets is that, depending upon the organization, becoming a member of organized informal social safety nets usually requires some formal initiation or ritual.[30] Help is usually rendered to the members of such organizations, and is limited in scope and extent.[31] While such organizations do provide help to the needy non-member, such as flood and earthquake victims, the amount, duration, and scope of help are limited.

So for the purposes of our discussion, I will place family, friends, and neighbors into the "casual" informal category. Religious organizations associated with one's church, synagogue, mosque, temple, or other place of worship, fraternities, and sororities fall into the "organized" informal category. I will discuss more about the recent history of FBOs in Chapter 8. In fact, because religious organizations wield enormous power in the social, political, and economic arenas in the United States, I devote Chapter 8 to the discussion of FBOs. In that chapter I also compare FBOs with secular non-profit organizations in providing social safety nets.

Let me now turn to the main distinguishing features of informal (both casual and organized) and formal social safety nets.

1.2.2. Relationship Capital and Informal versus Formal Social Safety Nets

One factor that distinguishes informal social safety nets from formal social safety nets is the relationship capital. By "relationship capital" I mean the resources (time, energy, as well as finances) spent on building a relationship. It needs not only the frequency but also the extent of contact. That is, how helpful one has been to the other person on a given occasion and how often the help has been extended. For instance, while family members are genetically related, genetic relationship, however, may not be enough to build up relationship capital. Same is true of neighbors—just living next door may not be enough. It is also true for friendships. Indeed, that is one difference between a "friend" and an "acquaintance." An informal social safety net requires relationship capital. Without the relationship capital, there is no informal social safety net.

In a formal social safety net, relationship capital is not a requirement. One becomes a member of a formal social safety net by virtue of being a part of the body politic, regardless of age, gender, race, income status, or other such demographic markers. Membership is much broader and does not require a relationship history. It is not relationship dependent in the sense described above in the case of an informal social safety net. The criteria for membership are objective in the formal social safety net. They do not require subscribing a particular belief system either, as in the case of a religious organization.

This is an important point. As I discuss in a lot more detail in Chapter 8, while gender, racial, social, ethnic, and religious diversities are extremely important for economic growth and are inevitable in a globalized economy, these diversities also lead to divisions along these very lines. Individuals are discriminated along these lines and even persecuted. In a formal social safety net, subscription to a particular belief system or being member of a particular ethnic group is not required.

Take the example of unemployment insurance. In the event of one losing one's job, the individual applies for unemployment benefits. The state gives the person certain amount of money, regardless of race, gender, age, or religious affiliation, which helps one pay for food and other necessities of life for a certain period of time. In the United States, examples of formal social safety nets include unemployment benefits, food stamps, or as it is now known, Supplemental Nutrition Assistance Program (SNAP),[32] Medicaid, etc.

1.2.3. Geographic Portability and Informal versus Formal Social Safety Nets

Another major difference between informal and formal social safety nets is geographic portability. I define geographic portability as the ability to untie oneself from the geographic proximity. That is, the ability to move from one geographic area in a country to another geographic area in the same country without losing the membership benefits. For instance, in the case of the United States, it may mean moving from one state to another. While informal social safety nets are effective and indeed important, these are not portable.[33] For instance, in an informal setup, where safety net is a function of one's knowing the neighbors, it requires, well, knowing the neighbors. This constraint may keep one from moving to a place where one's resources are valued higher, lest one loses the safety net. A geographic immobility of this sort may hurt economic growth.

1.2.4. Monitoring and Informal versus Formal Social Safety Nets

Another difference is the monitoring mechanism of participants so that free-rider problems are eliminated or at least minimized. In an informal social safety net, neighbors perform the monitoring by physically watching the participants' behavior. While the ability to physically monitor participants ensures that participants do not engage in behaviors that are not in the interest of the community, this very feature limits the viability of informal social safety nets. The moment a participant moves to a place far enough where he/she cannot be watched, the system breaks down. The fear of the breakdown of the system may also affect contributions from the members. Participants may not contribute for fear of not being able to monitor other participants and for fear of not being able to take advantage of contributions by others or what they have contributed in the past, should the need arise. Just the expectation of breakdown may very well lead the actual breakdown.

In a formal setup, however, the monitoring function is performed by relatively sophisticated tracking systems. Individual income, tax, credit reports, and criminal records are a few examples.

1.2.5. Anonymity and Informal versus Formal Social Safety Nets

An important point is that of anonymity and the possible loss of self-respect of the recipient. In an informal social safety net, anonymity is not possible. It is a teleological issue. Informal social safety nets are built upon knowing the participants. One has to be visible to be known. Formal social safety nets, however, do not require visibility of this kind. In a formal social safety net, there is higher probability that the recipient's neighbors, friends, and family may not find out about his/her plight. While it is true that one's circle of family and friends may not be able to extend any help due to the lack of knowledge about one's predicament, this may also serve to save one's dignity in the eyes of one's friends. The value of human dignity cannot be overlooked.

1.3. The State of Formal Social Safety Nets in the United States and Other Countries

One way to look at the presence and extent of formal social safety nets is to see the spending patterns of various countries on social services. Figure 1.1 plots data of public spending from 1960 to 2012, as a percentage of gross domestic product (GDP),[34] by selected Organization for Economic Co-Operation and Development (OECD) member countries. The data source is the OECD website.[35]

As can be seen from the figure, there is quite a bit of variation among countries' public social expenditure. As is, perhaps, common knowledge,

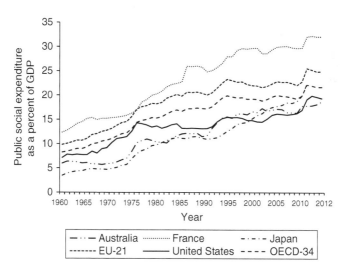

Figure 1.1 Public social spending in selected OECD countries as a percentage of GDP
Source: OECD social expenditure database.

Western European countries, as compared with the United States, spend a higher percentage of their GDP on social services. "Why doesn't the United States have a social safety net as the Western European countries?" Alberto Alesina et al. (2001)[36] ask this very question and find some interesting answers. I will turn to this issue in Chapter 7, where I discuss the financing of formal social safety nets. In chapters 6 and 7, I also provide a more detailed discussion of the differences in this arena between various developed countries.

1.4. The Roles of Research and Development, Innovation, Economic Growth, and Formal Social Safety Nets

Generations of economists, and policy makers alike, have spent lifetimes on deciphering the secrets of economic growth.[37] Economist and policy makers want to know the reasons behind the observed differences in the income levels of countries, and areas within countries. So much so that Adam Smith titled his seminal 1776 book *An Inquiry into the Nature and Causes of the Wealth of Nations*. With much effort and research, economists agree that one of the main determinants of economic growth is research and development (R&D). R&D adds to the pool of knowledge and leads to inventions and innovations that drive the engine of economic growth. I argue in this book that inventions and innovations, key ingredients of economic progress, may be enhanced by the presence of formal social safety nets. Here is why?

Innovative activities are inherently expensive and risky; outcomes are uncertain. Recognizing this fact and the potential benefits of R&D governments provide grants and subsidies through various source. Applying for these grants and subsidies, however, requires an extensive infrastructure on the part of the applicants. One need not look any further than the local universities and colleges; separate departments with fulltime staff are in place to help faculty members apply for grants. It goes without saying that establishing such paraphernalia may not be for individual inventors. Formal social safety nets lower the downside risk of undertaking uncertain activities by individuals. I present this argument in greater detail in chapters 3 and 4, and show that formal social safety nets may have substantial positive externalities in the form of increased innovation and economic growth. Using data from 19 OECD member countries for the past three decades, I show that formal social safety nets indeed enhance innovative activities. These results and a detailed discussion are presented in Chapter 4.

1.5. Income Distribution, Poverty, the Economy, and the Social Safety Nets

Studies show that unequal income distribution and rampant poverty tear at the fabric of a society. Inequality of income quite possibly leads to the inequality of opportunity. Furthermore, inequality of income distribution also impedes income mobility: A child born to poor parents has a lot lower likelihood of moving up the income distribution.[38] Not only do unequal income distribution and poverty take a toll on the poor, depending upon the state of the economy they may not be growth inducing either.[39] My own empirical findings, presented and discussed in Chapter 4, show that income inequality has a negative impact on innovative activities. Studies also show that formal social safety nets not only reduce poverty, they also tend to make income distribution less unequal. I turn to these issues in chapters 5 and 6. I argue that formal social safety nets not only make sense because they reduce poverty and preserve human dignity due to anonymity, they also make economic sense as they make income distribution relatively less unequal and make opportunities available to a broader segment of the society.

1.6. Financing of Social Safety Nets

One point that is often raised in public debates is the financing of social safety nets. It is, indeed, an extremely important point and deserves much attention. The provision of formal social safety nets is expensive. However, it is perhaps not as expensive as usually thought.[40] Also, the question whether or not the provision of social safety nets is expensive is missing an important part. The question has to include: expensive compared to what? I argue that on purely economic basis, once we take into account the positive externalities, in the long run formal social safety nets may turn out to be a bargain for the economy. Findings of my own empirical exercise point out that taxes, after they have been in effect for five years, have a positive impact on innovative activities. Viewed this way, considering taxes to finance formal social safety nets as "expenditure," as opposed to an "investment" in society, does not do justice.

1.7. Chapter Summary

In this introductory chapter of the book I have outlined the themes that I intend to cover. I have provided a snapshot of what a reader might expect in the coming chapters. I have argued that the need for social safety nets is not a partisan issue; even the most ardent libertarians like former congressman and presidential candidate Ron Paul agree that a society needs some sort of safety net to help the unfortunate. The question is: How does a society accomplish this task? I have presented an outline of the argument I intend to expand on in coming chapters of this book. I have argued that just as a modern economy needs a well-functioning monetary system and a legal tender, formal social safety nets provided by the government and financed by taxes are also needed for the long-term economic health of a country.

CHAPTER 2

The Need for Formal Social Safety Nets

A hypothetical situation: The economy of California is booming due to the public's renewed interest in movies. A plumber moves from Iowa to California. His skills are better suited for the kind and quality of plumbing done in California. As a result, his skills can carry a higher price in California as compared with Iowa. He is better off because he earns higher wages and the Californians are better off because they get the kind of service they want. His car breaks down, and he takes his car to a car mechanic. The car mechanic goes to a dentist when her tooth starts hurting. Her dentist finds that the cause of pain is her wisdom tooth and it needs extraction. Before extraction, the dentist gives the mechanic a sedative produced by a pharmaceutical firm. The owner of the pharmaceutical firm takes her kids to watch a movie made in a studio in Hollywood in which actors, directors, camera operators, and so on[1] from practically all over the world have participated.

The plumber hurts his back and has to take some time off. Being a smart individual he had purchased health insurance. He pays the health insurance premium every month. He also has some savings—a retirement account and some real estate. His illness, however, lingers on and gets worse as time passes. Bills pile up. He runs out of savings. He has to empty his retirement account. Not only that, he has to pay a penalty for early withdrawal. He also has to sell his real estate. His health worsens still, which keeps him from returning to work. He cannot afford to pay the monthly health insurance premium, so the insurance company cancels his insurance. To make matters worse, his car breaks down. He cannot get his car fixed due to financial troubles. The car mechanic's business suffers. She needs a tooth extraction. However, she cannot afford to pay the dentist. The dentist does not need the pharmaceutical firm to produce sedatives. The owner of the pharmaceutical firm now considers watching movies an avoidable expense. She cuts back. The Hollywood movie studio cannot recoup its investment and shuts down.

The above scenario is obviously highly exaggerated: A plumber hurting his back and taking down a successful movie studio? The odds are rather slim. However, once you add to the number of "plumbers hurting their backs," the odds improve. Modern economies are connected in ways that our brains, which evolved to escape sabre-toothed cats, find it hard to imagine. As long as life moves along smoothly, lack of formal social safety net does not matter. However, once hardship strikes, the need for such a safety net surfaces.

Perhaps the fall of this domino could have been avoided if only the plumber could get some financial support. Banks would not extend loans due to lack of collateral—he has run out of his savings and sold his real estate. Since the condition of his back is rather serious, they cannot expect him to get healthy soon, start working, and repay. And since he has moved to California relatively recently, he has not been able to establish an informal social safety net.

The trouble could also have been limited to the plumber if the dentist needed her car fixed and our mechanic was able to fix it, the owner of the pharmaceutical firm needed her child's tooth extracted and our dentist was the one who could extract the child's tooth, and movie theater owner needed some pain medication that the owner of the pharmaceutical firm could provide, and all the people involved in making the movie could . . .

My head hurts!

The dentist getting her car fixed in return for the dentist performing the tooth extraction, and so on, is an example of barter. It would not only require that one person needs what the other has to offer, but also in the exact quantities and qualities that each has to offer and wants. It's possible, but not probable in a modern economy. Paying for goods and services in terms of money makes an economy function much more smoothly and makes life much easier.

Just as the increased number of goods and services traded, the increased participants in the trade, and the increased complexity of societies led to the need and creation of a monetary system and a "legal tender," the same factors also call for a framework of formal social safety nets. I will provide more detail on legal tender shortly. It will suffice for now to note that a legal tender is the form of money that can be used legally.[2] Look at any denomination dollar bill and you will see the sentence "THIS NOTE IS LEGAL TENDER FOR ALL DEBTS, PUBLIC AND PRIVATE." (capital letters original).

And just as economies benefit from a well-functioning monetary system, as opposed to using a barter system, formal social safety nets prove beneficial, as compared with informal social safety nets. Indeed, as economies grow informal safety nets prove highly inadequate. I will discuss the inadequacies of informal social safety nets in detail later in this chapter and in later chapters. First, however, let's see how modern monetary system can help us understand the virtues of formal safety nets and serve as a guide in establishing such formal social safety nets.

2.1. Formal and Informal Social Safety Nets: Monetary System versus Barter

One way to look at the difference between informal and formal social safety nets is by comparing an economy where the predominant way to exchange goods and services is a barter system with the one where money is used to exchange goods and services. To get a better sense of this comparison, perhaps some explanatory comments are in order. Some readers may find these details tedious (but hopefully not unnecessary). Please bear with me. There is a method in this madness. It will become clear shortly.

2.1.1. Monetary System and the Concept of Money

First, what do we mean by "monetary system"? At its very basic level, a monetary system is an institutional arrangement that facilitates exchanging goods and services for money. *Financial Times* defines a monetary system as "[t]he system of money in a particular country or the world as a whole, and the way that it is controlled by governments and central banks."[3] *Cambridge Dictionary* defines a monetary system as "[t]he system used by a country to provide money and control the exchange of money."[4] If we are talking about a single country, "monetary system" and the establishment of "legal tender" become effectively the same.

According to the United States Code,[5] legal tender is defined as follows: "United States coins and currency (including Federal reserve notes and circulating notes of Federal reserve banks and national banks) are legal tender for all debts, public charges, taxes, and dues." Once a government has declared what counts as legal tender so that prices of goods and services may be established in legal tender, it requires institutions that monitor and control the supply of legal tenders so that prices of goods and service follow a predictable path over time. In modern economies, central banks perform the tasks of supplying and monitoring legal tenders.

In the United States, up until the creation of the Federal Reserve System, the central bank of the United States, "over 30,000" different entities issued money. Even drug stores would issue their own money.[6] Since so many entities issued their own currency, it made it almost impossible to figure out which currency was worth how much. The need for a central body that would regulate currency arose. The establishment of the Federal Reserve System, however, took over a century and a half of concerted efforts. There were several false starts and failures along the way. But these efforts eventually paid off on December 23, 1913, "when President Woodrow Wilson singed the Federal Reserve Act into law."[7]

It requires more agreed-upon rules when exchanging goods and services involves other countries. Edwin Truman (2010)[8] defines international monetary system as "the set of rules, conventions, and institutions that govern and condition official actions and policies affecting the international economy and financial system: exchange rate regimes, intervention policies, the size and composition of reserve holdings, mechanisms of official financial support, etc." (p.4).

Let us now see what is meant by "money." Every economy uses money in one form or another. We exchange billions and billions of goods and services in exchange for US dollars, British pounds, Euros, renminbis, and so on. We use currency, checks, credit cards, and a whole host of other forms of money, even bitcoins,[9] an electronic form of money. It is essentially a file on the bitcoin holder's computer. What is this thing called "money"? It may be instructive to go into a bit more detail. "Money," as defined in any principles-level economics textbook, refers to an asset that has certain characteristics. "And what is an asset?" one may ask. An asset is anything subject to ownership. Examples of an asset may include an egg; a bottle of olive oil; a share of stock, which represents partial ownership of the firm; a house; a boat; a piece of gold; and so on.

Money may be "commodity money" or it may be "fiat money." Commodity money has some intrinsic value—it can be used for some other purposes as well. For instance, a bottle of olive oil or an egg can be used as food. Fiat money, on the other hand, does not have any intrinsic value. The paper of a ten dollar bill does not have much use other than being used as money. Furthermore, two eggs are worth twice as much as one egg. A ten dollar bill, however, is worth ten times a one dollar bill because it says on the ten dollar bill that it is worth this much, even though the size, weight, and other physical properties of the paper of a ten dollar bill are the same as that of a one dollar bill.

Just as a historical footnote, paper currency first appeared in the United States around 1690. About the advent of paper money in the United States, Farley Grubb writes: "the legislatures of the various colonies (later states) directly issued their own paper money—called bills of credit—to pay for their own governments' expenses and as mortgage loans to their citizens, who pledged their lands as collateral."[10] Later, the power to issue money was taken away from the legislator of colonies at the Constitution Convention in 1787.

Now back to the characteristics that make an asset serve as money. I will list these characteristics one by one and provide some explanation.

2.1.1.1. A Medium of Exchange

Perhaps the most important characteristic of an asset that can serve as money is its ability to serve as a medium of exchange. If this asset is to function as money, people should be willing to accept it in exchange for their goods and services. While eggs are an asset, they may not serve as money. Say one is in need of millet, but the millet seller is not willing to accept eggs, then we cannot say that eggs are "money." One cannot exchange eggs for millet, and thus cannot serve as a medium of exchange. There has to exist, what economists call, "double co-incidence of wants." The seller has to want what the buyer has to offer in exchange. It may be argued that if the buyer offered high enough a quantity of the product—5,000 eggs for a pound of millet?—the seller may be persuaded to sell after all. While true, this may leave the realm of practicality.

A related point is the geographic mobility. Not only would one want to be able to buy goods and services with money in, say town A, but if one moved to town B, one would expect that money does not lose its value. Even if one moved to another country, one would expect that currency from one country would be exchangeable with another country's currency. Of course the amount of one country's currency that one gets depends upon the exchange rate—the price of a unit of one country's currency in another country's currency. On July 30, 2012, at 11:36 A.M., for instance, the price of one British pound, known as pound sterling, in terms of US dollars was $1.5694.[11]

Geographic mobility and the ability to exchange one country's currency into another country's currency is an important one. As we will see shortly, informal social safety nets lack this quality, which makes them rather inadequate in modern economies. So let us talk a bit more about it. What are the factors that determine the price of one country's currency in terms of another country's currency? As with most other questions in economics, the answer is supply and demand. Why would one country's residents demand another country's currency, and why would the residents of the other country supply their country's currency? While residents of one country may also hold currency of another country as an asset, the main reason for demanding another country's currency is to purchase that country's goods and services. This creates both the demand for and the supply of currencies of different countries. It may be easier to understand with an example. Suppose you are going to visit the United Kingdom and someone from the United Kingdom is visiting the United States. Let's start with you visiting the United Kingdom.

Assume that you arrive in London. Once there, you will need British pounds to pay for the hotel, food, travel, and so on. Why not pay with US dollars? The reason is that individuals in the United Kingdom will usually accept only British pounds. When they pay for goods and services they purchase, the sellers of those goods and services usually will accept only British pounds. I have used the word "usually." This is because the British residents may accept, say, US dollars from you if they have a reasonable expectation of being able to exchange US dollars for British pounds. You, by visiting the United Kingdom and buying various goods and services there, created the demand for British pounds, and since you bought British pounds with US dollars, you also created the supply of US dollars.

This raises another question: Why would British residents accept US dollars or exchange British pounds for US dollars? The answer is that just as you are visiting the United Kingdom, there are British residents who are visiting the United States. They need US dollars to make transactions once they arrive in the United States. This creates the demand for US dollars and the supply of British pounds. The US and British residents buy and sell goods and services to each other worth billions of US dollars each month. During the month of May 2012 alone, the United States sold to the United Kingdom goods worth $4,437.5 million and bought goods worth $4,851.9 million from the United Kingdom.[12] The interaction of demand for and supply of US dollar determines the price of US dollar in terms of British pound. In general, the interaction of supply of, and demand for, one country's currency determines its price in terms of another country's currency.

Going back to "A Medium of Exchange" characteristic, US dollar (or British pound) is a good medium of exchange. Eggs? Not so much!

2.1.1.2. A Unit of Account

"A Unit of Account" characteristic refers to the quality that an asset can be used to evaluate goods and services. That is, it serves as a yardstick. A horse is an asset, but to evaluate computers in terms of a horse, or vice versa, is a hard proposition. One has to know the values of all the different kinds of computers—make, processor speed, size of memory, and so on—and have knowledge about different kinds of horses—age, pedigree, and so on—to make an informed judgment.

A related quality is "divisibility." For an asset to serve as money, it has to be divisible in smaller units. Take the example of trading a horse for a computer again. Suppose both parties are able to establish that one horse is worth two computers—each computer is worth one-half of a horse. The buyer of computer, however, needs only one computer. Slicing the horse into two is obviously not a viable option. Depending upon how much glue can be produced, a horse sliced into two may lose most of its value.

In the United States and, to my knowledge, perhaps almost everywhere in the world, governments use the decimal system to divide money units. Alexander Hamilton, in his *Report on the Establishment of the Mint* argued that[13]

> it is certain that nothing can be more simple and convenient than the decimal subdivisions. There is every reason to expect that the method will speedily grow into general use, when it shall be seconded by corresponding coins. On this plan the unit in the money of account will continue to be, as established by that resolution [of August 8, 1786], a dollar, and its multiples, dimes, cents, and mills, or tenths, hundreths [sic], and thousands.

2.1.1.3. A Store of Value
The next quality is that of "A Store of Value." This refers to the ability to store and transfer purchasing power from one time period to the next. Tomatoes are an asset. They carry a certain value. Suppose a farmer has two tons of tomatoes. She wants to buy a new tractor, but she wants to wait till next year. Her current tractor is expected to run fine for another year. If she leaves this crop of tomatoes in the field, they will rot and become worthless by next year. She may want to store tomatoes in a cold storage facility, but this is an expensive option. At least some of the value of tomatoes will be used up in storage fees. Currency, by the way, runs into the same problems if prices are increasing rapidly. It is still a prevalent form of money because its other characteristics outweigh this drawback (more on this shortly).

2.1.1.4. Limited in Quantity
Another quality to which Paul Seabright (2010)[14] refers is that an asset has to be limited in quantity. Any asset that is being used as money

> must be scarce, either naturally (like gold) or artificially through the restricted printing of bank notes that are difficult to forge. If it were not, there would be easier way to obtain money than by offering valuable goods in exchange. If acorns functioned as money, for instance, people would stop producing other goods and start collecting acorns instead. (p.95)

I mentioned bitcoins above as a form of money. One hurdle bitcoins (or more precisely the issuers of bitcoins) have to overcome before they can become viable and widely accepted is figuring out how to make sure that the holders of bitcoins do not just copy the bitcoin files without limit.

Usually when one thinks about money these days, one invariably gets the image of currency. By "currency" I mean paper currency and coins. Depending upon one's country of residence, it may be a dollar bill in the United States, a pound in the United Kingdom, a rupee in India, a renminbi in China, a Euro in the Euro area, and so on. Currency, however, is just one particular form of money. Humans have used different objects as money, ranging from sea shells to precious stones and metals.[15] An oft-cited example is that of stone discs used as money in the Island of Yap. The inhabitants of the Island of Yap call these stone discs *fei*.[16]

Another famous example of using commodities as money is provided by R. A. Radford (1945) of a prisoner of war camp where prisoners used cigarettes, along with other commodities, as money.[17] Lest one thinks these practices belonged to the ancients, Seabright (2010) cites examples of "cans or pouches of mackerel fillets" being used as money in the US federal prisons by the inmates. The US federal prison inmates switched from the use of cigarettes as money to the use of mackerel fillets due to the ban on cigarettes instituted in 2004. As recently as 2008, residents of the Solomon Islands have used dolphin teeth as money.[18]

What made currency so popular and ubiquitous? The answer lies in the qualities that an asset needs to have to function as money. For instance, paper currency and coins have the quality that, depending upon the issuing agency, everyone is willing to accept them in exchange for their goods and services. This makes currency a good medium of exchange. Furthermore, governments require that taxes and fines be paid in terms of that country's currency, either in cash or with checks, debit cards, credit cards, and so on, denominated in that currency. This requirement further strengthens a currency's status as a medium of exchange.

Another reason that currency has become so ubiquitous is that people can easily evaluate various goods and services in terms of currency, making currency a good unit of account. It also makes exchange easier. In order to use currency to make transactions, one does not need special skills, other than the very basic ability to read, to distinguish between a five dollar bill and a ten dollar bill. In fact, in countries where literacy rates are low, governments have bills of different denominations in different sizes and colors to make it easier to distinguish. India is one such example. Furthermore, currency is divisible into very small units, while each unit maintaining its proportional value.[19]

The quality of transferring purchasing power—A Store of Value—is perhaps the weakest quality in currency. Purchasing power may erode rather quickly during times of inflation and hyper-inflation—usually defined as inflation rate higher than 13,000 percent per year. Examples of Germany during the early 1920s and Zimbabwe during 2008 are often presented to undergraduate students when professors want to emphasize how quickly money can lose its value in certain situations.[20] Another example is that of the "continentals." The Continental Congress during 1775–1791 "to finance the American Revolution" started issuing money.[21] These notes were known as "continentals." Soon the number of continentals got out of control as the war dragged on. So many continentals were issued that the word "continental" became synonymous with worthless. In maintaining purchasing power, perhaps precious metals like gold or silver or other tangibles like a house are better suited. However, since currency's other attributes—a medium of exchange and a unit of account—outweigh it being a relatively poor store of value, it has become far more popular.

After this rather lengthy discussion about money and exchange rates, let's look at the similarities between formal social safety nets and money, and informal social safety nets and barter system. At first blush the concepts of safety nets and money may seem completely different. Upon reflection, however, one finds that the differences are only superficial and that similarities run deep. As we go through this chapter, we'll be able to appreciate the similarities. As I will show, factors that made money necessary for the modern society also make formal social safety nets necessary.

2.1.2. Conditions for Informal Social Safety Nets to Stay Viable

As noted above, in a barter system people trade goods and services for goods and services. Under a system of informal social safety nets, when need arises, people trade favors for favors. For this system to work, however, following conditions have to hold.

2.1.2.1. Reciprocity

If one falls on hard times, one's neighbor may step in to help, expecting that when he/she will need help in the future, the favor will be returned. Whether or not this expectation is made explicit does not make much difference. (And whether or not the intrinsic value and the reverence attached to an act of kindness is diminished by mentioning it in an overt fashion, to a great extent, is perhaps a matter of taste and cultural mores.) The person receiving the favor today has, at least, to be willing to return the favor in the future. If the recipient of the favor today is not expected to return the favor at a later date, the provider of the favor today may not be willing to help out. This may be called the social safety net counterpart of the "store of value" quality of money. The benefactor is "storing the value" of the favor to be used at a later date.

In other words, for informal social safety nets to function, there has to be a reliable system of reciprocity such that free riding—taking advantage of a common good without making necessary contribution—is eliminated or at least minimized. While an overt expectation of returned favor from the recipient may be considered in bad taste, the fact remains that a reasonable expectation of reciprocity, and realization of this expectation should the need arise, is needed for an informal social safety net to function. Note, by the way, that the expectation of reciprocity and the realization of this expectation are negatively affected with the increase in geographical distance between the recipient and the grantor of a favor. (Recall the point about geographic portability mentioned in Chapter 1.) I will have more discussion about this point shortly.

2.1.2.2. Measurability of Favors Granted and Received
Both participants have to know the "quantity" and the "quality" of the favor rendered and received. This may be termed as the social safety net counterpart of "unit of account" property of money discussed above. The system may break down if either the quality or the quantity of the favors is not easily discernible, and the receiver and the grantor of the favor need special skills to evaluate the favor.

Let me give an example. Suppose one received a monetary help of, say, $10,000 and later on the recipient donated a pint of blood to his/her neighbor when she had surgery; are they even? Who is to say? What if it was a pint of blood versus a pint of blood? Or what if it was $10,000 versus $10,000? Would this simplify the situation? Not necessarily. Let us take the relatively simple scenario of one individual helping out another individual by loaning $10,000. I will argue that even this seemingly simple scenario is not without complications. Let me explain why that may be the case.

It is quite possible that the receiver of the sum had, what economists call, "borrowing constraints." The strength of the constraint will depend upon and reflected in, among other factors, the interest rate being charged. Simply put, having a borrowing constraint means that one cannot borrow from, say, a bank at a reasonable interest rate. A reasonable interest rate refers to an interest rate that makes borrowing feasible. It may vary between not being able to borrow at *any* interest rate to between significantly higher-than-a-given-benchmark interest rate such that it makes borrowing infeasible. This constraint may exist due to the lack of collateral, a tainted or a non-existent borrower history so that the bank cannot determine whether the borrower is trustworthy, gender and racial discrimination, and a whole host of other reasons. It may also be that in that geographic area such formal infrastructure or market does not exist. Indeed, the existence of the borrowing constraint was the very reason that he/she needed a non-bank entity's help. Under these conditions, it is reasonable to conclude that the recipient and the benefactor valued the sum at higher than its face value of $10,000. What complicates the situation is measuring the *perceived* value. Note that this is a rather simple scenario where $10,000 is loaned and borrowed. The first scenario where we compared donating a pint of blood versus loaning $10,000 adds yet another dimension. Some may consider assigning a monetary value to the act of donating blood rather vulgar. This negative connotation may exist even if charging for blood were legal, which it is not in the United States.

Just as trading goods and service for goods and services becomes unnecessarily complicated and even infeasible as economies grow and goods and services increase in number and in complexity, the same way trading favors for favors becomes impractical as the types of favors increase in number and in complexity.

2.2. Increasing Population Size, Specialization, and Formal Social Safety Nets

Another way to look at the need for formal social safety nets is from the vantage point of increasing population sizes and specialization of various activities. Indeed, increasing population size made it possible to gain from specialization. For a better understanding of the phenomenon of specialization, a simple example often used in principles-level economics classes may be instructive. It relies on the Theory of Comparative Advantage. David Ricardo, the nineteenth-century English economist, is given credit for this theory.[22]

2.2.1. Comparative Advantage and Specialization

Imagine a hunter-gatherer economy and a situation where there is only one individual. Let us call her Sara. To survive, Sara will need food and shelter. Imagine that she spends half of the day gathering food and the rest of the day gathering wood to build shelter. For the purposes of this example, assume that the shelter is temporary and is used only for one night; in the morning she moves on in search of food and abandons the shelter she built the night before. Assume that on a typical day Sara gathers five bushels of food and five tree branches to build shelter. Sara has to engage in both activities to survive. If she wants one more bushel of food, she has to give up one branch. On the other hand, if she wants one more tree branch, she will have to give up one bushel of food.

Let us now introduce another individual to this hypothetical economy. One day while Sara is searching for food and tree branches to build shelter, she runs into Anna. As you would have expected, Anna also needs both shelter and food for survival. Just like Sara, Anna spends part of her day gathering food and the remainder on gathering tree branches. Anna, however, finds it relatively easier to gather food than looking for tree branches. In one-half of a typical day, Anna can gather eight bushels of food, but only four branches during the remainder of the day. That is, if Anna tries to gather one more tree branch, she has to give up two bushels of food. Or conversely, if Anna wants one more bushel of food, she has to give up only one-half of a tree branch.

Economists call what one gives up to get something the "opportunity cost" of what one gets. More formally it is defined as the next best alternative forgone. In this simple example, for Sara, the opportunity cost of one more bushel of food is one tree branch, and the opportunity cost of more additional tree branch is one bushel of food. And for Anna, the opportunity cost of each tree branch is two bushels of food. Anna has a lower opportunity cost of gathering food than Sara, and Sara has a lower opportunity cost of gathering tree branches than Anna. This is because if Sara opts for one additional tree branch, she has to give up only one bushel of food, and if Anna gathers one more tree branch, she has to give up two bushels of food. Conversely, if Sara opts for one additional bushel of food, she has to give up one tree branch, and if Anna gathers one more bushel of food, she has to give up only one-half of a tree branch. One is said to have a comparative advantage in the production of a product if one can produce that product at a lower opportunity cost than the other. In this example, Anna has a "comparative advantage" in gathering food, and Sara has a "comparative advantage" in gathering tree branches.

Let's say that both Sara and Anna realize this and decide that both should specialize in one product—Sara in gathering tree branches and Anna in gathering food—and trade with each other. If Sara gets more than one bushel of food for each tree branch, she will be better off, and if Anna gets more than one-half of a tree branch for each bushel of food, she will be better off.

A related concept is that of "absolute advantage." One has an absolute advantage if one can produce all the goods and services at a lower cost than the other. Put another way, one has an absolute advantage if one can produce more of all the goods and services than the other person for a given amount of inputs used. As an example suppose that Anna could gather eight bushels of food and six tree branches in a day. In this scenario Anna would have an absolute advantage in both food and branches—she is better at both the activities. However, Anna would have a comparative advantage in food—her opportunity cost for each bushel of food is 0.75 tree branches and 1.33

bushels of food for each tree branch. Sara, on the other hand, would have a comparative advantage in gathering tree branches. Sara's opportunity cost of each tree branch is only one bushel of food. What matters for trade to take place, however, is comparative advantage. This is the reason that even rich countries trade with poor countries.

Note that in this example, neither Sara nor Anna would have been able to specialize and gain from trading with each other had there been only one individual. All else constant, what made this gain possible is the increase in the number of individuals. Stated much more eloquently by Adam Smith, "As it is the power of exchanging that gives occasion to the division of labour, so the extent of division must always be limited by the extent of that power, or, in other words, by the extent of the market."[23]

While the example of Anna and Sara is admittedly simplified, it is far from simplistic. This example has all the constitutive elements of a modern-day economy with millions, if not billions, of individuals participating in exchange. In a modern economy we accept specialization and trade as normal activities. Just as Sara and Anna both benefited from specialization and trade, we, the denizens of modern world, are all the beneficiaries of the gains from specialization and trade.

Over the past three centuries, world population increased exponentially, and so have economic activities.[24] Around the middle of the eighteenth century, usually considered to be the start of the Industrial Revolution in Europe, world population is estimated to be about 800,000,000.[25] By 1800 there were 1,000,000,000 individuals in the world. Within the next 130 years our planet was inhabited by 2,000,000,000 humans. In July 2012, for instance, world population stood at 7,025,613,011.[26] It is expected to reach 9,000,000,000 by 2048.[27] With this increase in population, demand for housing and jobs also increased. One way to meet this increased job and housing demands was to venture outside of one's immediate family, social, and geographic environments.

Changes in travel technology also came along during the seventeenth, eighteenth, and nineteenth centuries: steam engine powered ships to explore the seas, locomotive engine, railroads, and internal combustion engine powered automobiles, which transformed land travel, and then airplanes, which made traveling over long distances easy. Furthermore, during the nineteenth and twentieth centuries, income levels also increased. This increased prosperity, itself a result of technological changes, made traveling more affordable.

"But what does this lengthy discussion have to do with social safety nets?" you may ask. The answer is: a lot. Let me explain. As economies grow, specialization takes place, which further enhances economic growth, and so on. In this process a few things happen. One, individuals move to where their skills are valued the most. They leave their informal safety nets behind. The plumber, in our example, could have just stayed in Iowa where he knew people—he had an informal social safety net. In that case, however, the benefits from trade would not have occurred and both parties, the plumber and the Californians, would have been worse off. No one would have realized their comparative advantages.

Second, in a specialized economy one needs goods and services for which one has to rely upon other providers. We rely on grocers for groceries, car mechanics for car repairs, doctors for health-related issues, attorneys for legal issues, and so on. A formal institutional arrangement is required to organize the production and distribution of various goods and services. Services provided by social safety nets are no different; a formal institutional arrangement is required for the provision of these services.

This, however, still does not answer the question of why does the institutional arrangement, which provides social safety nets, has to be run by the government? Why can't informal safety nets, both casual and organized—neighborhood associations, fraternal orders, religious organizations, and so on—do the job? The reason is that limitations of informal social safety nets get in the way. I address this issue in some detail below. I go into a lot more detail in Chapter 7, where I discuss financing of social safety nets, and in Chapter 8, where I show why religious organizations may not be suited for the delivery of social safety nets.

2.3. Limitations of Informal Social Safety Nets

One often finds people romantically talking about the "good old days" when neighbors used to know one another. They would help out each other in time of need. It is, however, not uncommon these days for one to move into and out of a neighborhood without even meeting the next door neighbor, let alone having learned their names and the names of their children, and their birthdays. This means that if your neighbor is in need, you may not even be aware of it. After all, depending upon the need, it is hard to ask a stranger for help. It is true that a stranger might give a hand if you need a jumpstart on a particularly snowy evening, or provide a ride to a grocery store or to a hospital to an elderly person. Usually, however, this is how far it goes.

In Chapter 1, I outlined some of the factors that distinguish formal social safety nets from informal social safety nets. Let's revisit those factors in a bit more detail, and see how informal social safety nets prove to be deficient for the modern economies.

2.3.1. Relationship Capital

As I pointed out in Chapter 1, informal social safety nets are relationship dependent. For informal social safety net to be formulated, relationships have to be cultivated, either familial, or friendly, or neighborly, and so on. (A combination of these may also exist; siblings, who are friendly to each other, may live next door and belong to the same fraternal order.) I called this "relationship capital" in Chapter 1. Perhaps at the risk of belaboring the point, let me give an example that may be helpful.

Suppose I lose my job. In an informal setting I may go to my relative or my friend or my next-door neighbor who helps me get by. She gives me food and/or money to meet my needs. This is an example of an informal social safety net. They helped out because they knew me. We had a relationship—a familial, or a friendship, or a neighborly relationship. I had to accumulate this relationship capital. No such relationship capital is required for a formal social safety net. Neither do I have to develop a deep friendship with my neighbor nor belong to the same political, social, or religious organizations as my neighbor does. I might have just moved next door a few days ago and not even know the names or even faces of my neighbors. If, however, need arises and I have to seek help, I could apply for assistance from a formal social safety net to get by. And while developing friendships with neighbors and helping each other in times of need are, indeed, invaluable and make life more palatable, this relationship capital comes at a (material) cost: had our plumber decided to stay in Iowa and maintain his relationship capital, he would have had to give up his material gains. The Californians would also have missed out on the services of a skilled plumber, and so would have the economy as a whole.

2.3.2. Geographic Portability

This point is linked to the relationship capital point just discussed. There are, however, vital differences. Refer, again, to the example of losing my job, and seeking assistance from a formal social safety net as opposed to an informal social safety net. I was able to apply for assistance, say, unemployment insurance, or Medicaid, or food stamps (now formally called "Supplemental Nutritional Assistance Program," or SNAP), because the safety net was portable. I would not, however, have been able to seek assistance from an informal social safety net. This is because there is no record of how much relationship capital I had, if any, in my previous place of residence, and I had not had enough time to build relationship capital with my new neighbors, and so on. As mentioned in Chapter 1, in a formal social safety net, membership criteria are much more objective. Take the example of a US citizen. One becomes a member of formal social safety net by virtue of being part of the body politic. And since body politic is much larger and inclusive, geographic boundaries matter less, if at all. For instance, in the United States, while there are state-level differences for how long one can collect unemployment insurance, federal assistance is available to all (usually)[28] for the same length of time no matter where one lives.

2.3.3. Monitoring

How does one make sure that participants are not abusing the system? That is, how does a plan avoid free riders? One more free rider, and before you know, the plan is not viable: more people are taking advantage without making the necessary contributions. One option is to monitor the activities of the participants. Take the example of neighbors and friends. In an informal social safety net, the same neighbors and friends who are watching out for each other are also watching each other. For this to happen, however, it is important that the participants live close enough that they can monitor. The system breaks down when one participant moves to a far enough location where she/he can neither watch nor be watched. In a formal social safety net, monitoring is done via thorough record keeping. Income and tax records and credit reports are examples of such monitoring. And while close geographic proximity and the ability to watch prove beneficial in an informal social safety net setting, they also raise some concerns, namely, lack of anonymity and loss of dignity.

2.3.4. Lack of Anonymity and Loss of Dignity

In an informal social safety net, one cannot remain anonymous. This is an important point. Asking for help is not easy. One may not ask for help for fear of losing one's dignity, perhaps the most valued asset.[29] If I lose my job and apply for unemployment insurance or food stamps, I may be able to keep my situation secret from my family, friends, and neighbors, and maintain some semblance of dignity. This, however, by design is not possible in an informal social safety net. Furthermore, while knowing a participant at a personal level may be an efficient way of monitoring and keeping the free riders out, it may refute the basic purpose of having a social safety net—participants may not ask for help for fear of losing their dignity.

2.3.5. Geographic Mobility and Investment in Informal Social Safety Nets

General Social Survey collects data on a number of social issues.[30] One of the questions asks respondents their likelihood of seeking a new job next year. Respondents in the 2006 survey said they were about 38.2 percent "very likely" or "somewhat likely" to look for a new job next year. About 13.2 percent of respondents in the 2006 survey were at the job less than a year.[31] According to the US Census Bureau's 2010 estimates, about 2.2 percent of the US population (one year and older) lived in a different state a year ago. Only about 84.6 percent lived in the same house a year ago.[32]

Anticipating moving to a different town or a different state (or even a different country) in search of better opportunities, individuals may invest less in informal social safety nets. This leads to a decline in the number of participants in informal social safety nets, making them even less workable. For example, for an insurance plan to work and stay viable it has to have a large number of participants so that risk can be spread.

These limitations of informal social safety nets have a paralyzing effect. They are rendered perilously impractical in a modern economy. Imagine having a currency whose value is not quantifiable, which you can use only at a given location, and to buy goods only from certain individuals. Such a currency will not be suitable in a dynamic economy. Having a formal social safety net is akin to having a well-functioning monetary system. It is akin to having legal tender. No matter where one lives, one can use it, if need arises. It serves as "A Medium of Exchange," "A Unit of Account," and "A Store of Value."

2.4. Chapter Summary

Given that there is a positive probability, however small it may be for some and not so small for others depending upon the socioeconomic conditions of the individual, of falling on hard times, it stands to reason that we, as individuals and as a society, prepare for such an event. We need safety nets. In this chapter I have made the argument that having formal social safety nets is no different than having a monetary system and that informal social safety nets are akin to having a barter system. While informal safety nets have served their purpose, and in some instances still do, they are limited in their scope and extent in a modern society. Increasing population sizes, more footloose individuals in search of better economic and social environments, more racially diverse demographics, technological advances in healthcare coupled with increasing healthcare costs, to name just a few, are all the factors that require that social safety nets be provided in a more formal setting.

In Chapter 3 I look at the role of research and development, the resulting innovations and economic growth, and argue that formal social safety nets may enhance research and development, and innovative activities, resulting in higher economic growth.

CHAPTER 3

Research and Development, Innovation, and Economic Growth

What prompted Galileo Galilei to question the geocentric model of the universe, so much so that he would spend years in prison for this "heresy," as the Roman Catholic Church at the time would have it? Indeed, what prompted Aristotle, Ptolemy, Copernicus, and many others, before and after them, to spend time and effort to make any such pronouncements, in the first place? Why did it matter? One answer is curiosity: an artifact of the evolved human brain. They wanted to know how the world around them worked. How did the celestial bodies move and what role did they play in the changing of seasons, and much more? They wanted to figure out the laws of nature.

An effect of research and development, whether it is the intended purpose or a side effect, is the betterment of human race. Developments in medical science bring us perhaps the most obvious examples. One such example is the human papillomavirus (HPV) vaccine. HPV is a main cause of cervical cancer. The vaccine was introduced in 2006 in the United States. According to a recent report,[1] the vaccine has had tremendous success: the incidence of HPV has dropped by half among teenage girls. This is despite the growing resistance against the vaccine.[2] Apparently some parents fear that their teenage offsprings, especially females, will become promiscuous if they knew that there were fewer consequences of sexual activities.

In this chapter I start with what we mean by research and development, innovation, and economic growth. Then I turn to the role of research and development in promoting economic growth. Given that research and development and innovative endeavors are risky enterprises, but have a proven record of promoting economic growth, governments subsidize the conduct of research and development. I argue that the presence of formal social safety nets may be considered as a subsidy for conducting research and development. I also spend a part of this chapter on the competing needs a modern society may have and how it may allocate its resources.

3.1. What Is meant by Research and Development, and Innovation?

The System of National Accounts, a branch of the United Nations Statistics Division, defines research and development as follows:[3]

> Research and development is creative work undertaken on a systematic basis to increase the stock of knowledge, and use this stock of knowledge for the purpose of discovering or developing new products, including improved versions or qualities of existing products, or discovering or developing new or more efficient processes of production.
>
> (p.119, paragraph 6.207)[4]

The story of economic growth is intimately tied to the story of acquisition and dissemination of knowledge. Indeed, often the two are indistinguishable.[5] Humans have devoted lifetimes to answer questions that interested them. Millions of years of evolution, which led to the development of human brain, also led to efforts to figure out what surrounds us and what is within us? We want to figure out what it is and, then, why it is whatever it is. These efforts range from making basic survival possible to making life more meaningful and perhaps even entertaining once survival is assured—from the mundane to the sublime.

At the risk of over-simplification, pick a point in the evolutionary timeline and picture a group of early humans. One may imagine how they learned, by trial and error, to sharpen the ends of a tree branch so that it may be used as a weapon, both against the predator and the prey. A sharpened tree branch used to guard against an attacking animal made survival possible and the same tree branch used to hunt made sustenance possible. Overtime they figured out the appropriate length and the kind of tree branch to use and the ways to sharpen it. They found out that the chances of survival and a successful hunt were higher when more members of the group had weapons. Once survived and satiated, lying under the night sky, they wondered about the celestial bodies. And so it began.

Simply put, the urge to discover and innovate and invent, be it guided by curiosity about the world around us or the need to find a solution to a problem in hopes of financial riches and professional accolade, or to help fellow humans (more on this shortly), is what leads to research and development. Engaging in research and development is trying to figure out. Our early ancestors wanted to figure out how to guard against predators or how to hunt more effectively. Safety of environment and a full belly meant relatively healthy and longer lives, which in turn, provided more resources and further fueled the urge to discover, invent, and innovate.

And it continues till today. We try to find better ways to build houses to guard against the elements; faster planes to fly places—from one country to another, from the Earth to the Moon, to the Mars, and beyond. We try to develop better ways to grow more and better food so that more people may be able to have plentiful and nutritious meals. While different individuals in a society and different societies may have varied objective for engaging in research and development—ranging from satisfying a curiosity and learning for the sake of learning to raise self-worth, to alleviate the sufferings of fellow humans in the spirit of altruism, to gaining notoriety and accumulate wealth with the acquired knowledge—one engages in research and development to figure out the "hows" and "whys." Interestingly, satisfaction of curiosity, however, was not always an admirable endeavor. As late as the sixteenth century, it was regarded as "vanity," unsuitable for gentlemen (Mokyr, 2005, p.293, footnote 23).

3.2. Research and Development, Innovation, and Economic Growth and Development

Before going further, let us distinguish between "economic growth" and "economic development." While intimately related, these are distinct concepts. When we talk about economic growth, we are referring to increases in total per capita output of an economy. That is, an increase in the number of goods and services produced in an economy divided by the population. One popular measure of total output is gross domestic product (GDP). Perhaps a bit more explanation of GDP will be helpful to the non-economists.

3.2.1. A Measure of Total Output: Gross Domestic Product

In the United States, the Bureau of Economic Analysis (BEA) is the government agency that collects, analyzes, and disseminates data about economic conditions.[6] According to its website:

> BEA produces economic accounts statistics that enable government and business decision-makers, researchers, and the American public to follow and understand the performance of the Nation's economy. To do this, BEA collects source data, conducts research and analysis, develops and implements estimation methodologies, and disseminates statistics to the public.

The BEA defines (real) GDP as "the output of goods and services produced by labor and property located in the United States."[7] Furthermore, "real" GDP is distinguished from "nominal" GDP in that nominal GDP is the market value—the prices at which they are bought and sold—of those goods and services. When GDP is divided by the population of a country, it is called per capita GDP. If the real GDP is divided by the population, it will be called real per capita GDP, and if the nominal GDP is divided by the population, it will be called nominal per capita GDP.

This measure of output, however, has come under increasing scrutiny, and in the opinions of many economists, rightly so.[8] One reason is that GDP does not measure goods and services that are not traded in the market. Suppose I have a vegetable garden in my backyard. I grow vegetables for my own consumption, and perhaps give some of the vegetables as gifts to my neighbors. Since these vegetables are not being traded in the market, their value will not be added to GDP. Note also that GDP will not account for the neighborly feelings between my neighbor and me because these feelings are not traded in the market. GDP does not measure goodwill. Even if a product is traded in the market but not reported, perhaps to avoid tax, or the product is not legal in that state, GDP will not account for that trade.

Take another example. Suppose that a parent takes time off from work or cuts down the number of hours she/he works to spend more family time. Assuming that her/his income is tied to the output she/he produces, which is a function of number of hours worked, her/his income will decline, and GDP figures will show a decline accordingly. The individual, however, may be happier. In this case happiness and GDP are moving in the opposite direction.

Even with these deficiencies, GDP as a measure of output, however, is not useless either. Refer back to the example of a parent taking time off from work or cutting down hours to spend time with family: the parent is able to take time off from work or cut down the number of hours only because she/he has enough income that she/he can afford to do so. Such a possibility most likely exists only in countries that have high enough output. GDP thus provides a valuable snapshot of an economy, albeit at times missing some details. While concerted efforts are being made to account for the welfare and happiness of people,[9] we do not yet have an agreed-upon objective measure to do so. As a result, economists and policymakers still use GDP to measure an economy's material health.

3.2.2. Economic Growth versus Economic Development

Let's get back to the distinction between "economic growth" and "economic development." We will see that the concept of economic development helps, to some extent, fill in some of the gaps left by GDP as a measure of wellbeing. Whereas economic growth refers to an increase in total output, economic development, on the other hand, relates to having better healthcare outcomes, better educational opportunities, and better living standards of the general populace. In this sense economic development is a "distributional" concept. Whereas economic growth refers to an increase in the total output, economic development deals with the question of how the output is distributed among people. While economic growth is essential to have more goods and services, it does not guarantee that the living standard of the masses will increase. It is quite possible that those who are already well off may get most of the increase in output. Economic development, on the other hand, refers to the improvement of the living standards of the masses.

This distinction is made perhaps most eloquently by the economist and philosopher Amartya Sen, a Nobel laureate.[10] Sen argues that certain "freedoms" and "capabilities" are most basic. In his book *Development as Freedom* he focuses on five types of "instrumental freedoms" (Sen, 1999, p.38). He names them:

(1) "political freedoms"—the freedom to express one's views in the political arena, to decide who represents, and the ability to criticize without fear of retribution;
(2) "economic facilities"—an atmosphere that makes the pursuit of economic wellbeing possible and allows one to use the economic resources one has;
(3) "social opportunities"—the provision of opportunities in a society that allow all members to prosper. These include societal institutional arrangements that allow one to acquire education and healthy living. "These facilities are important not only for the conduct of private lives . . . , but also for more effective participation in economic and political activities" (p.39);
(4) "transparency guarantees"—rules of game that are transparent so that "trust" among the participants can be established, and room for capriciousness is eliminated; and
(5) "protective security"—provision of safety nets in case certain members of the society fall on hard times.

Economic growth, then, is important not in itself, but for what it brings in terms of economic development—in terms of, what Sen (1999) calls, increased "freedoms" and "capabilities." The distinction is between "means" and "ends." Such sentiments have a rich tradition. Anand and Ravallion (1993) quote from Aristotle's *Nicomachean Ethics*: "The life of money-making is one undertaken under compulsion, and wealth is evidently not the good we are seeking; for it is merely useful and for the sake of something else" (p.135, footnote 5).[11]

3.2.3. The Study of Economic Growth

The next question is: Which factors affect economic growth? Philosophers, economists, and public policy makers, of today and the centuries past, have indeed spent lifetimes trying to answer this question.[12] Reading the newspaper or watching news on TV, especially in the aftermath of the Great Recession, which started in 2007, to some it may seem like that the modern-day pundits are the ones who unlocked the secrets of economic growth. It will, however, be a mistake and a testament to our short memories. The history and the formal study of economic growth go at least as far back as the mid-eighteenth century.[13]

While it is common to think of modern growth starting with the Industrial Revolution, Joel Mokyr (2005) argues that the roots of the Industrial Revolution are set in the scientific revolution of the sixteenth century and the ideals of the Enlightenment movement of the seventeenth century.[14] Mokyr argues that it was the teachings of philosophers like Francis Bacon (1561–1626),[15] who relied upon and demanded empirical evidence, that laid the foundations of the advances to come. Mokyr writes that Bacon was of the view that "the main purpose of knowledge was to improve mankind's condition rather than the mere satisfaction of that most creative of human characteristics, curiosity" (p.293). This also led to the development of what Mokyr calls "useful knowledge"—aiming at the development and spread of skills that could be applied to "solve technological problems." These solutions, in turn, led to economic growth.

In the West, the ideas of the Enlightenment movement were instrumental in generating and spreading knowledge to the masses. This, according to Mokyr, also explains why societies in the West are richer today than they were during the 1700s and before, and why the societies in the West are richer as compared with the rest of the world. The main reason is that these societies now have more knowledge. Of course, the mere possession of knowledge and solutions to technological problems, in and of itself, does not guarantee widespread economic growth. Indeed, philosophers of the antiquity had knowledge and wisdom from which we derive life lessons even today. And the Chinese had developed techniques to make a product that survived thousands of years after its invention, that is, paper. Same goes for the Mesopotamian civilizations. Economic prosperity and knowledge, however, were hardly widespread in those societies. The difference, Mokyr argues, is that by the mid-eighteenth century due to declining costs, knowledge was made more transferable to the masses and to the coming generations. Suddenly, knowledge and solutions to problems of the day were no longer the domain of only the elites and those living in cities. Furthermore, it did not die with the individuals who possessed them.[16]

Formal study of economic growth in the twentieth century owes a great deal to the economist Robert M. Solow, a Nobel laureate. In his 1956 paper[17] he formalized the theory of economic growth. He showed that the output of a country depended upon, along with the amount of "physical" capital (that is, roads, bridges, buildings, machinery, software, and so on),[18] on labor, and technology. By "technology" we mean the pool of knowledge—recipes, formulae, the knowhow to combine various inputs, and so on. This pool of knowledge about how to combine various inputs so that a given level of output is produced is the reason for economic growth. Holding other factors constant, as our pool of knowledge increases and we learn better ways to combine various inputs, so does our output.

To understand this, think of the development of the machine called "computer." At its very basic level it is just a combination of silicon, petrochemicals, and metal. What converts these rather mundane and uninteresting ingredients into an exotic machine that can crunch numbers at lightening speeds, take pictures, videos, provide us directions, and provide access to the books, once available only to the extremely wealthy, to pretty much anyone who has the desire to read, is the knowledge of how to combine these inputs. Furthermore, technological advances in the form of increases in the processing speeds and functionality and other attributes are the artifacts of better knowledge.[19]

Economists following Robert Solow built upon his formal framework and his insights. Indeed one would be hard-pressed to find economists trained during last quarter of the twentieth century and later for whom Robert Solow's 1956 paper was not a required reading in their graduate-level macroeconomics courses. In fact, even the undergraduate-level macroeconomics textbooks rely on Robert Solow's model to introduce students with economic growth. The Solow (1956) paper has been so influential in the discipline of economics that the model and its implications are being studied well into the twenty-first century.[20]

3.2.4. How Is Knowledge Created?

Knowledge may be of various "kinds." It may range from, say, learning how to build an arrow that travels straight and how to hunt a deer to the deeper epistemological questions about "what we know, and how we know what we know." The latter kind is beyond the scope of this book, and more importantly, beyond the expertise of this author. My focus here is the former, and perhaps more mundane kind of knowledge, which Moykr calls "useful knowledge." I will avoid this label though. It may lead one to think that the generation and dissemination of "propositional" knowledge is not useful.

The question of how "technical knowledge"—how to build a better arrow, how to gather and store enough food to last through the winter, how to build a machine that can fly—is created and disseminated is perhaps as old as the human species. It would not be too wild a speculation on our part to say that our ancestors most likely found out, say, the proper length of an arrow and which tree branch is most suitable, by trial and error. And how did our ancestors pass this information on? While we do not have a written record—writing was invented only about 5,000 years ago[21]—it is safe to say that the passage of this knowledge from one person to another or one generation to another was mostly oral.

The British economist Alfred Marshall (1842–1924) in his book *Principles of Economics*, first published in 1890, argued that knowledge acquired by producers, by producing their widgets, spilled over. As these "spillovers" accumulated and kept on spilling over, the overall pool of knowledge kept on increasing. He referred to this phenomenon as "external economies."[22]

Kenneth J. Arrow, another Nobel laureate, in his 1962 paper[23] presented a formal framework for the accumulation of knowledge and economic growth. The models in this class came to be known as "learning-by-doing" models. Dexterity is the key, these models argue. Producers of widgets learn by producing widgets. As producers specialize in producing a certain kind of widget, they learn better ways to produce these widgets.

The Allied Social Science Association held its 1986 annual meeting in New Orleans, LA. Paul Romer presented a paper titled "Growth Based on Increasing Returns Due to Specialization."[24] In this paper he presented a formal model of knowledge generation. Philippe Aghion and Peter Howitt[25] explain the main crux of this model (and other models in this genre) as "the growth of knowledge . . . being the result, not of learning externalities among individual firms, but of the continuous increase in the variety of inputs" (p.35). While there had been efforts at "endogenizing" technological knowledge,[26] Paul Romer's (1987) paper is perhaps one of the most influential paper that formalized the knowledge production function of this kind where firms added to the pool of knowledge without intentionally trying.

Firms, of course, engage in research and development (R&D) explicitly. It makes economic sense to engage in R&D as long as it is profitable. Indeed, according to the National Science Foundation, during 2009, companies in the United States spent $291 billion on R&D.[27] During 2009 "companies in manufacturing industries" alone spent $189 billion on domestic R&D. Of that $189 billion, 81 percent was out of companies' own pockets. Most of the remaining 19 percent was from federal sources.[28]

This is a world-wide phenomenon. According to the Organization for Economic Co-operation and Development (OECD),[29] during 2009, Israel spent 4.46 percent of its GDP on R&D, followed by Finland (3.92 percent) and Sweden (3.61 percent). Recall that GDP is a measure of an economy's total output. Table 3.1 presents data for selected countries. And this is in a year when R&D spending had declined due to sluggish economic conditions world-wide by 4.5 percent, a record according to the OECD report.[30]

Firms spend on generating knowledge because, as pointed out earlier, increased knowhow increases their output, and as long as firms can safeguard their production secrets, it is well worth the expense. Perhaps the most common way firms protect their knowledge is by acquiring patents. Patents prohibit other firms to use the techniques developed by one firm, even if other firms happen to get their hands on the developing firm's secrets, thereby providing incentives for firms to invest in R&D and innovate.

Whether or not keeping production techniques secret is welfare enhancing from a social point of view is a hotly debated question in economics and other disciplines.[31] There is evidence, however, that patents "may influence the direction of technological change and help to encourage the diffusion of knowledge" (p.33).[32] The reason for the diffusion of knowledge, argues Petra Moser (2013, p.32), is that inventors may feel safe sharing if their intellectual property is protected. Inventors and innovators are more willing to share their

Table 3.1   R&D expenditure as a percentage of GDP during 2009

Country	R&D expenditure as a percentage of GDP
Canada	1.92
Denmark	3.06
Finland	3.92
France	2.26
Germany	2.82
Israel	4.46
Japan	3.36
Korea	3.56
Sweden	3.61
United Kingdom	1.85
United States	2.90

Source: OECD website[33].

knowledge with competitors and advertise their accomplishments if they feel that their techniques will not be stolen.

3.2.5. Governments and the Support for Research and Development

While firms may spend on R&D to enhance their profits, the question arises: Why would governments provide support for R&D activities? One main purpose of government R&D support is to increase economic growth and enhance living standards of the body politic. This is true at least in democracies. Other purposes, however, have been pervasive throughout history, even in democracies. The most ominous ones, of course, are supremacy in war—the Manhattan Project (1942–1945), a US government research project that exploited the nuclear technology to produce the atomic bomb, is one such example.[34] Even government support for the development of the Internet was in part militarily motivated.[35]

R&D leads to increases in productivity growth—increases in output per input unit. Estimates are as high as 123 percent.[36] Since the positive impact of knowledge on economic progress is well established,[37] it stands to reason, then, that governments, especially in times of economic downturn when private firms cut back on R&D expenditure,[38] boost R&D expenditure to make up for the loss.

All types of R&D expenditure by the government are not equal, however. Broadly speaking, a government may spend its resources on particular projects or it may provide assistance in general. In economics literature, the former type of R&D support is referred to as "targeted" support, and the latter type is referred to as "passive" support.[39] Examples of targeted support may include government assistance to firms to, say, develop and promote fuel cell electric cars,[40] or to sequence human genes.[41] Passive R&D support, on the other hand, does not focus on any particular project. Its main purpose is to provide incentives for greater R&D. These may include tax incentives to firms for engaging in R&D,[42] or grants to academic institutions.[43]

Should governments provide passive R&D support or targeted? The answer to this question depends upon which type of support results in the proverbial "biggest bang for the buck." How does one evaluate the "bang"? Keeping the ethical question—whether or not research should be performed to build military hardware, which may end up destroying life on this planet—aside for now, and focusing just on the efficiency part, Richard Gretz et al. (2010)[44] argue that government will be better off using

passive incentives when the spillover benefits of all projects are equal. The government should use targeted R&D support when spillover benefits to risky projects are larger than safe projects. And spillover benefits must be larger as a project becomes riskier in order to justify targeted R&D support. (p.82)

When we talk about "spillovers," given that we are living in a globalized world, how does the government of one country make sure that firms of other countries do not "free ride"? Should the subsidizing government even care about this question when making subsidy decisions? Note that subsides are negative taxes—government pays the firms/individuals for participating in an activity. Richard Gretz et al. (2009)[45] developed a two-country two-firm model to get some insight. Their results lead them to conclude that the firms of the "home country"—the country that is subsidizing its firms—will benefit whether or not the other country provides subsidies to its firms.

To get a deeper insight, one may create a finer division of government support for R&D into a number of sub-categories. These may include tax relief/credit to the R&D performing firms, accelerated depreciation of building and equipment used in R&D, public-private partnership, subsides, conducting research in government agencies and public universities, and making the results available to the private sector, among others. Economists and policy makers, of course, have explored which of these methods is a better use of tax payer funds.

Martin Falk (2006, table 1, p.537)[46] provides a summary of the estimated impact of various government policies and other institutional factors. These institutional factors include patent protection, openness of the economy, high-tech versus low-tech industry, technological education of the workforce, quality of research institutions, and overall size of the economy, among others.

Starting with government subsidies, there is strong evidence that government subsidies lead to an increased R&D spending by private firms. Furthermore, R&D funding provided to universities and R&D expenditures by private firms are also found to be complements. Martin Falk (2006) estimates that "[i]n terms of marginal impacts of public funding a dollar increase in R&D performed by universities leads to an additional industry R&D of about $0.6 in the short-run and $3.0 in the long-run" (p.544). Martin Falk (2006) reports that there is a "mixed evidence on the relationship between government funded R&D in the business sector and total business-sector R&D intensity" (p.544). In summarizing his study, Falk (2006) writes,

Estimates using static fixed effects and dynamic panel data models suggest that tax incentives for R&D have a significant and positive impact on business R&D spending in OECD countries regardless of specification and estimation techniques. The long-run elasticity is approximately –0.9 indicating that a 1% reduction in the price of R&D (i.e. increase in generosity of tax incentives for R&D) leads to a 0.9% increase in the amount of R&D spending in the long-run. (p.545)

3.2.6. Formal Social Safety Nets as R&D Support

"Where do formal social safety nets fit in this picture?" one may ask. A short answer is: right in the middle. Allow me to explain. While the payoffs of successful experiments are high, innovative activities are expensive and outcomes are uncertain. This is why firms spend billions on R&D and governments provide incentives for such activities. Firms, especially large ones, for instance, have separate departments and staff dedicated to this very task where they conduct several experiments on various projects simultaneously. This allows them to spread the risk; even if one experiment fails, the other may succeed, allowing the firm to recoup its investments and establish its position in the market.

Individuals, on the other hand, do not have the financial depth to conduct several experiments simultaneously so that the risk may be spread, unless, of course, one is independently wealthy. While they may apply for government grants, however, as discussed above, the process of application alone requires paraphernalia beyond the reach of most individuals and small firms. Individuals and small firms have to conduct experiment using their own resources. If they succeed, financial fortune and celebrity follow. If they fail, the opposite is the case. Most of us, however, are risk averse. Evolutionary biologists argue that those who took unnecessary risks did not live to spread their genes.[47] A large majority of us take calculated risks. Even those who dropped out of Ivey League schools to develop computers did so because they had reasonable expectations that they would not become homeless if they failed. Indeed, the very fact that they were able to attend an Ivey League school shows that they had certain level of financial depth. There aren't that many, if any at all, "daredevils" out there who will risk it all. Even the tightrope walkers practice and have calculated the risks, and at least have poles to maintain the balance,[48] or those who attach a jet engine to a car wear a helmet.[49] Whether or not calculations turn out to be correct is a different matter.

The benefits of an extensive pool of knowledge are enjoyed by the society at large. Advances in medical technology, the Internet, and the global positioning system (commonly known as GPS) are only a few examples of present-day inventions from which society at large gains enormous benefits. The more individuals there are, who are involved in the creation of knowledge, the larger the pool of knowledge, and the greater the benefits that society receives. Recall the earlier discussion about the impact of the Enlightenment movement on the Industrial Revolution: While independently wealthy individuals may be able to provide education to their offsprings, the knowledge stays confined and does not spread to the society at large. Indeed, this is the reason for the creation of public universities and the stress on the provision of education to general public.

How does a society involve more individuals to engage in the creation of knowledge? One way to obtain this objective is to lower the cost of knowledge creation. One may have enough resources to conduct an experiment and generate knowledge, and if one succeeds, all is well. Success, however, is not guaranteed. This makes it an expensive and risky undertaking, which resource-constrained, risk-averse individuals will likely avoid. While perfectly rational on the part of the individual, society on the whole is not better off. From the point of view of the society as a whole, the larger the number of individuals engaged in knowledge creation, the better. Formal social safety nets do just that; they lower the cost of engaging in the creation of knowledge. Yes, one can seek government grants, but as discussed earlier, seeking government grants is not as simple as it sounds. Universities and colleges, for instance, have separate well-staffed departments whose sole purpose is to help faculty members secure grants.

Recall the research findings of Richard Gretz et al. (2010), cited above. They argued that passive R&D incentives—general R&D support—are better than targeted ones—R&D support for a particular project—"when the spillover benefits of all projects are equal" (p.82). Targeted incentives, on the other hand, are recommended if the government thinks that firms will not engage in a given project if left to themselves. Put another way, in the latter case, the government is picking the "winners and losers" and in the former case it is leaving it to the firms. Politically it may be risky to pick "winners and losers." It may not be a good idea for a government to pick one project over the other even if it did not face any political backlash. This is because government may not have the expertise to do that. Leaving it to the individuals and firms may be a better economic choice. Formal social safety nets solve this problem as well; they provide support in the most general form possible and let individuals decide on which projects to focus.

A related point, with regard to picking winners and losers, is that of possible government corruption. Indeed, various firms and industry groups spend billions on lobbying government officials. According to OpenSecrets.org,[50] a total of $3.3 billion were spent on lobbying during 2012 alone. Of this, the share of the top 20 clients was over $481 million.[51] The biggest spender in this "top-twenty" list was, perhaps not surprisingly, the US Chamber of Commerce, which spent over $136 million on lobbying during 2012. Other notable spenders included the National Association of Realtors, which spent over $41 million; the health insurance provider, Blue Cross and Blue Shield, which spent over $22 million; and General Electric, closely following behind, which spent to the tune of $21 million. Boeing and Lockheed Martin each spent over $15 million during 2012, and the Royal Dutch Shell spent over $14 million.

The purpose of this expenditure, of course, is to influence the decisions of government officials and policy makers, including the decisions regarding who gets lucrative contracts and grants. That such activities lead to corruption is not a secret. The case of Jack Abramoff during 2008 highlighted the extent of such corruption.[52]

While the presence of formal social safety nets does not mitigate the ills of lobbying, it does allow individuals who cannot get government grants to engage in innovative activities. In the process, the society benefits from the knowledge generated by enterprising individuals.

3.3. Research and Development, and Innovation in the United States over Time

Let me now turn to trends regarding R&D and innovation in the United States and provide a brief discussion of the various measures used to proxy innovation. First, let us look at some data.

One measure of R&D in a country is the percentage of a country's total output spent on R&D. In Table 3.1 I presented figures for 2009 for selected countries. What has been the trend in the United States over the years? Figure 3.1 plots data for total, private, and government R&D investment in the United States since 1959.[53]

A measure of the "output" of R&D is the number of patents granted/obtained in a country. Figure 3.2 plots the number of patents granted in the United States to inventors in the United States since 1963.[54]

In Figure 3.3 I plot both total real R&D spending and total number of patents granted in the United States in the same diagram for comparison purposes.[55] Both measures indicate that the overall trend in the United States has been positive.

3.3.1. Some Concerns with the Use of R&D Expenditure and Patents Data

Why do economists use R&D expenditure and patent data to measure innovative activity? Perhaps a few comments are in order. First, the correlation between R&D expenditure and patent is positive—as R&D expenditure

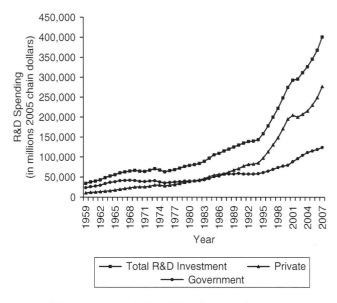

Figure 3.1   Real R&D spending in the United States by source of spending

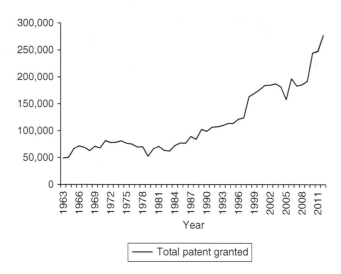

Figure 3.2   Number of patents granted in the United States

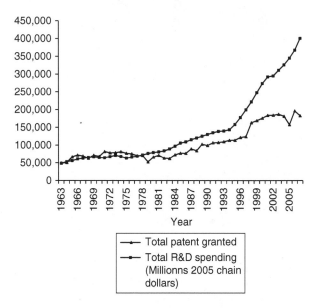

Figure 3.3   Total real R&D spending and total patents granted in the United States

increases, so do the number of patents, and vice versa. For example, the US data from 1963 to 2007 indicate that the correlation is 0.96 and highly significant.[56] Because of this high correlation, one may use the two terms—patents and R&D spending—interchangeably. The use of patents and/or R&D spending to proxy for innovative activities is not without its critics, however. So it is worth spending a few paragraphs exploring these issues and getting a better understanding of the matter. Let's first look at concerns raised on the use of R&D expenditure data as a proxy for innovative activities.

One concern that is raised about the use of R&D expenditure data is that only large firms keep a detailed record of their expenditure on R&D. It is, indeed, highly unlikely that small firms and individuals engaged in innovation and inventions will keep a separate record of their expenditure on these activities. Famous, and perhaps over-used, examples of students working in their dorm rooms and car garages—Mark Zuckerberg, Steve Jobs, Bill Gates, and others—on the development of computer programs and applications highlight this flaw of the use of R&D expenditure data. Furthermore, as mentioned earlier, a lot of innovation takes place in the process of production, that is, "learning-by-doing." It is extremely hard, if not impossible, to determine which marginal improvements were the result of just engaging in production and having an "epiphany" and which were the artifact of explicit effort to improve a process. Looked at this way, R&D expenditure records may underestimate the actual innovative activities.

On the other hand, it will also strain credulity to say that all R&D expenditures lead to some innovation. It is quite possible that at least some part of the R&D expenditure—salaries of experts, equipment and material purchases, and so on—will not bear fruit, and a given experiment may reach a dead end. From this vantage point, R&D expenditure may lead to an overestimation of innovative activity.

It gets even more complicated. Assume that researchers engaged in an innovative activity, say activity A, reached a dead end. However, they documented their steps in great detail. It is possible that this roadmap may prove helpful to future researchers engaged in some other innovative activity, say, activity B. Since researchers performing activity B learned from their predecessors—researchers of activity A—the R&D costs of activity B are lowered. Assume now that activity B is successful. In this case, the R&D expenditures on activity B are overestimating innovative activity.

Let's now turn to the use of patent data to proxy for innovation. We find that similar problems arise in the case of the patent data. First, not all inventions and innovations are patented. The inventor has to decide whether to patent an invention or keep it secret and reap the benefits. Second, even if the inventor decides to obtain a patent, she/he may not be able to get one. Patenting authorities have certain standards that have to be met in terms of whether the inventions and innovations are "non-trivial" and "groundbreaking." This is especially the case if the improvements, while vital, are marginal and not easily quantifiable. If this is the case then patents are underestimating inventions and innovations.

Second, for patents to represent the underlying innovative activities, institutions protecting intellectual property rights have to be in place. While this is largely true in developed economies, in less-developed economies, such institutions are practically non-existent. As mentioned above while discussing diffusion of knowledge and the role of patents, if the inventor happens to live in an economy where such institutions are present, he/she may benefit from patenting and selling the rights to use the invention. On the other hand, an individual living in an economy where either such institutions and laws do not exist or they are not enforced may be better off keeping the invention secret. In the latter case patents will lead to an underestimation of innovative activities.

Another issue, perhaps mostly in the high-tech sector, is that of firms acquiring patents, not so much as to produce the product, but to sue other firms who happen to have a similar product. These firms are often known as "Patent Trolls."[57] In June 2013 President Obama signed several executive orders to protect firms from such frivolous lawsuits. In a similar vein, firms often achieve patents so that their competitors cannot enter the market segment. When companies buy other companies, often a main reason, if not the main reason, is the number of patents the company that is being bought holds. Take the example of Google acquiring Motorola Mobility. In 2011 Google paid $12.5 billion to buy Motorola Mobility. According to a *Forbes* article,[58] one reason for buying Motorola Mobility was "Access to the Motorola patent portfolio which it could then license to partners like HTC and Samsung to protect against the long arm of Apple's lawyers."

While it is widely acknowledged that R&D spending as reported in the Bureau of Economic Analysis in the National Income and Product Accounts (and other government agencies across the world), and patents data to measure innovative endeavors, are not perfect tools, there also seems to be a consensus among the experts that the benefits of using these proxies to measure innovation outweigh the problems associated.[59] There is hope and some evidence[60] that the overestimations and underestimations of innovative activity cancel each other out. This is not to say that the variations at the micro-level are all accounted for. At the aggregate level, however, R&D expenditure and patent data represent the innovations and inventions rather well.

3.4. Economic Growth and Modern Society: Some Competing Needs

Economic growth—increasing output—requires running machines, and running machines requires energy. Not surprisingly, studies show that increasing growth requires increasing use of energy.[61] So far most of the energy used in production activities comes from traditional sources—coal, oil, and natural gas. According to the OECD website, as of 2010, the latest year for which complete data are available, only about 13 percent of world-wide energy supply comes from renewable sources.[62] Some countries are, of course, more reliant on traditional sources of energy than others. According to the OECD data, during 2010 the highest percentage of renewable energy supply was in Iceland (82.5 percent), and the lowest was in Korea (0.7 percent). In the United States, during 2010, about 5.6 percent energy supply came from renewable sources.

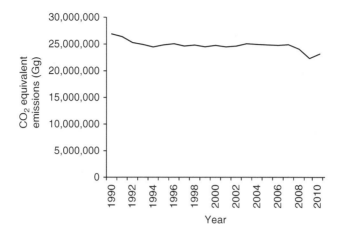

Figure 3.4 Total CO_2 equivalent emissions with land use, land-use change, and forestry[63]
Source: United Nations framework convention on climate change.

3.4.1. Environmental Costs of Economic Growth

The problem, however, is that traditional sources of energy also lead to environmental degradation. In mainstream science there is consensus that Earth's temperature is rising and that the reasons for this are human-made.[64] Due to industrial processes, emissions of greenhouse gasses—carbon dioxide (CO_2), methane (CH_4), nitrous oxide (N_2O), perfluorocarbons (PFCs), hydrofluorocarbons (HFCs), and sulphur hexafluoride (SF_6)—the main source of global warming and climate change, after declining somewhat, has been on the rise again.[65] I plot total greenhouse gas emissions data since 1991 in Figure 3.4.

These climatic changes can have catastrophic impact on life on Earth: A headline in the May 28, 2013, issue of *Scientific American* read, "Sea Level Could Rise 5 Feet in New York City by 2100."[66]

In a study about the possible impact of global warming, Martin Weitzman[67] notes:

> Global average warming of 10°C–20°C masks tremendous local and seasonal variation, which can be expected to produce temperature increases *much* [italics original] greater than this at particular times in particular places. Because these hypothetical temperature changes would be geologically instantaneous, they would effectively destroy planet Earth as we know it. At a minimum such temperatures would trigger mass species extinctions and biosphere ecosystem disintegration matching or exceeding the immense planetary die-offs associated in Earth's history with a handful of previous geoenvironmental

mega-catastrophes. There exist some truly terrifying consequences of mean temperature increases, 10°C–20°C, such as disintegration of Greenland's and at least the western part of the Antarctic's ice sheets with dramatic raising of sea level by perhaps thirty meters or so, critically important changes in ocean heat transport systems associated with thermohaline circulations, complete disruption of weather, moisture and precipitation patterns at every planetary scale, highly consequential geographic changes in freshwater availability, and regional desertification. (p.5)

While to some readers the preceding warnings may seem hyperbole, this, however, is not the case. The more we learn about climate change and global warming, the more we realize the extent of the possible damage to the environment.

3.4.2. Human Costs of Economic Growth

Another dimension along which economic growth may take its toll is the very direct and immediately observable human cost. In 2009 a news item in *The New York Times* revealed the deplorable working conditions of workers at Foxconn, a Taiwanese firm that supplied Apple's, highly profitable, iPhone, among other Apple gadgets.[68] It pointed to the human cost of increasing output and competing in the world markets. A worker had committed suicide.

This was hardly an isolated incident though. Soon picture of factories that showed net installations around factories started appearing. A quick Google search results in hundreds of such pictures. Apparently the purpose behind these net installations was to catch workers who tried to jump off the factory buildings to commit suicide. The causes of suicides were reported to be extreme pressure accompanied by long working hours, low pay, and mistreatment of workers by the management.

In 1979 the Chinese leader Deng Xiaoping introduced a policy known as One-Child Policy. As the name suggests, it limited the number of children a couple may have to one.[69] The rationale behind this policy was to lower the population growth rate in China so that economic growth rate could increase: Resources could be diverted from consumption to investment, which would lead to increased economic growth. While the birth rate has indeed declined to 1.8 (official estimates),[70] the policy has had unintended consequences. Reports of sex-selective abortions, female infanticide, and forced abortions abound.[71] A recent study in the journal *Science* reported behavioral differences between individuals born before and after the policy was instituted.[72]

The study found that individuals born after the institution of the one-child policy were "significantly less trusting, less trustworthy, more risk-averse, less competitive, more pessimistic, and less conscientious" than their counterparts born before the institution of the policy (p.953).

Globalization is another example. While the benefits of globalization and trade are numerous and well documented,[73] the challenges posed by globalization are also quite a few. Dani Rodrik, in his book *The Globalization Paradox: Democracy and the Future of the World Economy*, paints a vivid picture of the costs and benefits of globalization.[74] Not all the world residents are better off all the time, as the basic economic theory will predict. Left unregulated, globalization and trade may very well accomplish exactly the opposite of what they are supposed to accomplish.

And therein rests the conundrum. Given our current state of knowledge, if we, humans, want to decrease the adverse effects of economic growth, we need to cut down the production activity tremendously. On the other hand, however, at least for now, decreasing production does not seem to be a viable choice. This is especially so when one thinks from the point of view of the emerging and developing economies. "How can developed countries ask us to slow down our economic growth when most of the environmental problems have been created by the developed economies?" they ask.

3.5. Chapter Summary

In this chapter I have reviewed the research showing that R&D and the resulting knowledge are the main ingredients of economic growth. All else constant, the deeper and wider the pool of knowledge is, the better are prospects for economic growth, and the better off a society is. While firms invest in R&D to increase profits, governments across the globe provide support for R&D to enhance overall economic growth. I have argued that formal social safety nets are a form of this support, only better in that they do not require extensive infrastructure on the part of the individual. Furthermore, because knowledge generated in this form is more widespread, the whole society benefits as opposed to just a few. I have also discussed the competing needs that a society and, indeed, the world as a whole face. That is, the need to grow, on the one hand, and the problems of global warming, increased stress levels, and the resulting suicides, on the other hand.

Note, however, that the awareness about climate change and global warming, and other problems related to economic growth, was possible only through our increased knowledge. Formal social safety nets may very well provide answers to these problems by widening the circle of individuals involved in the generation of knowledge. Not only that, when whole communities and cities are suffering as in the case of Hurricane Katrina in New Orleans and Hurricane Sandy in New Jersey, and the whole informal social safety net infrastructure is wiped out, the need for formal social safety nets is further highlighted. In the next chapter I look at the empirical evidence of whether or not tax-finance social safety nets increase innovation.

CHAPTER 4

Innovation and Formal Social Safety Nets

In Chapter 3 I provided discussion about the role of research and development (R&D) in enhancing innovation and, in turn, economic growth and economic development. I presented studies that show that one main ingredient in the recipe of economic growth is R&D, and the resulting innovation. In this chapter I look at the empirical evidence of the link between formal social safety nets and innovation. I argue that because innovative activities are resource intensive and have uncertain outcomes, social safety nets provide an insurance against the negative outcome. This sense of security not only allows the freedom to continue on this path to those who are already involved in such endeavors, but also invites others to join in. As a result of this increased innovation, higher economic growth results and the whole society enjoys the fruits. The premium for this insurance is, of course, paid by taxes: The society as a whole foots the bill and gets higher economic growth in return. From the point of view of the society as a whole and over a longer period, the path to riches is made a lot smoother. Looking, however, at the resources expended toward the provision of formal social safety nets as expenditure with no return to the society unnecessarily limits the scope of formal social safety nets.

Recall that invention and innovation refer to the development of new goods and services, or improving the processes that produce goods and services. When we talk about "technology," we are basically talking about our pool of knowledge, our recipes, our formulae, and our knowhow about how "things" work. Those "things" may be the stars and planets and galaxies, or they may be at the quantum level, and everything in between. Furthermore, "things" may not be tangible at all. They may be intangible like different languages and their various components or discovering mathematics—discovering the rules of the universe and developing a system to express them. As I discussed in earlier chapters, and perhaps it bears repeating, often the artifacts of technology—computers and other gadgets, cars, submarines, space crafts, artificial heart valves, flu vaccines, and so on—are confused with technology, which is our understanding about how to combine various inputs to produce these gadgets and medical devices. I could go on but you get the point. An improvement in technology, then, is adding depth and breadth to the pool of knowledge so that, as a result of added depth and breadth, new products are developed and improvements are made to the processes that are being used to produce goods and services.

The material in this chapter is based on my research on this topic and the resulting articles presented at various academic conferences. Because some of the details of the topic are of technical nature, and may not be of interest to everyone, I will provide a discussion of the main results in the beginning of the chapter, and then present the details of the analysis. In this way, if a reader, who is not interested in the details, were to skip the latter part of the chapter, he/she would not miss the main points made in this chapter.

4.1. The Objective of Empirical Study

The question I want to answer in this empirical exercise is to what extent formal social safety nets impact innovation. As we saw in Chapter 3, since innovative activities are a major ingredient in the recipe of economic growth, formal social safety nets, via their impact on innovation, may affect economic growth of a country. In order to see the impact of the provision of formal social safety nets on innovation, one would want to compare innovative activities in countries that have government-provided formal social safety nets with those countries that do not have an institutional arrangement in which people rely on government-provided formal social safety nets. One may also be able to ascertain the impact of government-provided formal social safety nets on innovation by looking at innovative activities in a country before such social safety nets existed and compare innovation after such a plan is implemented.

Furthermore, to add precision to the estimated effects, ideally one would want to separate innovations made by the research departments of corporations and other entities, be it government or private, versus innovations made by individuals. The reason is that individuals are the ones who would be the potential beneficiaries of such an insurance policy. Individuals will be the ones who may embark on an innovative adventure encouraged by the presence of formal social safety nets.

Another point is related to the measurement of innovation. Technological advances are not discrete, they are continuous. Knowledge increases a "bit" at a time—an infinitesimally small bit. Without the discovery of mathematics and the understanding of physical laws of nature, centuries ago, which, over time, allowed us to solve (some of) the riddles of nature, the path to modern-day computer technology, at least this particular path, would not have been possible. How does one decide at which particular point on the continuous line of technological progress is worth stopping and taking note? Not only that, how does one decide that the point at which we have arrived is due to a particular event that took place earlier in time? What led to the discovery of mathematics, which helped us later, centuries later, to develop computers? Are all increments of knowledge equally important or some realizations are more valuable than others? Were the theories of relativity and special relativity by Einstein breakthrough events or the use of those theories a century later in the development of global positioning system, commonly known as GPS (which possibly saved a teenager a parent's yelling on a road trip because roadmaps were not folded just so), a notable point? These are important questions to ask. In empirical economic research, however, one is constrained by the availability of data. As I will discuss shortly, all is not lost however.

4.1.1. A Brief (and Non-Technical) Discussion of Methodology

(Note to the reader: In this sub-section I present some basics of the methodology used, which may be of interest to the lay reader. I provide detailed discussion of the methodology used later in the chapter.)

As mentioned earlier, while conducting empirical research in economics, one is always constrained by the availability of data. While one wants to conduct controlled experiments to see the impact of a given policy without the effects of other confounding factors that may affect the results, this is not usually, if ever, possible. In empirical economic research, such ideal situations do not present themselves. Harder still is the establishment of causation—determining that, say, event A *caused* event B.

This, however, does not mean that we are completely helpless. Econometricians, with help from mathematicians, over the years, have developed methods to deal with such problems. They have developed tools that minimize, if not completely eliminate, the impacts of external factors. And while we cannot establish causality in a classical sense—I push the table and it moves—we are certainly able to establish correlation—event A and event B took place, depending upon the time stamp, either concurrently or sequentially. For instance, using the fact that events taking place later in time could not have caused events taking place earlier in time—a child could not have given birth to her parents—we can narrow down, to some extent, the number of candidate events that *may* have caused a given event—two individuals, one male and one female, *may* have participated in the procreation of a child.

How do we narrow down the number of candidate events that may have caused an event? Let us conduct a thought experiment. Let us say that we want to figure out which factors affect the number of miles driven in a car by a typical individual in a given year. Some factors that may affect the number of miles driven include price of gas; distance from work; distance from stores; availability of alternative modes of transportation, such as public transportation; personal preferences, that is, driving verses taking public transportation or walking; and so on. For the sake of this example, let me also add two other factors: the color of one's car and whether or not one has hardwood floors in one's house. (The reason for adding the last two factors in this example will become clear shortly.) While there may be a number of other factors that may or may not affect the number of miles driven, for the sake of this example let us focus on these.

It is easy to see that if the price of gas changes, one may change his or her driving habits; if price increases, all else constant, one may be tempted to drive fewer mile—one may combine trips by, say, getting grocery shopping done while driving back from work (assuming, of course that there is a grocery store on the way), or one may start using a cheaper mode of transportation, such as public transportation, or one may start carpooling with co-workers, and so on.

We can also see how distance from work or from shopping places may affect number of miles driven. All else constant, the further away one lives from work or from shopping stores, the more likely it is that one would end up driving more miles. Similarly, one's preference for driving may also affect the total number of miles driven. If one gets pleasure out of the act of driving itself, one may be tempted to drive more. The opposite may be the case for someone who abhors driving.

What about the color of one's car? Would the car's color affect number of miles driven? Or how about whether or not one has hardwood floors in his/her house? Would having hardwood floor in one's house affect the number of miles driven? It can safely be said that the color of one's car and the presence or absence of hardwood floors in one's house are very unlikely to have any impact on the number of miles driven. I suppose one can argue that the individual happens to like or dislike the color of his or her car, which affects his/her driving habits. Or that one likes to look at the beautiful hardwood floor one has in his or her house, and that this makes him or her stay at home as much as possible. While this is possible, it is not very likely that the number of miles driven can be affected in this indirect way, at least not in any significant way. So right from the start, we can delete these two factors from the list of our possible candidates.

The next step, after we have narrowed down the number of factors that may affect the number of miles driven, is to collect data on all these factors—individuals' number of miles driven, (average) gas prices during the year, distances from work and shopping stores, availability of public transportation, and individual preferences for driving. One may want to use already available data. For instance, one may want to use the data that have already been collected by the US Census Bureau. Except, perhaps, for personal preferences for driving, the rest of the data are publically available.

It goes without saying that there may be some variation among individuals' miles driven, distances from work and shopping stores, and so on. How does one make some coherent statement about the effects of each of these factors on number of miles driven? This is where the tools developed by econometricians, with the help of mathematicians, come in handy. Indeed, the very variation, which was keeping us from making a coherent statement, is one of the characteristic that helps us draw conclusions. Furthermore, the more individuals about whom we have data, the more precision there will be in our results, and the more coherent and applicable will be our statement about the matter.

Tools developed by mathematicians—calculus to be precise—also allow us to hold "all else constant"—a phrase notoriously used by economists and the bane of non-economists and those who are not mathematically inclined. These methods allow us to separate the effects of each of the factors considered. For instance, in the present example, we can separate the effects of changes in gas prices from the effects of distance to work, distance to shopping stores, availability of public transportation, and individual preferences for driving, on miles driven. Not only that, tools developed by econometricians—again, with the help of mathematicians—also allow us to see the relative importance of each of these factors. We can see which factor contributes relatively more to the miles driven. Is it the price of gas or availability of public transportation or distance from work or distance from shopping, and so on? This analysis is referred to as "regression analysis."

So far, in this example, we have talked about the impact of various factors on the number of miles driven in a given year. We may also be interested in learning how the effects of these factors have changed over time. That is, we can add the time dimension to our analysis. Adding the time dimension will provide us a richer and more detailed picture. The terminology used for the former type of analysis, where we look at the impact of various factors on another factor, is "cross-sectional" regression analysis. The term used for the latter type of analysis, where we look at the effects of a number of different factors on another factor over time, is "panel" regression analysis. In this study, I have made use of panel regression analysis to see the impact of formal social safety nets—holding all else constant, of course—on innovation.

4.1.2. A Discussion of Factors Affecting Innovation

Let us now turn to the discussion of which factors are the likely candidates that may affect R&D and innovation. My main factor of interest, of course, is formal social safety nets. I want to see how the presence of formal social safety nets may affect innovation. And, as discussed in Chapter 3, since innovation is one of the most important sources of economic growth and development, factors that enhance innovative activities will quite likely lead to economic growth and development. Innovation, however, may also be affected by other factors, that is, other than the presence or absence of formal social safety nets. So we need to separate the effects of those factors from the effects of formal social safety nets on innovation.

One factor that may have an impact on individuals' and firms' decisions to invest in R&D and engage in innovative activities is how equally or unequally income is distributed among the citizenry. I go into much more detail about the link between income inequality and R&D investment, and as a result, on economic growth and development in Chapter 5. Here I briefly outline the channels through which income inequality may affect innovation. As discussed earlier, R&D investments and innovative activities are resource intensive and inherently risky. For someone to invest in R&D, they must have the financial resources to do so. Not only do they need enough resources to get started, they must have deep enough pockets to absorb the shock should the project turn sour. From this point of view, if a society has a relatively unequal distribution of income, those with a larger resource base are in a better position to invest in R&D and innovative adventures.

On the other hand, inequality of income may lead to social unrest. Indeed, the Occupy Wall Street movement,[1] which started in the fall of 2011, remains a vivid example of such public outcries. This type of social and political unrest may deter individuals and firms to invest, including investments in R&D. A decreased level of investment due to social and political unrest can have long-lasting effects on the economy. Not only will present-day workers have fewer machines to use, which may lower their productivity, future generations of workers will also have fewer machines to start with, and as a result may have lower productivity. From a theoretical stand point, it is not clear whether or not the positive effects of income inequality, which may give some the resources needed to embark on risky adventures, outweigh the negative social and political environments created by unequal distribution of income, which may reduce investment. Economic theory does not have a definitive answer with regard to the impact of income inequality on economic growth. Empirical evidence is needed to resolve the issue. Another factor that may have an impact on R&D investment and innovative activities is tax. To finance government-provided formal social safety nets, a government may need to raise taxes. I discuss the relationship between taxes and economic activity in a bit more detail in chapters 6 and 7, and provide empirical evidence. Here I provide a brief overview.

Let us take the example of tax on income. Basic economic theory tells us that, all else constant, increased taxes reduce after-tax income. Reduced after-tax income may also lower the incentive to invest, including investment in R&D, and earn the additional dollar. On the other hand, increased tax revenue may be used to build and improve infrastructure, provide education, reduce crime, and provide social services. These factors may enhance societal cohesion and lead to peaceful and stable socio-political and economic environments. Not only that, a country may also use tax revenue to invest in basic research for which the private sector may be ill-suited. All these factors have been shown to create an investment-friendly atmosphere. Which effect, positive or negative, will outweigh is not known *a priori*. Economic theory does not provide a definitive answer and empirical evidence is needed.

These are the factors that I have included in my empirical model. That is, I look at the effects of formal social safety nets, income distribution, and taxes on innovative activities. In the next sub-section I provide a brief discussion of the data used to perform statistical analysis.

4.1.3. Data Used to Test the Hypotheses

In order to perform statistical analysis, I use data for 19 Organization for Economic Co-Operation and Development (OECD) member countries. The data period is from 1980 to 2005 and the data are quinquennial. Why 19 OCED countries, why the data period from 1980 to 2005, and why quinquennial data? The answers to all three questions are the availability of data: This is the largest number of countries for which comparable data are available at this time. The names of the countries included are provided in Table 4.1.

Firms and individuals invest in R&D to understand a phenomenon. But not all R&D expenditure bears fruit. Some research projects invariably end up at dead ends. Is R&D expenditure a good measure of innovation? What if we only looked at the research that turned out to be successful? How about the number of patents that firms and individuals obtain for their inventions? But, then again, not all inventions are patented. Not only that, just because a

Table 4.1 Countries included in empirical estimation

Australia	France	Japan	Sweden
Austria	Germany	Netherlands	Switzerland
Canada	Iceland	Norway	United Kingdom
Denmark	Ireland	Portugal	United States
Finland	Italy	Spain	

certain project ends up at a dead end does not mean that it is not helpful to the proceeding researchers. It tells the other researchers which road to avoid. In this way, even those projects that do not yield successful results add to the existing pool of knowledge. But how does one measure the contribution of such projects? As I discussed in Chapter 3, these are all valid questions without any good answers, which address all concerns. One way out of this quandary is to use various measures of innovative activity. And this is the route I take. I use three different measures of innovative activity. The first one is real R&D expenditure as a percentage of real GDP incurred in a country, both in per capita terms. This measure can be thought of as "input" in the innovation production function. The second measure I use is the number of patents granted to, or applied by, the residents of a country in per capita terms. This measure can be thought of as the "output" of the innovation production function. The third measure is calculated by dividing total patents per capita by the real R&D expenditure per capita for each country. This measure can be thought of as "innovative productivity."

As a measure of the depth and breadth of social safety nets, I use the total amount of real per capita public and mandatory private saving as a percentage of real GDP per capita for the 19 OECD member countries listed in Table 4.1. To measure taxes in a country, I use real per capita revenue as a percentage of real per capita GDP.

A commonly used measure of income inequality is Gini coefficient.[2] This coefficient indicates what percentage of income is distributed among what percentage of population. The value of Gini ranges between zero and one. A value of zero indicates perfect equality ("for example, if each fifth of the population, ranked by income, received one-fifth of total income"), and a value of one indicates perfect inequality ("for example, if one household received all the income").[3] I use Gini coefficients of the 19 OECD member countries to measure inequality.

It seems reasonable to assume that economic agents may need some time to form their expectations about formal social safety nets. That is, if a given country establishes formal social safety nets at time t, the citizens may need some time to form expectations about how it might affect them in the future. Not only that, it may take some time for other factors that I have included in the model—taxes and income inequality—to have an impact on the behavior of economic agents with regard to engaging in innovative activities and, in turn, on the economy. I use a five-year lag between formal social safety nets, taxes, and income inequality, and their impact on innovative activities. The choice of using a five-year lag is restricted by the availability of data. Recall that these data are available on quinquennial basis.

4.1.4. Main Findings of the Empirical Analysis

While I postpone a detailed discussion of the results till the next part of the chapter where I present regression results and other technical details, here I provide a summary of the findings. First, recall that the effects of formal social safety nets, taxes, and income inequality on innovative activities are estimated after they have been in effect for five years. Or, using the econometric terminology, all three variables—formal social safety nets, taxes, and income inequality—are lagged by five years. Using this dataset and the methodology, both of which I detail below, I find rather strong evidence of the beneficial effects of formal social safety nets on innovation. The results also indicate that taxes have a positive impact on innovative activities, and income inequality has a negative impact on innovation. It is also important to note that while the strength of the results changes depending upon which variable is included in the model, the overall message of the results stays relatively robust to the changing model specifications.

As promised, in the next section of the chapter I provide technical details of the model and the dataset used, the methodology applied, and the results. Readers uninterested in these details may skip this section.

4.2. Details of the Empirical Analysis (Optional)

I start this section by presenting the model used to conduct empirical analysis. Then I turn to the dataset details, followed by presentation and discussion of results. In an effort to make this section self-contained, I have provided details and discussions that, at times, may seem redundant because some of these points have already been discussed in the previous section.

4.2.1. Model

The panel regression model used in the empirical analysis takes the following form.

$$lninv_{i,t} = \beta_0 + \beta_1 lnssn_{i,t-k} + \Sigma_j \beta_j ln X_{i,t-k} + \varepsilon_{i,t}, \text{ for } j = 2, \ldots, J \quad (1)$$

Where $lninv_{i,t}$ is the natural log of the measure of innovation. I use three measures of innovation. One, total real per capita R&D expenditure as a percentage of real per capita GDP in country i at time t; two, per capita patents taken/granted (more on this point in the Data section) by country i at time t; and three, following Jacob Madsen (2007, Equation 3, p.164)[4] a ratio of patents per capita divided by real R&D per capita as a percentage of real GDP per capita—more precisely, $ln(Pat/R\&D)$. I call this variable "R&D intensity" hereafter. $lnssn_{i,t-k}$ is the natural log of a measure of formal social safety nets in country i at time $t-k$, $lnX_{i,t-k}$ are the control variables in country i at time $t-k$, and the value of lag length, k, is five. The control variables included in the model are $lntax_{i,t-k}$, which represents the natural log of real per capita tax revenue as a percentage of real per capita GDP, and $lngini_{i,t-k}$ is the Gini coefficient to measure income distribution. βs are the coefficients to be estimated, and ε is the error term.

4.2.2. Data and Data Sources

I use quinquennial data for 19 OECD countries from 1980 to 2005. The number of countries and the time period are limited by the availability of comparable data for the largest number of OECD countries. The names of countries included in this study are provided in Table 4.1, which I provided in the previous section of this chapter.

Variables included in this study are the number of patents granted/applied for in per capita terms (per 1 million population), and real per capita R&D expenditure as a percentage of real per capita GDP to measure the innovative activities in a country. To measure the magnitude of social safety net, I use the total amount of real per capita public and mandatory private saving as a percentage of real GDP per capita. I control for taxes by including real per capita tax revenue as a percentage of real per capita GDP. To control for income inequality I use Gini coefficients.

As mentioned earlier, it may take some time for economic agents to formulate their expectations about how the presence of formal social safety nets may affect them. To allow for this possibility, the right-hand-side variables are lagged by five years. The choice of using a five-year lag is dictated by the availability of data, which are available quinquennially. The data source is the OECD website.[5] R&D and GDP data come from OECD Factbook 2009.[6]

Patent data come from the so-called Triadic Patent Families published by OECD. As the OECD document titled *Compendium of Patents Statistics* notes:

Triadic Patent Families are defined at the OECD as a set of patents taken at the European Patent Office (EPO), the Japan Patent Office (JPO), and granted by the US Patent and Trademark Office (USPTO), to protect the same invention.... In terms of statistical analysis, indicators on triadic patent families improve the international comparability of patent-based statistics (no "home advantage"). Furthermore, patents that belong to the family are typically of higher value (as regards additional costs and delays involved in extending protection to other countries).

The criteria for counting triadic patent families are the earliest priority date (first application of the patent worldwide), the inventor's country of residence, and fractional counts. Owing to time lag between the priority date and the availability of information (especially for USPTO grants), 1999 is the latest year for which triadic patent families are almost completely available. Therefore, data for the latest years are OECD estimates based on more recent series....

(OECD, 2008, p.7)[7]

4.2.3. Empirical Findings and Discussion

I start by presenting descriptive statistics in Table 4.2.

Note that $n = 19 \times 5 = 95$, where the number of countries included in the analysis is 19 and the length of time series is five. Also note that the Gini coefficient ranges between 0 and 1. As a result, the natural log values are negative.

In Table 4.3, I present Pearson correlation coefficient estimates of the variable used.

I tested the stationarity of the panel dataset used. I use panel unit root test proposed by Jörg Breitung and M. Hashem Pesaran (2008; their Equation 9.37, p.296).[8] In the present case, the test takes the following form.

$$\Delta y_{it} = \alpha_i + \varphi_i y_{i,t-k} + u_{it} \text{ for } i = 1,\ldots,n; t = 1,\ldots,T \qquad (2)$$

Table 4.2 Descriptive statistics

Variable	n	Mean	Std. Dev.	Sum	Minimum	Maximum
lnR&D	95	5.145	0.493	488.817	3.555	5.964
lnpat	95	7.591	1.449	721.134	1.91	9.369
ln(Pat/R&D)	95	1.462	0.193	138.898	0.493	1.703
lnssn	95	7.582	0.286	720.249	6.953	8.086
lntax	95	3.553	0.21	337.563	3.1	3.956
lngini	95	−1.253	0.162	−119.015	−1.609	−0.994

Table 4.3   Pearson correlation coefficient estimates (p-values in parentheses)

	lnR&D	lnpat	ln(Pat/R&D)	lnssn	lntax	lngini
lnR&D	1.000	0.916	0.719	0.353	0.333	−0.407
		(0.000)	(0.000)	(0.000)	(0.001)	(0.000)
lnpat	0.916	1.000	0.93299	0.43343	0.35314	−0.42474
	(0.000)		(0.000)	(0.000)	(0.000)	(0.000)
ln(Pat/R&D)	0.719	0.933	1.000	0.448	0.355	−0.383
	(0.000)	(0.000)		(0.000)	(0.000)	(0.000)
lnssn	0.353	0.433	0.448	1.000	0.834	−0.573
	(0.000)	(0.000)	(0.000)		(0.000)	(0.000)
lntax	0.333	0.353	0.355	0.834	1.000	−0.678
	(0.001)	(0.000)	(0.000)	(0.000)		(0.000)
lngini	−0.407	−0.425	−0.383	−0.573	−0.678	1.00000
	(0.000)	(0.000)	(0.000)	(0.000)	(0.000)	

Note: Pearson correlation coefficients, $n = 95$; Prob > $|r|$ under H$_0$: $\rho = 0$.

Where y represents any given time series, and $k = 5$. I test the null:

$H_0\colon \varphi_i = 0;\quad \forall\, i$, against the alternative[9]

$H_0\colon \varphi_i < 0;\quad \forall\, i = 1,\dots,N_1;$ and $\varphi_i = 0;\quad \forall\, i = N_1 + 1,\dots,N.$

Applying this panel unit root test I did not find evidence of unit roots.

Now I turn to the regression results. I start with the simplest model specifications where there is only one independent variable. Results using the natural log of a measure of formal social safety nets in country i at time $t-5$, $lnssn_{i,t-5}$, are presented in Table 4.4. Table 4.5 presents results using natural log of the total amount of real per capita tax revenue as a percentage of real per capita GDP in country i at time $t-5$, $lntax_{i,t-5}$, as the independent variable. And Table 4.6 presents results using the natural log of Gini coefficient in country i at time $t-5$, $lngini_{i,t-5}$, which measures income distribution.

The layout of Table 4.4 is as follows. (The layouts of Tables 4.5 through Table 4.9 are the same as that of Table 4.4, except that independent variables included in the model change.) The first row of the table lists the column numbers. The second row lists the dependent variable used to measure the innovative activity, $lninv_{i,t}$, in Equation (1). Recall that I use three different measures of innovative activity, $lnR\&D$, $lnPat$, and $ln(Pat/R\&D)$. Column 1, row 4, lists the name of the independent variable, in this case, $lnssn_{i,t-5}$. I do not provide estimated values of the intercepts to avoid clutter in the table. Columns 2 and 3 provide estimates of a fixed-effects, β_{FE}-est, and a random-effects, β_{RE}-est, model, respectively, where the dependent variable is

Table 4.4 Regression results (Regression equation: $lninv_{i,t} = \beta_0 + \beta_1 lnssn_{i,t-5} + \varepsilon_{i,t}$)

[1]	[2]	[3]	[4]	[5]	[6]	[7]
Dependent variable	lnR&D		lnPat		ln(Pat/R&D)	
Variable	β_{FE}-est (p-value)	β_{RE}-est (p-value)	β_{FE}-est (p-value)	β_{RE}-est (p-value)	β_{FE}-est (p-value)	β_{RE}-est (p-value)
$lnssn_{i,t-5}$	0.289[c]	0.48[a]	0.841[b]	1.153[b]	0.148	0.218[b]
	(0.06)	(0.009)	(0.037)	(0.015)	(0.11)	(0.01)
R^2	0.89	0.09	0.96	0.12	0.93	0.18
F-stat	22.07[a]		61.76[a]		32.52[a]	
(p-value)	(0.000)		(0.000)		(0.000)	
H-m	6.57[b]	6.57[b]	1.0	1.0	1.59	1.59
	(0.01)	(0.01)	(0.317)	(0.317)	(0.207)	(0.207)
BP-stat	123.46[a]	123.46[a]	158.71[a]	158.71[a]	146.61[a]	146.61[a]
	(0.000)	(0.000)	(0.000)	(0.000)	(0.000)	(0.000)

Note: Significance Levels: [a] = 1 percent; [b] = 5 percent; [c] = 10 percent. *F-stat* tests for no fixed effects. *H-m* is the Hausman test for random effects. (A non-rejection of the null indicates preferences for random effects model.) *BP-stat* is the Breusch-Pagan test for two-way random effects. (The null is of no random effects).

Table 4.5 Regression results (Regression equation: $lninv_{i,t} = \beta_0 + \beta_1 lntax_{i,t-5} + \varepsilon_t$)

[1]	[2]	[3]	[4]	[5]	[6]	[7]
Dependent variable	$lnR\&D$		$lnPat$		$ln(Pat/R\&D)$	
Variable	β_{FE}-est (p-value)	β_{RE}-est (p-value)	β_{FE}-est (p-value)	β_{RE}-est (p-value)	β_{FE}-est (p-value)	β_{RE}-est (p-value)
$lntax_{i,t-5}$	1.199[a] (0.000)	1.323[a] (0.000)	1.573[b] (0.014)	1.986[a] (0.007)	0.115 (0.376)	0.234[c] (0.084)
R^2	0.9	0.23	0.96	0.12	0.92	0.06
F-stat (p-value)	26.54[a] (0.000)		67.42[a] (0.000)		33.45[a] (0.000)	
H-m	0.69 (0.405)	0.69 (0.405)	1.24 (0.265)	1.24 (0.265)	2.78[c] (0.095)	2.78[c] (0.095)
BP-stat	126.67[a] (0.000)	126.67[a] (0.000)	157.56[a] (0.000)	157.56[a] (0.000)	145.4[a] (0.000)	145.4[a] (0.000)

Note: Significance Levels: [a] = 1 percent; [b] = 5 percent; [c] = 10 percent. *F-stat* tests for no fixed effects. *H-m* is the Hausman test for random effects. (A non-rejection of the null indicates preferences for random effects model.) *BP-stat* is the Breusch-Pagan test for two-way random effects. (The null is of no random effects).

Table 4.6 Regression results (Regression equation: $lninv_{i,t} = \beta_0 + \beta_1 lngini_{i,t-5} + \varepsilon_t$)

[1]	[2]	[3]	[4]	[5]	[6]	[7]
Dependent variable	lnR&D		lnPat		ln(Pat/R&D)	
Variable	β_{FE}-est (p-value)	β_{RE}-est (p-value)	β_{FE}-est (p-value)	β_{RE}-est (p-value)	B_{FE}-est (p-value)	β_{RE}-est (p-value)
$lngini_{i,t-5}$	−0.936[b]	−1.012[a]	−1.082[b]	−1.467[a]	0.008	−0.085
	(0.022)	(0.003)	(0.031)	(0.009)	(0.917)	(0.409)
R^2	0.89	0.08	0.96	0.04	0.92	0.00
F-stat	21.6[a]		58.74[a]		32.09[a]	
(p-value)	(0.000)		(0.000)		(0.000)	
H-m	0.06	0.06	0.38	0.38	0.74	0.74
	(0804)	(0804)	(0.536)	(0.536)	(0.391)	(0.391)
BP-stat	95.78[a]	95.78[a]	125.07[a]	125[a]	121.39[a]	121.39[a]
	(0.000)	(0.000)	(0.000)	(0.000)	(0.000)	(0.000)

Note: Significance Levels: [a] = 1 percent; [b] = 5 percent; [c] = 10 percent. *F-stat* tests for no fixed effects. *H-m* is the Hausman test for random effects. (A non-rejection of the null indicates preferences for random effects model.) *BP-stat* is the Breusch-Pagan test for two-way random effects. (The null is of no random effects).

the natural log of R&D as a percentage of GDP, *lnR&D*. Columns 4 and 5 provide the fixed effects and random effects estimates for the model where the dependent variable is the natural log of the number of per capita patents, *lnPat*. And finally Columns 6 and 7 provide the fixed-effects and random-effects model estimates, respectively, with the R&D intensity, *ln(Pat/R&D)*, being the dependent variable.

To choose between a fixed-effects approach and a random-effects approach, Jack Johnson and John DiNardo (1997, p.403)[10] note that in datasets such as this, it is preferable to use a fixed-effects model even if the Hausman test statistic turns out to be insignificant. On the other hand, Robert Barro (2000)[11] prefers a random effects model to a fixed-effects model. He argues that using a fixed-effects approach will filter out the cross-sectional sources of variation among countries. I provide regression results using both a random-effects model and a fixed-effects model. In addition to the Hausman test results, I also provide the Breusch-Pagan test for two-way random effects.

The results present an interesting picture. Using all three measures of innovative activity as dependent variable, *lnR&D*, *lnPat*, and *ln(Pat/R&D)*, I find that formal social safety nets, lagged five years, as measured by $lnssn_{i,t-5}$, have positive significant impact. This is true for five of the six variations of the basic model. In the case of R&D intensity, *ln(Pat/R&D)*, as the dependent variable using a fixed effect model, the coefficient estimate is positive but insignificant. Furthermore, for four out of the six iterations, the coefficient estimates are significant at least at the 5 percent level, with respectable R^2 values.

The implication of these results is that the presence of formal social safety nets indeed increases innovation. This is true whether one measures innovative activities by the amount of real per capita R&D expenditure as a percentage of real per capita GDP, *lnR&D*, by the number of patents, *lnPat*, or by the R&D intensity, *ln(Pat/R&D)*.

As mentioned above, a government may pay for the provision of formal social safety nets with tax revenue. However, taxes add to the costs of production which may lead to a decreased output. One may argue that taxes may also increase the costs of innovative activities as well. This may happen by lowering the amount of funds firms and individuals have at their disposal to invest in R&D. However, as I argued above, it is possible that formal social safety nets provided by tax revenue may have positive externalities which outweigh the costs imposed by higher taxes. To test this hypothesis I run regressions using the three measures of innovative activities as the dependent variables and the total amount of real per capita tax revenue as a percentage of real per capita GDP, *lntax*, as the independent variable. The results are presented in Table 4.5.

Quite interestingly, we find that tax revenues lagged five years, $lntax_{i,t-5}$, have a positive significant impact on innovative activities. Except in the case where the dependent variable is R&D intensity, the coefficient estimates are significant at least at the 5 percent level. In the model where the dependent variable is R&D intensity, $ln(Pat/R\&D)$, the coefficient estimate using the fixed effect model is positive but insignificant, and using the random effects model it is positive significant at the 10 percent level. Furthermore, as compared with the results in Table 4.4, where the independent variable measures formal social safety nets, $lnssn_{i,t-5}$, the magnitude of estimates is larger with relatively higher R^2 values.

The implication of these results is that contrary to the common belief that taxes may make an economy less innovative, we find that, at least for this dataset and this time period, this is not the case. The five-year lagged impact of taxes is an increase in innovative activity. This may be due to the positive externalities associated with the government services provided by the tax revenues.

Next I provide results using income inequality, as measured by the natural log of the Gini coefficient lagged five years, $lngini_{i,t-5}$, as the right-hand-side variable. The results are presented in Table 4.6.

The results indicate that inequality of income, indeed, has a negative impact on innovative activities. The coefficient estimates are negative and significant at least at the 5 percent significance level, except in models where the innovative activities are measured as R&D intensity, $ln(Pat/R\&D)$—Column 6 and Column 7. The R^2 values are also respectable by conventional standards. In models where the dependent variable is R&D intensity, the coefficient estimate using the fixed-effects model is positive but insignificant, and the coefficient estimate using the random-effects model is negative but insignificant.

The implication of these results is that the argument against policies which tend to equalize income distribution may not be valid. A relatively equal income distribution may not lead to the erosion of incentives as conventional wisdom would have it, at least not to the point where the negative effects of a relatively equally distributed income outweigh the beneficial effects.

So far I have presented and discussed results using the simplest forms of the model where there is only one right-hand-side variable. Now I provide regression estimates of the effect of formal social safety nets on innovative activities after controlling for taxes and income inequality. The results in Table 4.7 are after controlling for taxes, and the results in Table 4.8 are after controlling for income inequality. Then finally I control for both taxes and income inequality in the same model. These results are presented in Table 4.9. Again, the

Table 4.7 Regression results (Regression equation: $lninv_{i,t} = \beta_0 + \beta_1 lnssn_{i,t-5} + \beta_2 lntax_{i,t-5} + \varepsilon_t$)

[1]	[2]	[3]	[4]	[5]	[6]	[7]
Dependent variable	lnR&D		lnPat		ln(Pat/R&D)	
Variable	β_{FE}-est (p-value)	β_{RE}-est (p-value)	β_{FE}-est (p-value)	β_{RE}-est (p-value)	β_{FE}-est (p-value)	β_{RE}-est (p-value)
$lnssn_{i,t-5}$	−0.071 (0.653)	0.112 (0.548)	0.529 (0.161)	0.771[c] (0.083)	0.156[c] (0.076)	0.202[b] (0.012)
$lntax_{i,t-5}$	1.263[a] (0.001)	1.222[a] (0.001)	1.094[b] (0.049)	1.332[b] (0.042)	−0.026 (0.763)	0.05 (0.586)
R^2	0.9	0.24	0.96	0.17	0.93	0.18
F-stat (p-value)	25.59[a] (0.000)		63.06[a] (0.000)		32.03[a] (0.000)	
H-m		3.14 (0.208)		0.69 (0.408)		0.73 (0.392)
BP-stat	126.53[a] (0.000)	126.53[a] (0.000)	157.99[a] (0.000)	157.99[a] (0.000)	145.46[a] (0.000)	145.46[a] (0.000)

Note: Significance Levels: [a] = 1 percent; [b] = 5 percent; [c] = 10 percent. *F-stat* tests for no fixed effects. *H-m* is the Hausman test for random effects. *BP-stat* is the Breusch-Pagan test for two-way random effects. (The null is of no random effects for random effects model.) A non-rejection of the null indicates preferences for random effects model.) A non-rejection of the null indicates preferences for random effects model. (The null is of no random effects).

Table 4.8 Regression results (Regression equation: $lninv_{i,t} = \beta_0 + \beta_1 lnssn_{i,t-5} + \beta_2 lngini_{i,t-5} + \varepsilon_{i,t}$)

[1]	[2]	[3]	[4]	[5]	[6]	[7]
Dependent variable	lnR&D		lnPat		ln(Pat/R&D)	
Variable	β_{FE}-est (p-value)	β_{RE}-est (p-value)	β_{FE}-est (p-value)	β_{RE}-est (p-value)	β_{FE}-est (p-value)	β_{RE}-est (p-value)
$lnssn_{i,t-5}$	0.269[b] (0.048)	0.393[b] (0.024)	0.82[b] (0.039)	1.109[b] (0.018)	0.149 (0.109)	0.224[a] (0.006)
$lngini_{i,t-5}$	−0.905[b] (0.027)	−0.768[b] (0.023)	−0.985[c] (0.057)	−1.027[c] (0.059)	0.026 (0.762)	0.023 (0.803)
R^2	0.89	0.12	0.96	0.14	0.93	0.19
F-stat (p-value)	21.34[a] (0.000)		58.52[a] (0.000)		31.04[a] (0.000)	
H-m	2.21 (0.331)		0.00 (0.944)		0.00 (0.977)	
BP-stat (p-value)	107.62[a] (0.000)		147.5[a] (0.000)		142.07[a] (0.000)	

Note: Significance Levels: [a] = 1 percent; [b] = 5 percent; [c] = 10 percent. *F-stat* tests for no fixed effects. *H-m* is the Hausman test for random effects. (A non-rejection of the null indicates preferences for random effects model.) *BP-stat* is the Breusch-Pagan test for two-way random effects. (The null is of no random effects).

Table 4.9 Regression results (Regression equation: $lninv_{i,t} = \beta_0 + \beta_1 lnssn_{i,t-5} + \beta_2 lntax_{i,t-5} + \beta_3 lngini_{i,t-5} + \varepsilon_{i,t}$)

[1]	[2]	[3]	[4]	[5]	[6]	[7]
Dependent variable	$ln R\&D$		$ln Pat$		$ln(Pat/R\&D)$	
Variable	β_{FE}-est (p-value)	β_{RE}-est (p-value)	β_{FE}-est (p-value)	β_{RE}-est (p-value)	β_{FE}-est (p-value)	β_{RE}-est (p-value)
$lnssn_{i,t-5}$	−0.057 (0.702)	0.093 (0.621)	0.546 (0.144)	0.789[c] (0.077)	0.155[c] (0.076)	0.203[a] (0.009)
$lntax_{i,t-5}$	1.161[a] (0.002)	1.106[a] (0.004)	0.974[c] (0.081)	1.204[c] (0.064)	−0.023 (0.8)	0.063 (0.484)
$lngini_{i,t-5}$	−0.68[c] (0.068)	−0.353 (0.281)	−0.796 (0.132)	−0.666 (0.193)	0.022 (0.808)	0.039 (0.663)
R^2	0.91	0.22	0.96	0.18	0.93	0.2
F-stat (p-value)	24.23[a] (0.000)		58.08[a] (0.000)		30.05[a] (0.000)	
H-m	4.02 (0.259)	4.02 (0.259)	0.51 (0.777)	0.51 (0.777)	0.85 (0.654)	0.85 (0.654)
BP-stat	103.82[a] (0.000)	103.82[a] (0.000)	137.00[a] (0.000)	137.00[a] (0.000)	135.51[a] (0.000)	135.51[a] (0.000)

Note: Significance Levels: [a] = 1 percent; [b] = 5 percent; [c] = 10 percent. *F-stat* tests for no fixed effects. *H-m* is the Hausman test for random effects. (A non-rejection of the null indicates preferences for random effects model.) *BP-stat* is the Breusch-Pagan test for two-way random effects. (The null is of no random effects).

layouts of these tables are the same at those of Tables 4.4 through 4.6, except for the changes in the right-hand-side variables.

Looking at the results presented in Table 4.7, a few points jump out. One, when the dependent variable is *lnR&D*, and when the dependent variable is *lnPat* in the case of the fixed-effects model, the coefficient estimates for the formal social safety nets variable, *lnssn*$_{i,t-5}$, become insignificant. The coefficient estimate of *lnssn*$_{i,t-5}$ is negative and insignificant when the dependent variable is *lnR&D* and the estimation is performed using a fixed-effects model—Column 2. However, the coefficient estimates for *lnssn*$_{i,t-5}$ stay significant when the dependent variable is either *lnPat* (using the random-effects model) or *ln(Pat/R&D)*, at least at the 10 percent levels. The coefficient estimate of *lnssn*$_{i,t-5}$ is positive and significant at the 5 percent level using a random-effects estimation procedure—Column 7.

Second, the coefficient estimates of the tax variable, *lntax*$_{i,t-5}$, remain significant at least at the 5 percent level with relatively large magnitudes when the dependent variable is either *lnR&D* or *lnPat*. The coefficient estimate of *lntax*$_{i,t-5}$ become insignificant when the dependent variable is R&D intensity, *ln(Pat/R&D)*, with a negative insignificant estimate using the fixed-effects model and a positive insignificant estimate using the random-effects model.

The implications of these results in most estimations is that formal social safety nets have a positive impact on innovative activities even after we control for taxes; and that taxes have a positive impact on innoative activities even after we control for expenditure on formal social safety nets. These positive impacts may be due to the positive externalities, as discussed earlier. The R^2 stats are relatively high for all estimations.

In Table 4.8 I provide coefficient estimates of the impact of formal social safety nets on innovative activities after controlling for income inequality as measured by the natural log of the Gini coefficient, *lngini*$_{i,t-5}$.

Once again we find that formal social safety nets have a positive impact on innovation. The coefficient estimates for *lnssn*$_{i,t-5}$ are positive and significant at least at the 5 percent level, except when the dependent variable is R&D intensity and the estimation method is fixed-effects model—Column 6. In this case the coefficient estimate is positive but insignificant.

In four out of the six models, the coefficient estimates of *lngini*$_{i,t-5}$, which measure the effects of income inequality with a five-year lag is negative and significant at least at the 10 percent level. The coefficient estimates of *lngini*$_{i,t-5}$ are negative and significant at the 5 percent level when the dependent variable is *lnR&D*—Columns 2 and 3. In the remaining two models, where the dependent variable is R&D intensity, *ln(Pat/R&D)*, the coefficient estimate of *lngini*$_{i,t-5}$ is positive but insignificant. Again, contrary to the contention that a country needs inequality of income to create incentive, the implication of these results is that inequality of income does not bode well for innovation.

Next, in Table 4.9, I present regression results of the "full" model where all three variables, $lnssn_{i,t-5}$, $lntax_{i,t-5}$, and $lngini_{i,t-5}$ are included in the model, Equation (1).

Using the full model I find that out of the six estimations, coefficient estimates for $lnssn_{i,t-5}$, the term used to measure formal social safety nets, three estimations carry a positive significant estimate. The coefficient estimate is significant at the 5 percent level in one estimation—random-effects model using R&D intensity, $ln(Pat/R\&D)$, as the dependent variable, under Column 7—and it is significant at the 10 percent level in the remaining two estimations—fixed-effects model using R&D intensity, $ln(Pat/R\&D)$, as the dependent variable—Column 6—and random-effects model when the dependent variable is the natural log of the number of per capita patents, $lnPat$—Column 5.

The coefficient estimates of the tax variable, $lntax_{i,t-5}$, are positive significant in four out of the six estimations. The coefficient estimate is positive and significant at the 1 percent level when the dependent variable is natural log of per capita real R&D expenditure as a percentage of per capita real GDP, $lnR\&D$. This is true whether one uses the fixed-effects model or the random-effects model, Column 2 and Column 3, respectively. The coefficient estimate of $lntax_{i,t-5}$ is positive significant at the 10 percent level when the dependent variable is the natural log of the number of per capita patents, $lnPat$. The significance level stays the same in both the fixed-effects model as well as the random-effects model, Column 4 and Column 5, respectively.

Using the full model, the coefficient estimate of $lngini_{i,t-5}$, the variable measuring income inequality, is negative and significant in only one estimation. It is negative and significant when the dependent variable is natural log of per capita real R&D expenditure as a percentage of per capita real GDP, $lnR\&D$, and the estimation is performed using the fixed-effects approach—Column [2]. Furthermore, the significance level is only 10 percent. The R^2 values in all the estimations are rather large by conventional standards, indicating a good fit of the model.

As can be seen by comparing the results presented in Table 4.9 with those presented in Table 4.4 through Table 4.8, the strength of the results as measured by the significance levels of the estimates in Table 4.9 where all three variables are included in the model, has dropped. What explains the change in the significance levels of coefficient estimates? I will suggest that the reason for drop in significance levels is the strength of correlations between the right-hand-side variable—$lnssn$, $lntax$, and $lngini$.

Refer to Table 4.3 where I present the Pearson correlation coefficient estimates. Note that the estimate of correlation between *lnssn* and *lntax* is positive, with a value of 0.834. The correlation coefficient estimate between *lnssn* and *lngini* is –0.573, and the correlation coefficient estimate between *lntax* and *lngini* is –0.678. All these estimates are significant at the 1 percent level, and the magnitude of the estimates indicates a close fit. I argue that the drop in the significance level in the regression coefficient estimates is due to the presence of high correlations between the right-hand-side variables, and not due to the lack of the hypothesized relationship between innovative activities and formal social safety nets, innovative activities and taxes, and innovative activities and income inequality.

4.3. Chapter Summary

In this chapter I have provided an empirical evidence of the positive impact of formal social safety nets on innovative activities. This positive impact of formal social safety nets may be due the positive externalities which formal social safety nets may carry. Given that engaging in innovative activities is a risky endeavor with uncertain outcomes, formal social safety nets may be thought of as insurance against unfavorable outcomes of innovative activities. Society pays the insurance premium in the form of higher taxes and reaps the benefits of innovation in the form of increased economic growth and development.

The results also show, that contrary to the conventional wisdom, taxes do not have a negative impact on innovative activities. I have also shown that innovative activities are affected negatively by income inequality. The last two results—a positive impact of taxes and a negative impact of income inequality—need further explanations. I take up this discussion in the next three chapters. In chapters 5 and 6, I delve deeper into the issues of income distribution and poverty. In Chapter 7, I take up the discussion about taxes.

CHAPTER 5

Income Distribution and Economic Growth and Development

I n this chapter, after providing definitions of basic concepts, I talk about some of the factors that may affect income distribution. I discuss the roles of historical, political, and social factors in determining income distribution. Then I turn to the links between income distribution and economic growth. The final section concludes the chapter.

5.1. Meaning of Income Distribution: Some Concepts

What does income distribution mean? Before we answer this question, it will be instructive to understand the meaning of "income." In common vernacular, by income one means the earnings one gets for whatever she/he produces, be it goods or services. When we think of income, we think in monetary terms. For instance, if individual A earns, say, $50,000 per year, we will say that his/her income is, well, $50,000 per year. To make more sense of this statement that individual A's income is $50,000 per year, we need to go back to Chapter 2.

Recall from Chapter 2 that for an asset to be called "money," it has to have three basic characteristics. To refresh our memories, these are: (1) A Medium of Exchange, (2) A Unit of Account, and (3) A Store of Value. In saying that the individual has an income of $50,000 per year, we are using the "Unit of Account" characteristic. The individual produced certain amount of goods and services during the year and those goods and services were considered to be worth $50,000. If the individual, then, accepts $50,000 for those goods and services—exchanges goods and services for $50,000—we are using the "Medium of Exchange" characteristic. If the individual takes those $50,000 and puts them in a bank (or under a mattress, for that matter) to be used at a later date, she/he is using money as a "Store of Value." She/he is transferring the purchasing power of what she/he produced from one time period to another.

Economists distinguish between "real" income and "nominal" income. By real income we mean the actual amount of goods and services that can be bought with the paycheck. Nominal income, on the other hand, refers to the earnings in monetary terms. That is, the amount on the paycheck. Changes in income are measured accordingly. Suppose that the individual in our example earned $50,000 during 2011, and she/he could purchase two cars of a given quality/brand during 2011, with nothing left over. She/he earned $55,000 during 2012, and she/he could, again, purchase two cars of the same quality/brand, and again with nothing left over. While her/his nominal income increased from $50,000 in 2011 to $55,000 in 2012, her/his real income stayed the same: the number of cars purchased has not changed. The change in nominal income is just enough to compensate for the change in car prices.

What really matters, then, is the amount of goods and services one can purchase with one's earnings, and not the zeros in the paycheck. This leads to another point: In economics, "income" and "output" refer to the same concept. Economists use income and output as synonyms. This is an important point, and it will become handy when we discuss income (or output) of a country and income distribution.

While we are discussing real versus nominal, another point worth mentioning is the meaning of "constant" dollars (or euros, or pesos, or renminbies, etc.). One often hears or reads income/output mentioned in, say, 2005 "constant" dollars. What it means is the output evaluated in prices, which prevailed in 2005. We do this so that we can compare the amount of output produced during different years. This conversion takes out the impact of changes in prices—it "corrects" for inflation. In fact, we encountered "inflation corrected" output in Chapter 4 and elsewhere earlier in the book.

The total output or income that a country produces is called national income or output. One measure of output is gross domestic product (GDP).[1] Take a specific example: During 2012 the nominal GDP of the United States was over 15 trillion dollars—more accurately, $15,684.8 billion.[2] It was over 13 trillion in 2005 chained dollars—$13,593.2 billion to be more accurate.[3]

How was this income or output distributed among the residents of the United States during 2012? I turn to this topic next.

The Bureau of Economic Analysis (BEA), a federal agency that collects data, among a whole host of other variables, on the total output in the United States, reported that during 2012, the after-tax income, corrected for inflation and divided by the population, was $32,841.[4] This is the so-called real disposable per capita income. This, however, may be a bit misleading since the output or income is not equally distributed among all residents of a country. Let's take a few examples to drive home this point.

John H. Hammergren, the chief executive officer (CEO) of McKesson, a biotechnology company, earned $131.19 million during 2012.[5] Ralph Lauren, the CEO of eponymous cosmetics company, earned $66.65 million during 2012. Jamie Dimon, the CEO of JP Morgan Chase & Co., earned 41.99 million during 2012. He was ranked number 12th. These compensations included salary, bonuses, value of stock options, and so on.[6]

According to the website "Baseball Player Salaries," New York Yankee's player Alex Rodriguez's salary during 2013 was $28,000,000, followed by New York Met's Johan Santa, who earned $25,500,000.[7] I will leave it to the reader to check other players' salaries.

The US Census Bureau is a federal agency that collects data on a number of variables about the US economy and people.[8] According this source, the mean household income for the lowest quintile during 2010, the latest year for which these measures are available, was $11,034, and the mean household income for the top quintile during 2010 was $169,633.[9] Compare the $131.19 million compensation of Mr. Hammergren, CEO of McKesson, during 2012 with the mean income of $11,034 earned by a typical individual in the lowest quintile during 2011.

Mr. Hammergren made about 11,889.6 times the income of a typical individual in the bottom quintile. Looked at it another way, total personal income in the United States during 2012 was $13,431.1 billion (current dollars), and total population during 2012 (mid-period) was 314,278 thousand. If the total personal income were divided equally among all the individuals, it would be around $42,737 (current dollars). This is called "per capita" personal income. By this measure, Mr. Hammergren made about 3,069.7 times the per capita personal income.

Quite a difference! Wouldn't you say?

(Note that the BEA provides various measures of income. These include Gross Domestic Product, Gross National Product, Net National Product, National Income, and Personal Income (all in terms of nominal, or current dollar, as well as real, or constant dollar). Curious reader may also want to visit the bureau's website to learn about the rationale for these various measures as well as the methodology.[10])

Economists have developed several formal measures to estimate how proportionately, or disproportionately, income is distributed. These include the Gini coefficient, the Mean Logarithmic Deviation of Income (MLD), the Theil Index, and the Atkinson Index.[11] For instance, the Gini coefficient ranges between the value of 0, perfect equality where everyone gets equal share of national output or income, and 1, perfect inequality where only one unit

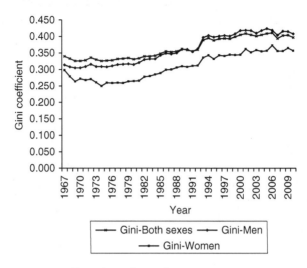

Figure 5.1   US Gini coefficients by sex from 1967 to 2010

Source: US Census Bureau, table IE-2: Measures of individual earnings inequality for full-time year-round workers by sex.

(individual, household, group of individuals) gets all the output or income. Perhaps Gini coefficient is the most commonly used measure of income distribution. So while discussing income distribution, I will primarily use Gini coefficient in this chapter. By the way, recall that I used Gini coefficient while conducting empirical analysis in Chapter 4 as well.

What does the profile of income distribution look like for the United States? In Figure 5.1, I plot Gini coefficient data published by the US Census Bureau from 1967 to 2010.[12] This figure, by way of comparison, also plots Gini coefficient data for men and women separately.

A few points need highlighting. One, throughout the late 1960s and early 1970s, income inequality, as measured by the Gini coefficient, declined and remained low up until the early 1980s. By the MLD measure (not plotted in this figure), however, income inequality started to increase around the mid-1970s.[13] The increase in income inequality during the 1980s shows up in both the Gini coefficient and the MLD. The US Census Bureau's analysis report, *The Changing Shape of the Nation's Income Distribution*, which came out in June 2000, reported that the Gini coefficient increased by 5.5 percent and the MLD increased by 10.9 percent between 1980 and 1986.[14] This report also pointed out that from 1973 to 1992, income inequality rose steadily; the Gini coefficient rose by 9.3 percent, and the MLD rose by

17.2 percent during this period.[15] After a visible jump around 1991–1992, the upward trend was dampened during the rest of the 1990s.

Second, high income inequality seems to have been a permanent feature of the US economy, especially since the 2000s. And lastly, income inequality is higher for men than it is for women through this time period. This difference became more pronounced around 1991–1992, and has been thus since then.

Another point worth mentioning is that while income inequality as measured by the Gini coefficient for women has been relatively lower as compared with their male counterparts, women earn only about 77 percent as compared with men. According to the US Census data, during 2011, female median annual earning was $37,118, while male median annual earning was $48,202. These data are for earnings of full-time year-round workers, 15 years or older.[16]

How does income inequality in the United States compare with rest of the developed world? In Figure 5.2, I plot Gini coefficient data for 25 Organization for Economic Co-operation and Development (OECD) countries for 2009.[17] These coefficients are calculated using after-tax and transfer income data.

Using these data (and definitions) for 2009, the United States ranks somewhere closer to the upper bound with a value of 0.379. The highest value of the Gini coefficient is 0.471 (Mexico) and the lowest value is 0.238 (Denmark). The median, mean, and mode values are 0.312, 0.311, and 0.331, respectively.

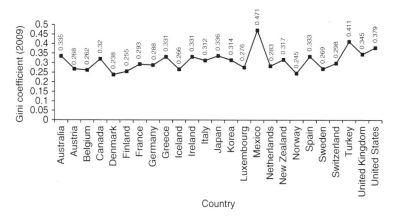

Figure 5.2 Gini coefficient for 25 OECD countries for 2009 (after-tax income)
Source: OECD website (www.oecd.org).

How do taxes affect income distribution? The answer, perhaps not surprisingly, is that taxes dampen income inequality, given that tax system is progressive.[18] The Gini coefficient value, for instance, for the United States for 2009, before taxes is 0.404 (Figure 5.1, both sexes), and after taxes is 0.379 (Figure 5.2). I will discuss this issue in greater detail in Chapter 6.

The purpose of these examples is to show that the total income or output of the United States, or any other country,[19] is not distributed equally. Some individuals get a larger share of the income than others. The question arises then, what determines who gets what? I turn to this question next.

5.2. Factors Affecting Income Distribution in an Economy

Purely from the neoclassical perspective, individuals whose widgets are valued more by the market have higher incomes, and in turn, are able to purchase a bigger share of the total output. The reason that, say, John H. Hammergren, the CEO of McKesson, whose example I cited above, had a compensation of $131.19 million during 2012 is that his skills were worth that much. His employers, the board members, and the shareholders of McKesson thought he was worth the price.

Or the Yankees' management agreed to pay the slugger, Alex Rodriguez, $28 million during 2013 because the management thought that his presence in the team will more than pay for his salary by the tickets, TV, and other revenue sources that will be generated. According to this viewpoint, the "median" male worker who earned $48,202 during 2011 had the skills that were worth only this much. The skills of the "median" female worker were less valuable still—worth only $37,118.

An underlying assumption here is that producers of goods and services do not care about factors other than maximizing profits. All else constant, whichever set of skills maximizes the profits, those skills would carry the highest price, and individuals who have those skills will earn the highest levels of incomes. By this logic, the reason that women earn only 77 percent of their male counterparts is that women's skills are only worth 77 percent of their male counterparts. Mr. Hammergren's widgets are worth over 3,534.4 times the widgets of a median female.

While a good start, this point of view leaves out a number of other factors that have come to light through years of research on labor markets.[20] The quality and the quantity of widgets produced by an individual are not the only determinants of how much income one earns. Just as in other facets of life, individuals are discriminated along racial, gender, religious, and sexual orientation lines. Humans have biases and fears, often because of lack of knowledge about other individuals. Even in the undoubtedly mundane and ordinary activities of commerce and trade, profit is hardly the only factor in human motivation. It would, indeed, be easier to understand and rectify the ill-effects of at least labor market discrimination, if it were so. But it is not. Humans are multidimensional, as the cliché goes. And while this multiplicity of dimensions makes for interesting academic studies, it also makes remedies of the ill-effects of human activities harder to devise and implement. Let's look at some of the factors that have come to light so far.

5.2.1. Historical Factors and Income Distribution

The Industrial Revolution, which started around the mid-eighteenth century, changed the relationship between the worker, the machine, and the output or income.[21] While increased mechanization meant increased output, it also meant a decreased need for workers whose jobs could be performed by machines. That also meant that part of the income that went to workers now went to the owners of the machines. Income distribution changed forever. Skilled workers who had relatively well-paying jobs were not needed anymore.

One such example is that of the workers who were employed in the wool industry in Leeds, England. Once the "Scribbling-Machines" were adopted by firms, workers were out of jobs.[22] These workers were not unskilled. They apprenticed and had learned the trade with great effort. Using the modern vernacular, they were educated workers. Once the machines were able to do the job at a cheaper rate, however, workers were no longer needed. The share of income that wool workers used to get in the form of wages started going to the owners of machines in the form of rent.

The competition between the worker and the machine continues. Increased use of robotics in the auto industry for, say, welding led to a decreased need of welders. With the invention of Automatic Teller Machine (ATM), the need for bank tellers decreased. Increased use of gas pumps, which utilized the "pay at the pump" technology, led to a decreased need for gas station attendants. The adoption of computer technology in the service industry decreased the need for secretarial staff: Taking dictation and typing memos on typewriters nowadays is as quaint as using an abacus to do basic arithmetic calculations.

5.2.2. Economic, Social, and Political Institutions and Income Distribution

That discrimination is present in labor market is a settled question. Research about the US labor market shows that, all else constant, US employers prefer whites over blacks and other racial minorities, males over females, and straights over gays and lesbians.[23]

During June 2000, *The New York Times* published a series of reports under the title "How Race Is Lived in America."[24] These reports highlighted the state of racial relationships in the social, economic, and political arenas. One report focused on how jobs were assigned at a Smithfield slaughterhouse located in Tar Heels, North Carolina.[25] Whether workers were assigned the jobs of killing the animals, or cleaning the floors, or to supervisory positions depended upon the race and ethnicity of the workers.

Discrimination also exists in the output market. The US history is filled with records of how blacks were treated differently than whites at various business establishments. A quick search of the Web shows millions of images of signs indicating the separation of races in public swimming pools, and beaches, and water fountains, and buses, the list goes on. The harrowing story of Ms. Rosa Parks, a distinguished civil rights activist, highlights the nature of race relations in the United States.[26] Indeed, the realization and acceptance of this fact is what led to a number of legislative initiatives. Some of the more influential legislative acts include the Presidential Commission on the Status of Women in 1961, the Equal Pay Act of 1963, Title VII of the Civil Rights Act of 1964, the Executive Order 11375 in 1967, the Executive Order 11478 in 1969, Title IX of the Education Amendments of 1972, and Equal Employment Opportunity Act of 1972 and amendments to the Act. I present a few highlights of these legislative events below.

On December 14, 1961, President John F. Kennedy created a commission to review the status of women in the US labor market.[27] The commission was tasked to review and make recommendations in the following area.

1. Employment policies and practices of the Federal Government.

2. Employment policies and practices, including those on wages, under Federal contracts.

3. Effects of Federal social insurance programs and tax laws on the net earnings and other income of women.

4. Appraisal of Federal and State labor laws dealing with such matters as hours, night work, and wages, to determine whether they are accomplishing the purpose for which they were established and whether they need to be adapted to changing technological, economic, and social conditions.

5. Differences in legal treatment of men and women in regard to political and civil rights, and family relations.

6. New and expanded services that may be required for women as wives, mothers, and workers, including education, counseling, training, home services, and arrangements for care of children during working day.

The commission was chaired by the former first lady, Mrs. Eleanor Roosevelt. Vice Chairman was Dr. Richard A. Lester, a professor of economics at Princeton University. Interestingly, the original document text states "Chairman" as opposed to "Chairwoman" or "Chairperson." Same masculine noun was used for the executive vice chair, even though the seat was filled by a woman, Mrs. Esther Peterson, assistant secretary of Labor. It stated "Executive Vice Chairman."

The Equal Pay Act of 1963 barred wage discrimination on the basis of gender.[28] It noted that

> [n]o employer having employees subject to any provisions of this section shall discriminate, within any establishment in which such employees are employed, between employees on the basis of sex by paying wages to employees in such establishment at a rate less than the rate at which he pays wages to employees of the opposite sex in such establishment for equal work on jobs the performance of which requires equal skill, effort, and responsibility, and which are performed under similar working conditions, except where such payment is made pursuant to (i) a seniority system; (ii) a merit system; (iii) a system which measures earnings by quantity or quality of production; or (iv) a differential based on any other factor other than sex: *Provided* [Italics original], That an employer who is paying a wage rate differential in violation of this subsection shall not, in order to comply with the provisions of this subsection, reduce the wage rate of any employee.
>
> (SEC 206, Subsection d.1)

Title VII of the Civil Rights Act of 1964 prohibited "employment discrimination based on race, color, religion, sex and national origin."[29] There were exceptions though. For instance, firms hiring workers outside of the United States and religious organizations were exempted. The Act

> shall not apply to an employer with respect to the employment of aliens outside any State or to a religious corporation, association, educational institution, or society with respect to the employment of individuals of a particular religion to perform work connected with the carrying on by such corporation, association, educational institution, or society of its activities.
>
> (SEC 2000e-1)

The Executive Order 11376 signed by President Lyndon B. Johnson on October 13, 1967, prohibited gender discrimination in hiring by the federal government and federal contractors. It was amended[30] by the Executive Order 11478, Equal Employment Opportunity in the Federal Government, signed on August 8, 1969. The Executive Order 11478 noted that[31]

> [i]t is the policy of the Government of the United States to provide equal opportunity in Federal employment for all persons, to prohibit discrimination

in employment because of race, color, religion, sex, national origin, handicap, or age, and to promote the full realization of equal employment opportunity through a continuing affirmative program in each executive department and agency. This policy of equal opportunity applies to and must be an integral part of every aspect of personnel policy and practice in the employment, development, advancement, and treatment of civilian employees of the Federal Government.

Title IX of the Education Amendments of 1972 banned gender discrimination in educational institutions receiving federal assistance. It stated:[32]

No person in the United States shall, on the basis of sex, be excluded from participation in, be denied the benefits of, or be subjected to discrimination under any education program or activity receiving Federal financial assistance . . .

Certain organizations, including "Educational institutions of religious organizations with contrary religious tenets," Boy Scouts, Girl Scouts, and so on, were exempted.[33] Equal Employment Opportunity Act of 1972, and later amendments to the Act,[34] opened up opportunities for women and minorities in the labor market.

These acts of legislation have had enormous influence on the US social and economic landscapes. Studies show that racial and ethnic minorities and women have been the beneficiaries.[35] While it is true that women do not need their husbands' signatures to open a bank account or apply for a credit card anymore,[36] women still face significant challenges in the workplace and in life.

On March 1, 2011, the Whitehouse released the findings of a research report on the status of women.[37] The report found that

1. Women have not only caught up with men in college attendance but younger women are now more likely than younger men to have a college or a graduate degree. Women are also working more and the number of women and men in the labor force has nearly equalized in recent years. As women's work has increased, their earnings constitute a growing share of family income.

2. Gains in education and labor force involvement have not yet translated into wage and income equity. At all levels of education, women earned about 75 percent of what their male counterparts earned in 2009. In part because of these lower earnings and in part because unmarried and divorced women are the most likely to have responsibility for raising and supporting their children, women are more likely to be in poverty than men. These economic inequities are even more acute for women of color.

3. Women live longer than men but are more likely to face certain health problems, such as mobility impairments, arthritis, asthma, depression, and obesity.

Women also engage in lower levels of physical activity. Women are less likely than men to suffer from heart disease or diabetes. One out of seven women age 18–64 has no usual source of health care. The share of women in that age range without health insurance has also increased.

4. Women are less likely than in the past to be the target of violent crimes, including homicide. But women are victims of certain crimes, such as intimate partner violence and stalking, at higher rates than men.

Discrimination is also persistent in a number of other avenues. Discriminatory behavior against gays, lesbians, bi-sexual, and transgender Americans is one example of such follies. As I write these pages in the summer of 2013, after intense public pressure, the Boy Scouts of America has revised its policy.[38] According to the news report, starting January 2014, the organization will allow openly gay boys to join the organization. Openly gay adults and leaders, however, will not be allowed in.

Following the Supreme Court's ruling of June 26, 2013, which overturned the key provisions of the 1996 Defense of Marriage Act,[39] on August 29, 2013, the US Treasury Department and the Internal Revenue Service issued a statement that same-sex legally married couples would be allowed the same federal tax benefits as the straight married couples.[40] The ruling applied to legally married same-sex couples regardless of whether or not the state they lived in recognized same-sex marriage. As of late July 2013, there are only 13 states, plus District of Columbia, which recognize same-sex marriage. Indeed, 35 states actively ban same-sex marriage.[41] This means that the same-sex married couples who legally married in states that allowed same-sex marriage and then moved to the latter set of states do not enjoy the state citizenship rights enjoyed by straight married couples.

Whether this discrimination is the artifact of millions of years of evolution and a survival mechanism is an important but separate question. Indeed, scholars have identified several possible reasons for the existence of discrimination against those who "look different."[42] One reason for preferring the "familiar" over the "different" is the trust factor. People not only find "different" less trustworthy but at times even morally reprehensible and "disgusting." This is especially the case when it comes to sexuality and religiosity.[43]

Put yourself in the proverbial shoes of a primitive human ancestor with primitive tools to hunt, to communicate, and to ascertain the situation at hand. Imagine you are out to hunt or gather food and run into another human. If the other human happens to be your sibling, you relax. If, on the other hand, the other human is a stranger, you are on high alert. Why? This is because it is easier to decipher the mood of a sibling—a very familiar face—than to figure out if a stranger—a less familiar face—is happy or angry or "is on to something" or just walking around. It requires fewer mental resources and time in the former than in the latter case. And when survival is at stake, one needs to make such decisions rather quickly. Delay in processing the information can be a matter of life and death.

One quick way to deal with this uncertainty is to trust only those with whom you are familiar—members of your family, your group, your clan, who speak the same language, people who go to the same place of worship and practice the same religion and have same belief systems, and be suspicious of those who are "different." Why is that?

Let's revisit the encounter of our early ancestors from different clans who ran into each other. Given the rudimentary means of figuring out the other's motives, it is a better bet to be on alert and not trust the other. If the other person happens to be harmless, and you have put yourself on high alert for no reason, not much is lost, except momentary high heart rate and emotional distress—a false positive. If, on the other hand, you decided not to be alert and draw your spear, thinking that the other person is harmless, and she/he turns out to have illicit motives, you are out of your luck. Not only have you lost your belongings, but perhaps your life as well—a false negative. The latter is not a good strategy for survival.

Explanations, however, are not justifications!

While we have come a long way, suspicions about the "different" still remain. Just to highlight the point of the distrust of the different, take the example of the voting preferences. One finds a rather vivid snapshot of the attitudes toward the "different." A 2007 *USA Today/Gallup* poll asked the following question.[44]

> *Between now and the 2008 political conventions, there will be discussion about the qualifications of presidential candidates—their education, age, religion, race, and so on. If your party nominated a generally well-qualified person for president who happened to be . . . , would you vote for that person?*

(Italics original)

The survey pointed out that, while attitudes of the American public have been changing over time,[45] divisions remain along the gender, age, religious, racial, ethnic, and sexual orientation dimensions. For instance, while only 4 percent of the respondents said that they would not vote for a Catholic, 5 percent would not vote for an African American, and 7 percent said that they would not vote for a candidate who was Jewish; almost half of the respondents (43 percent) said that they would not vote for an individual who was a homosexual. Atheists were the most unlikely to get the respondents'

Table 5.1   Median weekly earnings by education (Current US dollars)

Year	Less than high school	High school	Some college	Bachelor's degree	Advanced degree
2000	362	505	596	827	1024
2001	382	520	617	858	1061
2002	388	535	629	877	1096
2003	396	554	639	900	1126
2004	401	574	661	916	1153
2005	409	583	670	937	1173
2006	419	595	692	962	1203
2007	428	604	704	987	1236
2008	453	618	722	1012	1287
2009	454	626	726	1025	1328
2010	444	626	734	1038	1351
2011	451	638	739	1053	1346
2012	471	652	749	1066	1373

Source: The Bureau of Labor Statistics (www.bls.gov).

votes: About 53 percent said that they would not vote for someone who was an atheist.[46]

Another factor that may explain earnings differentials is educational attainment. Education has been considered the key to obtaining a middle class living standard. Indeed, data show that there is a positive correlation between educational attainment and earnings. Just by way of an example, Table 5.1 shows median weekly salary data by year and by educational attainment.[47]

While true, there is an irony in all this. The wool workers of the 1780s were educated; they had apprenticed and made effort to learn the skills. The auto workers of the 1950s, 1960s, 1970s, and 1980s had spent time and effort in acquiring the skills. Same was true of the secretarial staff and others who learned the trade through formal vocational training. They made middle class living and sent their off-springs to obtain skills through apprenticeship and formal education so that they would be able to make a comfortable living.

And it worked. Each successive generation enjoyed a relatively better living standard than its predecessor.[48] Technological innovations made life a bit easier. Widespread use of electricity in factories and home meant fewer deaths due to smoke related illnesses. Housewives did not have to toil in front of coal and wood burning stoves. Washing machines could be used to do laundry and air conditioning and heating meant escape from extreme weather conditions. Each successive generation made technological advances and developed machines which made more and better quality widgets.

More and better quality widgets meant higher output and income which was divided between the owners of the machines and those running the machines. To make sure that workers' rights were not overlooked, institutional changes followed in the form of labor unions which bargained on the behalf of member workers. Reasonable working conditions and pay standards were established. It was a delicate balance though. Over time, however, the structure of the economy changed. On the one hand, as more and better machines were being used for production processes, the demand for workers decreased and so did the strength of the unions which bargained on the behalf of workers. On the other hand, the share of production workers in the overall labor force decreased as well, as economies of the developed countries became more and more service oriented. Workers in the service industry were less likely to form unions.[49]

With the increasing share of income came increased political clout. Politicians needed financial support to run for offices. Obviously those who had the financial means were courted, and gained access to the political infrastructure.[50] A couple of recent examples which have come to the fore and garnered national headlines about politicians selling access include former Illinois governor Rod Blagojevich who was convicted of corruption and sentenced to 14 years in prison in 2011,[51] and that of Tom Delay, a Texas congressman who was convicted of money laundering charges.[52] Indeed, the list of politicians selling access to the wealthy for campaign contributions is too long to mention in these pages. The list is so long that several Wikipedia pages have been created by the curious for the curious.[53]

Not surprisingly, as the owners of machines gained more political clout, favorable policies followed. Around the 1980s on both sides of the Atlantic, there was an increased effort to deregulate. Ronald W. Reagan, a Republican, won the presidential election in 1980 and then re-election in 1984.[54] In his first inaugural address he made the famous remark that "Government is not the solution to our problems, government is the problem."[55] He was followed by another Republican, George H. W. Bush, who had served as Vice President in both terms of President Reagan. They both ran on the platform of decreasing the size of the government in the form of decreased regulation and lowered taxes.

On the other side of the Atlantic in Great Britain, Margaret Hilda Thatcher won the election in 1979.[56] A candidate of the Conservative party, she advocated a smaller role of the government and more individual freedom. She led the wave of privatization of state-owned enterprises, reduced regulation in the industrial and financial markets, and championed the free-market capitalism.

The deregulation swept both in the labor as well as the financial markets. Recall that "money" is just a means to exchange goods and services. Goods and services markets and financial markets are very intimately related in a number of arenas. Regulations in the financial market have consequences in the goods and services market, and vice versa. As the twin recessions[57] of 1980 and 1981 brought a sense of urgency, improvement of economic conditions was on the top of political agenda. The owners of machines saw labor unions and their demands as constraints. Because of their increased political access they got their wishes and labor regulations, along with financial regulations, were relaxed.

The fragile balance between the worker and the machine had sifted in favor of the machine. The owners of machines started getting bigger and bigger share of the income, and the generations of workers who had developed better machines in hopes of increasing output and income were never to gain a foothold. And therein lies the irony: workers who added to the pool of knowledge and built better machines lost to the very machines. Figure 5.3 plots quarterly data on employment, output per hour, and real compensation per hour of manufacturing workers since 1987.

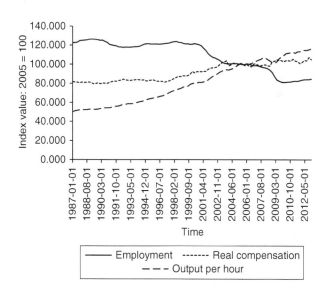

Figure 5.3 Manufacturing sector employment, output per hour, and real compensation per hour[58]

A few points stand out. First, while the overall level of employment (solid line) was relatively stable up until around 2000, it started to decline in early 2000s and fell precipitously during the Great Recession, which started in 2007. While the decline ended around 2009, the recovery has been minimal.

Second, the output per hour (broken line) has been increasing throughout this time period, but real compensation per hour (line represented by dashes) has not kept pace. Indeed, output per hour surpassed real compensation per hour around 2000. This second fact indicates that the share of output that a manufacturing worker can purchase with his/her income or output has been declining.

So far I have shown evidence of the changing shape of the income distribution. I have shown that income has been becoming more and more unequally distributed in the United States and elsewhere. I have also pointed to some of the reasons behind this worsening of income distribution. The question arises: So what? How does the worsening of income distribution affect economic growth over time? Now I turn to this question.

5.3. Evidence of Links between Income Distribution and Economic Growth

Imagine two countries with two different economic systems. Call them Countries A and B. For the ease of exposition, assume that these are the only two countries in the world, and that this is year zero. Both countries have the same aggregate output, same population size, same land area, same environmental factors, and so on. Everything is the same except that Country A divides its output equally among its residents. In Country A, everyone is equally well-fed, well-housed, well-clothed, well-educated, and well-cared for—a picture of egalitarianism. After feeding, housing, educating, and caring for its residents, Country A saves whatever is left over from consumption and build factories, roads, and other infrastructure, and invests in research and development, which adds to its pool of knowledge in expectation that the future consumption of its residents will increase.

In Country B, on the other hand, there is disparity. Output is not equally distributed among its residents. Some residents have a lot, whereas others can barely make their ends meet. There are "haves" and "have-nots." The haves consume to their hearts' content and still have plenty left over with which they build factories, roads, and other infrastructure, and invest in research and development, increasing their pool of knowledge, in hopes of increasing their future consumption.

Because of the differences in how income is divided among the residents of the two countries, Country A has relatively less left over after consumption as compared with Country B. In Country B, while the haves consume a lot more than their fellow residents, the have-nots, as well as more than the residents of Country A, there is only so much that can be consumed.[59] The "per capita" consumption in Country A is higher than that of Country B. As a result Country A has fewer total resources to build factories, and infrastructure, and invest in research and development.

You may ask: why can't Country A consume the way it does and still have the same resources left for building factories and infrastructure? Economists use the term "opportunity cost" to explain this phenomenon. We encountered the concept of opportunity cost briefly while discussing comparative advantage in Chapter 2. Since this is an important and often misunderstood concept, perhaps a bit more explanation is in order.

5.3.1. The Concept of Opportunity Cost Revisited

As we saw in Chapter 2, opportunity cost is defined as "what we give up to get something" or more precisely "the next best alternative forgone." The reason that opportunity cost exists is that resources are limited. Economists use the term "scarcity" to represent this limit on resources. An *accurate price* of a good or a service represents the true nature of its scarcity. In that case, if the resources are not sitting idle, we have to give up, part or all of, one thing to get something else.

To be even more precise, a product is scarce if it carries a price; it isn't scarce if it does not carry a price. Gas was scarce when the price was sometime in the past, say, ten cents per gallon, and it is scarce, now when the price is $3.272.[60] By this definition, the use of word "scarcer" to express a product becoming "expensive" is not exactly *kosher*. When one wants to express that a product has become expensive, one may say that its opportunity cost has increased. This is not to say that the word "scarcer" is not used at all by economist. Indeed, one finds "scarcer" used to express a product becoming expensive even in formal writings in the discipline.

Note the phrase "accurate price." By this we mean that the total opportunity cost is taken into account. If I buy a widget I am the one who is paying the full price, and no one else is picking the tab, in part or the whole. That is, there aren't any externalities, positive or negative. The concept of externalities is an important one. I will expand on this point shortly. Now back to opportunity cost.

I am writing these pages sitting on my desk which sits next to the window. As I look outside, it seems like a nice day. I could be riding my bicycle and enjoying the weather. I am, however, sitting inside and writing. In economic terms, the opportunity cost of writing these pages is enjoying a nice bicycle ride. I am giving up riding my bicycle in a nice weather. Why am I giving up a leisurely bicycle ride for working? I am doing this in hopes of getting this book published which will bring me professional accolades and perhaps some income as well. I am making a tradeoff. As individuals we make these tradeoffs all the time. When we save we give up present consumption for expected higher future consumption.

Firms and countries make similar tradeoffs. A firm may use its resources for research and development instead of production to have higher expected future production. A country may engage in research and development by diverting resources from the production of goods and services, in hopes of higher expected future production, and as a result, higher future consumption for its residents. In this case the opportunity cost of engaging in research and development is forgone current production of goods and services which the country could have produced using the resources now engaged in research and development. A country may also engage in the production of, say, military hardware in hopes of global dominance, and give up production of goods and services which its residents may be able to consume. Here the opportunity cost of gaining military power is the forgone current consumption. North Korea represents a vivid example of this phenomenon.

The question arises: In the long run which country is better off—Country A or Country B? In other words: Is equality conducive to economic growth? This is an empirical question. Economic theory does not have a definitive answer. There are economic, political, social, and philosophical dimensions to be considered. While Country B, in aggregate, will have a higher level of resources to invest in the factories, infrastructure, and knowledge, only a few will benefit from most of the development. Country B may have a larger portion of the population which is dissatisfied. This may lead to social unrest and political instability, which, in turn may lead to lower investment and lower subsequent output. In this case, while initially there was an abundance of resources to build factories and infrastructure which could increase output, the political and social climate did not allow for the investment to take place.

Not only that, even if the haves in Country B are able to produce a large amount of goods and services, they may run into an upper limit of what they can consume themselves. (For the sake of simplicity, assume that Country B could not sell its output to Country A's residents.) That is, aggregate demand may not be able to support what the haves are capable of producing. Remember most of the residents of Country B are barely making their ends meet. The majority cannot afford to buy what the haves produce. Eventually the need for more factories, roads, and other infrastructure may not be there. Indeed, even existing factories may be sitting idle.

Country A may face an incentive problem. In Country A, since everyone is relatively well-housed, well-fed, well-clothed, well-educated, and well-cared for, they may lack the incentive to work harder. The number of free-riders may overtake the number of people who contribute to the society their fair share. Social calm may lead to complacency at the national level, which may become the cause of decline.

On the other hand, since all residents of Country A can afford to purchase what it produces, the country's economy may be chugging along. That is, there is enough aggregate demand. Factories and other resources are not sitting idle. With education being more widespread in Country A, the overall pool of knowledge keeps on increasing, leading to broader and better understanding of "how things work." This increased understanding will improve production processes leading to more and better widgets for all. The living standard of an average resident in County A improves. Granted it may not be as high as the haves of Country B, but still a lot higher than the have-nots of Country B.

As the above scenario suggests, empirical evidence is needed to have a conclusive answer. So what do empirical studies suggest? Perhaps not surprisingly, the results depend upon the dataset analyzed, the time period considered, and the question asked.

For instance, Alberto Alesina and Roberto Perotti (1996) ask whether income distribution affect political instability, and in turn, whether political instability affects investment.[61] To answer these questions they use data from 1960 to 1985 for 71 countries. Their answer to both questions is "yes." They find that income inequality leads to political instability, which in turn adversely affects investment, leading to a decline in economic growth. They show that the results are statistically and economically significant.

Torsten Persson and Guido Tabellini (1994)[62] also found a negative impact of income inequality on economic growth. So did Grigor Sukiassyan (2007)[63] using data for "transition economies." Avner Greif and Murat Iyigun (2013)[64] looked at the impact of "Old Poor Laws" of 1601–1834. They argue that these laws were one of the major forces behind the economic development of England and the Industrial Revolution. (We will revisit Poor Laws in Chapter 6 where I discuss the role of formal social safety nets in alleviating poverty.)

Robert J. Barro (2000)[65] asked whether the effects of income inequality are dependent on the stages of economic development, and if so, which direction it might take. He found that the impacts of income inequality in rich versus poor countries differ. Rich countries benefit from income inequality when it comes to economic growth. In poor countries, however, income inequality retards economic growth.

Similar answers were found by Marta Bengoa and Blanca Sanchez-Robles (2005).[66] They found that

> ...first, the link equality-growth seems to change at the various stages of development. When a country has a low level of income, more equality will enhance growth by reducing sociopolitical unrest and institutional instability. For rich countries, instead, more equality may damage growth since it desincentivates the undertaking of risky projects by individuals. In addition, the social payments provided by the State to reduce inequality reduce the amount of resources that are available for investment in productive capital, thus affecting growth negatively. (p.483)

My own research, which I presented in Chapter 4, pointed to a detrimental effect of inequality on innovation. And since innovation is one of the key ingredients of the economic-growth recipe, lower innovation may lead to lower economic growth. Recall that in my empirical research I used data for the 19 countries which are members of the Organization for Economic Co-operation and Development. These countries fall in the rich category of countries.

The studies listed here barely scratch the surface of the vast and rich terrain on this topic. I have tried to present a (small) cross-section of the research which, I hope, captures an accurate picture. The evidence so far, of the link between inequality and economic growth is state-dependent. This is understandable. We want to understand a rather complex issue: how income distribution may affect economic growth. Not only economic growth is a long-run phenomenon, the factors which affect it are numerous. It is quite possible that some of the factors not only affect directly but also through other factors and with a considerable delay. And isolating the effects of various factors takes time and patience. Income distribution can shape social and political landscape which in turn can affect the formulation and functioning of social, political, and economic institutions, which in turn may affect economic growth with a lag of hundreds, if not thousands, of years.[67] As more data become available, empirical research follows. Some questions are answered and new questions arise, which, in turn, require more data. This is the nature of empirical research.

This inconclusive nature of the evidence, however, should not lead one to conclude that inequality of income, of any magnitude, in any state, and always is harmless. Far from it. Inequality has its price, as pointed out recently by Joseph Stiglitz in his book *The Price of Inequality*.[68] A poverty level which hinders one's ability to participate in social and economic activities can hardly be considered desirable. What Adam Smith 1776 (2010)[69] called "necessaries" of life; John Rawls (1973)[70] called "primary goods"; and Amartya Sen

(1999)[71] called "instrumental freedoms"; are needed for societies to thrive. (We will revisit these authors and these concepts in Chapter 6.)

5.3.2. Externalities and the Markets

Let me now turn to the question of externalities and how the presence of externalities may affect the functioning of markets. Externalities may be positive or negative. A positive externality will exist if the by-standers benefit from an activity taking place. An example may include my neighbor spending time and effort maintaining her yard and planting flowers. I enjoy the well-maintained yard by my neighbor, without having been engaged in the activity. That is, without having to spend time and effort to maintain the yard, not to mention money spent on buying flowers, shrubs, and other paraphernalia (the total price of having a beautiful yard).

By the same token, a negative externality will exist if by-standers' wellbeing is affected negatively from an activity. One may own a dog (with issues), who barks all the time. The owner of the dog benefits from the dog's presence as potential burglars avoid the house. He does not mind the noise due to, perhaps, being a fan of punk rock, or having a faulty hearing aid. The neighbor's peace, however, is destroyed. She has to wear noise cancelling headphones. She is the one who is paying part of the price of her neighbor owning the dog.

At the risk of belaboring, let's continue using the trite example of my enjoying my neighbor's yard without contributing to the upkeep, and see what other points we can make. Recall a term used earlier in this book to refer to a situation where one is taking advantage of a good or service without paying for it is called "free-riding." It would be nice, from her point of view, if I chipped in, at least equivalent to the "amount" of my visual satisfaction. Or perhaps she could stop me from enjoying the immaculately maintained yard. In this particular example, it is of course hard, if not impossible, for my neighbor to keep me from enjoying the yard. Some may argue that it is quite likely that she gets satisfaction when her neighbors admire her beautiful yard, so why would she want you to stop enjoying it in the first place?

This is true. However, my free-riding may have consequences. It is quite likely that since I get the required dose of visual satisfaction by looking at her yard, I let my yard deteriorate. I let bushes grow and weeds spread. Weeds spread, not only in my yard they also spread into my neighbor's yard as well. (Weeds tend to have a rather poor sense of neighborly boundaries.) My neighbor has to do extra work to keep her yard weed-free. On the one hand, this leads to increased effort on her part, and on the other hand, when she looks at my overgrown and un-kept yard, her enjoyment decreases. My neighbor may come to the conclusion that given her extra cost in terms of effort and time and her decreased enjoyment due to my poor yard maintenance, it is not worth maintaining her yard either. For a while I might have gotten away without putting in my fair share, it did not last long. Due to my poor neighborliness, not only did the whole neighborhood suffer, others who might have walked by and enjoyed the view suffer as well. A more formal way to explain my neighbor's decision not to maintain her yard is to say, using the economics terminology, my neighbor's marginal (or incremental) cost became greater than her marginal (or incremental) benefit.[72]

The requirement, that externalities should not be present, is an important requirement. Whenever there are externalities, markets will fail. They will not allocate resources to their most valued use. All else constant, if there are negative externalities, there will be an over production. This is because complete opportunity cost is not taken into account and the product is under-priced; part of the price is being paid by someone other than the consumer of the product. In our example of someone owning a noisy dog, part of the price of owning a noisy dog is being paid by the neighbor. Perhaps one way to assure that people do not own noisy dogs is to have an appropriate dog owning fee; the noisier the dog, the higher the fee. Since this will increase the true price of owning a noisy dog, fewer people will own such dogs.

On the other hand, if there are positive externalities, left to the market, all else constant, there will be an under production of the product. In our example of my neighbor's well-maintained yard, since I, along with others in the neighborhood enjoy a nicely maintained yard, it benefits the whole neighborhood. Maintaining a beautiful yard takes time, effort, and money. It is pricy. If the price of such an activity were somehow lowered, it is likely that more residents will start keeping an immaculate yard. One way may be to provide a subsidy (a negative tax) for maintaining the yard. This subsidy may be supported by taxes on neighbors like me who do not maintain their yards.

Why would providing a subsidy to my neighbor induce her to restart maintain her yard? Using the economics terminology, again, this will likely have two effects. One, since my neighbor is getting partially compensated for maintaining her yard, her marginal (or incremental) cost has gone down. Two, since I am paying higher taxes for not maintaining my yard, it may provide me an incentive to start cutting bushes and weeding[73] my own yard. Also, since I am paying higher taxes, my free-riding is remedied, at least partially.

Another way to induce my neighbor to restart the yard maintenance is raise her marginal (or incremental) benefit from doing so. If she gets satisfaction from her neighbors' praises of her yard, she may be induced to restart maintaining her yard if the social accolades can somehow be increased. In the US, in most suburban neighborhoods there are friendly competitions for "the most beautiful yard." The winners get the bragging rights and a sign placed on their yards. Which one of these methods—a subsidy to lower the marginal cost or social accolades to increase the marginal benefit—will work best depends upon the situation? In other words, this is an empirical question.

Keep on owning a noisy dog without having to pay to offset the negative externality, or stop maintaining the yard due to individual marginal (or incremental) benefit being less than individual marginal (or incremental) cost, are examples of market failures. In the former case, too much output is being produced. In the latter case, not enough output is being produced. In both cases, market has failed to allocate resources in efficient manner. In both cases, the whole society suffers as a result. Solutions suggested above were a noise-based dog-owning fee to mitigate the negative externality, and a subsidy to reward the positive externality and induce the maintenance of the yard.

The realizations that there are externalities and that markets fail in the presence of externalities, are hardly new. Economists have known it for quite some time. Indeed, Arthur Pigou, the early twentieth century British economist, suggested taxes to correct negative externalities and subsidies to encourage activities which benefit the society. Such corrective taxes are known as "Pigovian taxes" in his honor. A majority of modern day economists is in favor of Pigovian taxes to correct the ill-effects of fossil fuels on climate.[74]

Why do markets fail in the presence of externalities? Why is it that when there are positive externalities, markets under-produce, and when there are negative externalities, markets over-produce, except of course by random chance? The reason is that in a market, prices serve as signals. Both buyers and sellers use price signals to make their consumption and production decisions, respectively. Externalities distort price signals, and when price signals are distorted, markets fail. They fail to allocate resources in an efficient manner, that is, to the most valued use, when externalities exist. It is a teleological issue. I think this point is worth further explanation.

Let's start with the buyers. As buyers we look at the prices of various goods and services, and given our willingness and ability to purchase, holding all else constant, we decide which product to purchase and in how much quantity. We subjectively evaluate the expected benefit from the consumption of a product and put a monetary value on this benefit. Note that while the price of the product is quantitatively measureable—$5 per unit or $13 per unit, and so on—our benefit is not; hence the adverb "subjectively." We compare the price of an additional (or marginal or incremental) unit with the subjective monetary value that we place on the additional benefit.[75] Given our willingness and ability to purchase and holding all else constant, if the subjectively assigned monetary value to the additional benefit is at least as large as the price of the additional unit, we buy the additional unit, otherwise we do not. This is, of course assuming that no one is forcing us to purchase a product.

Now let's look at the suppliers of goods and service. For the ease of exposition we will take the example of firms which produce goods and services for profit. A large majority of the firms are for-profit firms. Plus, their examples are simpler and easier to grasp. The understanding developed here, however, also serves in the cases of non-profits and charities.

Suppliers also look at the prices of various goods and services, and depending upon their ability and willingness to produce they decide whether to produce a given good or service and in what quantity. Profit, of course, is just price of the product times how much of that product is sold, minus the total cost of producing that product.[76] All else constant, if the prices of the products the producers are producing and selling increase, profit increases, and vice versa. Conversely, holding all else constant, for a given price if the cost of production goes down, profit will increase, and vice versa. Stated another way, producers decide to produce the quantity which maximizes their profits. Note that costs of production are just the prices which producers pay. These may include prices of raw materials, wages of labor, interest on the funds borrowed to buy machines, taxes, and so on.

Externalities, as stated above, distort prices for both the buyers and the sellers. Take the example of using gasoline to run cars. As discussed in Chapter 3, one negative side effect of economic growth is environmental pollution. One major contributor to environmental pollution is the use of fossil fuels. Because the price of gas does not adequately account for the environmental cost, gas prices in the United States are low relative to the Western European countries and most other countries around the world.[77] This leads to consumers purchasing more gas than they would if gas prices accounted for environmental costs as well. If gas prices were higher consumers may drive fewer miles; perhaps fewer joyriding trips. They may also carpool or use public transportation more often while going to work or school. They may also combine grocery shopping trips.

Low gas prices affect car producers as well. Producing cars which are relatively less fuel efficient is cheaper than producing cars which go further on a gallon of gas. Producing fuel efficient cars with hybrid, electric, and hydrogen fuel cell engines, among others, is relatively expensive and the sticker prices of such cars are higher as compared with their traditional counterparts. This is because these technologies are relatively new. It takes time to work the kinks out and develop dexterity. In general, not only machines using newer technologies are expensive in the beginning, the skilled workers needed to run such machines are also just a handful and command higher wages. Overtime, however, these costs decline as technologies mature. Going back to the example of cars, in the meantime, however, these factors increase costs of production and lead to lower profits and lower quantity of such cars produced and sold. This is why there was such a push back from the auto industry when the Obama administration raised fuel efficiency standards.[78]

Just by way of a rough comparison I checked prices of Toyota cars at their website.[79] The price tag (Manufacturer's Suggested Retail Price) on Toyota Camry LE was $22,680. Its hybrid counter part's price tag (Manufacturer's Suggested Retail Price) was 26,140. The price difference, of course, does not represent only the cost of production. Other factors such as the buyers' preferences for a hybrid versus a traditional car, gas prices (hybrids versions tend to travel more miles per gallon as compared with their traditional counterparts), and tax incentives provided by the government to promote hybrid technology, et cetera. In other words, the "equilibrium price" is the result of both quantity supplied and quantity demanded.

With regard to tax incentives for instance, according the Internal Revenue Service's Website, businesses get a tax credit for using an electric vehicle. Depending upon the type of vehicle, the amount ranges between $2,500 and $7,500.[80] Interestingly, a number of states are either considering or have already imposed additional fees for driving a hybrid or an electric car.[81] The rationale provided for imposing tax on driving a fuel efficient car is that most states rely on gasoline tax for the maintenance of roads, and the more cars there are which use alternative fuels, the less gas is purchased, and the lower is the revenue collected by the states.

"How could the market participants just look at the price of the product they are trading, without any regard for the larger picture? Doesn't this narrow-mindedness hurt the society as a whole?" one may ask. As it turns out this "narrow-mindedness" is not a flaw, as it may seem at first blush. It is indeed a virtue. Paul Seabright (2010, Chapter 2)[82] gives the example of the production, sale, and purchase of an ordinary cotton shirt in a town in the United States. As he shows that this rather unassuming article of clothing needs a lot of planning and coordination among a large number of individuals; from the buyers willingness and ability to buy a shirt, to the merchants decision to order the shirt, to the shirt producer's decision, who probably is located in a different country, to decide to produce, to the textile mill owner's decision to weave cotton cloth, to the cotton mill owner's decision to spin cotton and make thread, to the cotton farmer's decision to grow cotton. I am, of course, brutally condensing Seabright's very eloquent description of the process of shirt production, sale, and purchase.

The coordination of so many participants even in the production and sale of an ordinary cotton shirt could be mind boggling. However, this coordination does take place; shirts are produced and bought and sold every day, many times. This "tunnel vision" as Seabright calls it, is the reason that millions and millions, if not billions, parts of this economic engine moving rather smoothly considering the coordination required. Each participant is only focused on the very small part that he/she is performing. The cotton farmer is only looking at the price of cotton and, given the prices of seeds, fertilizers, and other inputs, deciding whether to produce cotton or some other crop, and of what kind, and in which quantity. And so do other participants.

"But do our individual actions, collectively, not hurt the society? Are the polluted environment and warming globe not the results our collective carelessness?" One may ask. The answer to both these questions, I would argue, is "yes." As discussed in Chapter 3, there is little argument in the mainstream scientific community that human actions are responsible for global warming and climate change. Examples of very real human cost abound as well. I presented some examples in Chapter 3. However the answer, in my opinion, is not taking economic coordination completely out of the hands of the individuals either. Indeed, as recent history and current events show, efforts to coordinate the various economic decisions made in an economy by a central authority did not bear fruit. Experiments with central planning in the former Soviet Union, China, and other countries, failed. Present day Russia, China, and other countries are increasingly leaving it to individual economic participants to make decisions.

Note also that the choice between a centrally planned economy and a completely free market, so called, "laissez faire," is a false choice. As the Great Depression of 1930s and the Great Recession which started in 2007, (and many events before, in between, and since), and their aftermath show, markets need regulations to do their job of allocating resources efficiently. Government's role on the economic stage is to set the rules of the game, according to the advice of the scholars in a transparent manner, and let the market participants do the coordination.

5.4. Chapter Summary

In this chapter we started by looking at how economic growth may differ from economic development. We saw that income distribution is related to both economic growth and economic development. We also looked at the factors which may help us understand the state of income distribution. These included historical, economic, and social institutional factors. We spent time understanding the role of externalities in the ability of markets to allocate resources to their most efficient uses.

In the next chapter we will look at how social safety nets may affect income distribution and poverty. We will also see how poverty may persist over generations and what, if any, impact this persistence may have on the economy as a whole.

CHAPTER 6

Formal Social Safety Nets, Income Distribution, and the Society

In the previous chapter we looked at the income distribution and its impact on economic growth. In this chapter I focus on income distribution and poverty. To the extent that it is possible, I will try to define poverty, or at least highlight the broader contours of poverty. I will explain why defining poverty is not as simple as it may sound. I will also look at the state of poverty in the United State and in other countries. What impact, if any, do formal social safety nets have on income distribution and poverty? I will try to address this question. I will also provide some thoughts on why the rich should care about the poor.

6.1. Income Distribution and Poverty: Some Definitions

Poverty is distinct from unequal income distribution. While both concepts deal with income, the former refers to the *level* of resources in a *given context*, whereas the latter refers to how resources are distributed among individuals or groups of individuals. Furthermore, while poverty and unequal income distribution may co-exist and feed into each other, but not necessarily; poverty does not imply unequal income distribution, nor does unequal income distribution imply poverty. Poverty is much more nuanced, and hence harder to measure, than income inequality. With this in mind, let us look at some definitions of poverty.

The World Bank defines poverty as[1] "the absence of acceptable choices across a broad range of important life decisions—a severe lack of freedom to be or do what one wants." (p.1). Poverty manifests itself in[2] (p.1)

- Inadequate resources to buy the basic necessities of life
- Frequent bouts of illness and an early death

- Literacy and education levels that undermine adequate functioning and limit one's comprehension of the world and oneself
- Living conditions that imperil physical and mental health
- Jobs that are at best unfulfilling and at worst dangerous
- A pronounced absence of dignity, a lack of respect from others
- Exclusion from community affairs.

This way of thinking about poverty has a rich intellectual tradition. Adam Smith talked about various facets of poverty in 1776 in his masterpiece, *An Inquiry into the Nature and Causes of Wealth of Nations*, when he talked about the "necessaries" of life.[3]

> By necessaries I understand not only the commodities which are indispensably necessary for the support of life, but what ever the customs of the country renders it indecent for creditable people, even the lowest order to be without. A linen shirt, for example, is, strictly speaking, not a necessary of life. The Greeks and Romans lived, I suppose, very comfortably though they had no linen. But in the present times, through the greater part of Europe, a creditable day-labourer would be ashamed to appear in public without a linen shirt, the want of which would be supposed to denote that disgraceful degree of poverty which, it is presumed, nobody can well fall into without extreme bad conduct. Custom, in the same manner, has rendered leather shoes a necessary of life in England. The poorest creditable person of either sex would be ashamed to appear in public without them.
>
> (Part II, Book V, Chapter 2, Article 4, pp.399–400)

John Rawls (1973)[4] argues for the need for and the necessity of "primary goods," which include "rights and liberties, power and opportunities, income and wealth," and "health and vigor, intelligence and imagination," and the centrality of "self-respect" for human existence. (p.62). Amartya Sen (1983)[5] expands upon the idea and argues that "absolute deprivation in terms of a person's capabilities relates to relative deprivation in terms of commodities, incomes and resources" (p.153). In his book *Development as Freedom*,[6] Sen talks about "instrumental freedoms," lack of which spells poverty. These freedoms include, "(1) political freedom, (2) economic facilities, (3) social opportunities, (4) transparency guarantees and (5) protective security" (p.38).

Note that defined this way, poverty is very much time and space dependent along certain dimensions. While basic life sustaining "necessaries" such as adequate caloric intake and shelter from the element—"an irreducible absolutist core"[7]—are required everywhere and at all times, beyond that, what constitutes as poverty depends upon the environment in which one lives.

Healthy teeth are needed to chew food, brightness of teeth will probably also be a factor in getting work as an actor and the role she/he is required to play.

At first blush these definitions of poverty may sound "liberal" and "elitist."[8] Some may argue that "yes, 'inadequate resources to buy basic necessities of life' and 'frequent bouts of illness and an early death' "—the first two bullet points in World Bank definition provided above—"are veritable sings of poverty, but literacy, a fulfilling job, and ability to participate in public affairs are luxuries." Upon further reflection, however, as has been argued most notably by Adam Smith,[9] John Rawls,[10] and Amartya Sen,[11] it becomes clear that these are not luxuries, far from it, and that absence of these "freedoms" may very well lead to poverty. Basing my arguments on the insights of Adam Smith, John Rawls, and Amartya Sen, among others, I will further expand on this point later in this chapter.

6.2. The State of Poverty in the United States and Other Developed Countries

As a starting point, and just as a starting point, let's look at the data of overall poverty rates using income as a proxy. One measure of poverty, using income, is the share of people living on less than 50 percent of the median after-tax income—after-tax income earned by the middle most individual. Figure 6.1 plots data for the 21 Organization for Economic Co-operation and

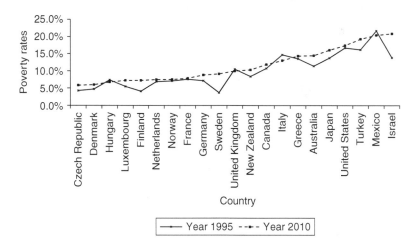

Figure 6.1 Overall poverty across the OECD countries
Source: OECD income distribution database.

Development (OECD) member countries. By way of comparison, the figure plots data for 1995 and 2010 (for countries for which data are available for both years).[12]

A few points stand out. One, using this measure, poverty seems to have increased between 1995 and 2010 in most of the OECD countries. Only four countries, for which data are available, had lower poverty rates during 2010 than they did during 1995. These countries are Hungary, United Kingdom, Italy, and Mexico.

During 2010, the average poverty rate was around 11.3 percent. And during 2010, 14 countries had poverty rate higher than the average poverty rate of 11.3 percent. These counties are (in increasing order of poverty rate) Portugal, Estonia, Canada, Italy, Greece, Australia, Korea, Spain, Japan, United States, Chile, Turkey, Mexico, and Israel.

Poverty rates, of course, are not the same across all ages. For instance, in the United States, the overall poverty rate during 2010 was 17.4 percent. Poverty rate for "working age" population, defined as 18–65 year olds, was 17.9 percent, and for retired individuals—over 65 year olds—was 14.6 percent during 2010.[13] (More on the poverty rates of children below).

Another measure of overall wellbeing in a country is life expectancy at birth. Figure 6.2 plots data for 2008 for the OECD countries.[14]

The mean life expectancy of the 30 OECD countries during 2008 was 79.42 years with a standard deviation of 2.48 years. Income level and life expectancy have a positive correlation. The estimated Pearson correlations between average disposable income and life expectancy is 0.73 (p-value = 0.000).

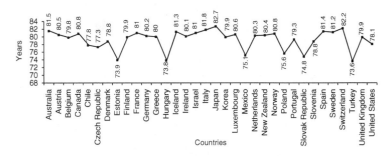

Figure 6.2 Life expectancy in years at birth (2008)
Source: OECD website.

6.2.1. Poverty and Children

The 2006 *Proceedings of the National Academy of Sciences* published the findings of a multidisciplinary study. The study was titled: Economic, Neurobiological, and Behavioral Perspectives on Building America's Future Workforce.[15] The study focused on the interaction between early childhood environment and lifetime achievements. In describing the reasons behind their focus the authors noted that:

> First, the architecture of the brain and the process of skill formation are both influenced by an inextricable interaction between genetics and individual experience. Second, both the mastery of skills that are essential for economic success and the development of their underlying neural pathways follow hierarchical rules in a bottom-up sequence such that later attainments build on foundations that are laid down earlier. Third, cognitive, linguistic, social, and emotional competencies are interdependent, all are shaped powerfully by the experiences of the developing child, and all contribute to success in the workplace. Fourth, although adaptation continues throughout life, human abilities are formed in a predictable sequence of sensitive periods, during which the development of specific neural circuits and the behaviors they mediate are most plastic and, therefore, optimally receptive to environmental influences. (p.10155)

Findings of the study led authors to the conclusion that " . . . the most efficient strategy for strengthening the future workforce, both economically and neurobiologically, and improving its quality of life is to invest in the environments of disadvantaged children during the early childhood years." (p.10155). And that " . . . the most cost-effective strategy for strengthening the future American workforce is to invest greater human and financial resources in the social and cognitive environments of children who are disadvantaged, beginning as early as possible."(p.10161).

Unfortunately children are the ones who get hit worst from poverty. In Table 6.1 through Table 6.3, I provide data, followed by discussion, for various OECD countries on a number of variables which highlight the various dimensions of child poverty.[16]

Column [1] in Table 6.1 lists the country names, Column [2] provides average disposable income of households with children up to 17-year, in thousands of 2005 constant US dollars, and Column [3] lists the percentage of children living in poor homes, where a poor home is defined as one which has income below 50 percent of the median income of the country. Column [4] lists educational deprivation. It is a measure which represents children's access to various educational paraphernalia, such as textbooks, dictionaries,

Table 6.1 Material well-being of children

[1]	[2]	[3]	[4]
Country	Average disposable income (in 000s of 2005 US $)	Children in poor homes (percent)	Educational deprivation
Australia	20.81	11.79	2.2
Austria	22.16	6.17	0.6
Belgium	21.40	9.97	1
Canada	25.61	15.06	2.1
Czech Republic	10.85	10.27	1.2
Denmark	23.18	2.74	0.7
Finland	22.03	4.17	1
France	18.96	7.64	1.2
Germany	19.89	16.29	0.5
Greece	17.18	13.23	6.1
Hungary	9.46	8.72	2.1
Iceland	22.29	8.25	0.4
Ireland	22.36	16.30	2.9
Italy	17.18	15.50	1.2
Japan	22.48	13.69	5.6
Korea	21.65	10.75	1.8
Luxembourg	34.24	12.39	1.1
Mexico	5.34	22.16	13.7
Netherlands	25.04	11.53	0.6
New Zealand	17.20	15.00	2.2
Norway	28.57	4.60	1.3
Poland	7.94	21.50	2.1
Portugal	13.84	16.55	1.4
Slovak Republic	7.80	10.93	3.8
Spain	16.43	17.30	0.9
Sweden	19.92	3.97	1.6
Switzerland	24.65	9.43	0.7
Turkey	5.07	24.59	13.6
United Kingdom	22.70	10.08	1.8
United States	29.20	20.59	4.8
OECD—Total	19.18	12.37	2.7

Note: See Table 6.A for variable definitions and detailed data sources.
Source: OECD website.[17]

desks, computers, Internet access, a suitable place to study, et cetera. It reports the percentage of children who had fewer than four of these items.[18]

A few points stand out. First, poverty rates for children are significantly higher than the total population poverty rates. Second, a higher average disposable income level is no guarantee that children will have basic tools for education. While the correlations between average disposable income and percent of children living in poor households, and average disposable income and educational deprivation are statistically significantly negative,[19] they are far from perfect, and countries like the United States stand out. The United States has the second highest average disposable income (Luxembourg has the highest average disposable income of $34.24 thousand US dollars) out of the 30 OECD countries, yet over 20 percent of children live in poor households and 4.8 percent of children report having fewer than four necessary tools to achieve proper education in the twenty-first century.

One dimension along which poverty may be measured is living conditions.[20] Table 6.2 provides data for the percent of children living in undesirable conditions, for various countries for which data are available.[21]

Table 6.2 Child housing conditions

[1]	[2]	[3]
Country	Overcrowding	Poor environmental conditions
Australia	19.70	10.50
Austria	34.01	20.15
Belgium	12.61	29.75
Czech Republic	58.90	29.75
Denmark	17.55	20.15
Finland	15.23	22.80
France	20.28	25.83
Germany	19.97	37.37
Greece	54.92	25.07
Hungary	73.31	22.21
Iceland	21.65	15.53
Ireland	16.43	19.30
Italy	47.85	32.58
Japan	22.54	32.38
Luxembourg	16.89	25.57
Netherlands	10.33	38.71
Norway	15.11	11.99
Poland	73.96	22.84
Portugal	31.95	33.46
Slovak Republic	68.36	27.35
Spain	10.83	31.68
Sweden	20.01	15.75
United Kingdom	21.50	29.07
United States	26.20	25.40
OECD—Total	31.95	25.22

Note: See Table 6.A for variable definitions and detailed data sources.
Source: OECD website.[22]

In Table 6.2, Column [1] lists the country names, Column [2] provides data on the percentage of children living in overcrowded homes, and Column [3] provides data on the percentage of children living in poor environmental conditions. The "Overcrowding" measure is based on the number of rooms in a house per family member, and the "Poor Living Conditions" measure is based on the crime rate, environmental pollution, traffic noise, among other factors. Please refer to Table 6.A for detailed definitions and data sources.

The correlation between "average disposable income" and "overcrowding," as one would expect, is negative.[23] There is, however, considerable variation.[24] The correlation between "average disposable income" and "poor environmental conditions" is essentially nonexistent.[25] As in the cases of child poverty and educational deprivation, (see discussion with regard to Table 6.1), a country having a higher income is no guarantee of its children having adequate living conditions.[26]

What do the data tell us about the educational wellbeing of children? Table 6.3 provides data about "average mean literacy score," a measure of the average performance of 15-year olds on mathematics, reading, and science tests; "literacy inequality," a measure of how 15-year old children of high income versus low income parents performed in mathematics, reading, and science test; and "youth NEET rates." It is the percentage of 15–19-year olds who are neither in school nor employed. The number of countries included in the table is limited by the availability of data.[27] Please refer to Table 6.A for detailed definitions and data sources.

"Average disposable income" and "average mean literacy score" are positively correlated,[28] and "average mean literacy score" and "literacy inequality" have a negative correlation.[29] The data do not show any statistically significant correlation between "average disposable income" and "literacy inequality."[30] The correlation between "youth NEET rates" and "average disposable income" is negative.[31]

Another dimension of poverty is the teenage pregnancy rates. Teen pregnancy decreases mother's chances of finishing high school and obtaining a college degree. College graduates tend to have significantly lower unemployment rates compared to individuals with high school or less than high school education.[32] Furthermore, unemployment spells last a lot longer for those without a college degree.[33] Add this to the fact that premiums of college education have been rising, teen mothers are very likely to get lower paying jobs and have lower lifetime earnings. This further exacerbates inequality and poverty. Miles Corak[34] highlights this facet of income inequality and poverty. His analysis shows that inequality and teenage fertility have a positive correlation.

Table 6.3 Child educational well-being

[1]	[2]	[3]	[4]
	Average mean literacy score	Literacy inequality	Youth NEET rates
Australia	520	1.61	7.4
Austria	502	1.72	6.9
Belgium	510.33	1.74	6.2
Canada	529.33	1.57	6.1
Czech Republic	502	1.74	5.3
Denmark	501	1.59	4.3
Finland	552.67	1.48	5.2
France	493	1.73	6.2
Germany	505	1.72	4.4
Greece	464	1.72	9.8
Hungary	492.33	1.62	6.4
Ireland	508.67	1.59	4.4
Italy	468.67	1.75	11.2
Japan	517.33	1.65	8.4
Luxembourg	485	1.70	2.2
Netherlands	521	1.61	3.9
New Zealand	524.33	1.68	8.5
Norway	487	1.69	2.5
Poland	500.33	1.63	1.7
Portugal	470.67	1.69	8.4
Slovak Republic	482	1.71	6.3
Spain	476.33	1.64	8.5
Sweden	504	1.63	4.7
Switzerland	513.67	1.65	7.2
Turkey	431.67	1.70	37.7
United Kingdom	501.67	1.69	9.3
United States	481.5	1.73	6.1
OECD—Total	496.32	1.67	7.38

Note: See Table 6.A for variable definitions and detailed data sources.
Source: OECD website.[35]

6.3. Income Inequality and Income Mobility

Alan Krueger, who was chairman of the Council of Economic Advisors from November 7, 2011 to August 2, 2013,[36] addressed the audience at Center for American Progress, on January 12, 2012.[37] After showing how income distribution had changed since the 1940s, he argued that:

> Higher income inequality would be less of a concern if low-income earners became high-income earners at some point in their career, or if children of

low-income parents had a good chance of climbing up the income scales when they grow up. In other words, if we had a high degree of income mobility we would be less concerned about the degree of inequality in any given year. But we do not. Moreover, as inequality has increased, evidence suggests that year-to-year or generation-to-generation economic mobility has decreased. (p.2)

And this is where income inequality has a long lasting impact; generation after generation low-income earners are trapped in the lower end of the income distribution. I will try to present this idea with the help of a simple diagram called "Production Possibilities Curve" (also called "Production Possibilities Frontier"). Economics students are introduced to this diagram in principles-level courses. A production possibilities curve is defined as a graph which shows all the possible combinations of two goods/services (or two sets of goods/services) which can be produced in an economy when resources are used in an efficient manner, holding all else constant. This model utilizes the concept of opportunity cost which we encountered in chapters 2 and 5.

6.3.1. Household Production Possibilities Curve

Suppose that a household spends its time and other resources "producing" two sets of activities, Work and Family. In "Work" I include all activities which generate income for the household. These activities may include the job(s) which the adult members of the household undertake, the savings and accumulated wealth which a household might have which generate interest income, et cetera.

"Family" includes activities ranging from time, effort, and financial resources spent on raising children to spending time with family members and friend. Resources spent on raising children may include the time parents spend with them in playful and in educational activities and the financial resources spent on formal education, that is, school, tutoring, books, and other related expenditure. They also include resources spent on extracurricular activities such as sending children to, say, summer camps and paying for piano lessons. Figures 6.3(a) and 6.3(b) plot production possibilities curves for "Rich Household" and "Poor Household," respectively.

For the ease of exposition assume that there are two consecutive generations at a time. The curves GEN_1 and GEN_2 represent the various combinations of the total production of the two generations, with the subscripts one and two representing the two generations, respectively. The first generation bears and raises children, who become adults in the second generation. The earning potential of the second generation depends upon a combination of its inherent capabilities and the "nurturing" it received

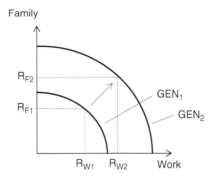

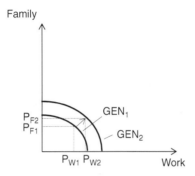

Figure 6.3 Household production possibilities curve
(a) Rich household; (b) Poor household

before it entered the workforce. Assume that at time t_1 two children are born; one to the rich household and one to the poor household. Assume also that both children are of the same gender and have equal physical and mental abilities. That is, there aren't any inherent differences between the two children. Another way to put it is that the "nature" part of the two children is identical. The only differences which may arise later in life are due to "nurture."

Both households, rich and poor, are using all their available resource in an efficient manner and, given their resources, choose the Work and Family bundle optimally. That is, they are not wasting any time or other financial resources on frivolous activities which do not contribute to the welfare of the household. Technically speaking, when a household is using its resources in an (allocatively) efficient manner, it is on its production possibilities curve *and* at a point on the production possibilities curve which produces the mix of Work and Family they consider optimal.

A bit of a sidetrack: Using the economics jargon, when a household, in this case, is not wasting any resources, that is, producing the maximum output given its resources, it will be on its production possibilities curve. The household will said to be "productively efficient." It is, however, possible that while a household is productively efficient, it not producing the mix of output which the members of the household want—which maximizes their welfare. Above I referred to that particular mix as optimal. When a household is producing the maximum output given its resources and producing that particular mix which its members want, the household is said to be "allocatively efficient." Note that allocative efficiency is a more stringent condition than productive efficiency. More formally, allocative efficiency is a *sufficient* condition, and productive efficiency is a *necessary* condition. If allocative efficiency has been achieved, productive efficiency must necessarily have been achieved. I mention this because these terms—necessary condition and sufficient condition—are often confused. Here "necessary" does not mean pre-requisite.

Now back to our households. If a household is not using its resources in a productively efficient manner—it is wasting at least part of its resources—it is to the left of its production possibilities curve, GEN_i, for $i = 1, 2$. Given that both households are using their resources in an efficient manner, when a household wants to, say, spend more time on Work it has to spend less time on Family. And when a household wants to spend more time on Family, it has to spend less time on Work.

Recall the concept of opportunity cost we encountered in chapters 2 and 5. The opportunity cost of Work, in this example, is Family. Work and Family, however, are not independent of each other. A household may decide to work more so that it can have an increase in income, which it can use to, say, pay for the school tuition, a part of the Family set of activities as defined above, of its child. But in order to do that, it will have to cut back on some other Family activity. It may have less time to spend with the child. It cannot increase income by working longer hours *and* spend more time with the child. There are limitations, and these limitations have impact on "nurture." (Recall that "nature" part is the same for the children of both households).

This presents a dilemma for the poor household. While a poor household may want to provide its child with the opportunities which the rich child enjoys, it cannot do so due to its resource constraints. As discussed earlier, certain level of basic necessities is required for survival. For a poor household to provide for those basic necessities, it may have to work longer hours to provide the basic necessities. In terms of our diagram for the poor household, this point may be represented by P_{W1} along the Work axis. By working these many hours it can provide the basics. Such a point may be represented by

P_{F1} along the Family axis in our diagram for the poor household. If a poor household wants to get to a different mix such that it reaches a point higher than P_{F1} while still remaining on GEN_1, it will have to decrease the hours, a point to the left of P_{W1}. This, however, may not be an option. Not only it may decrease take home paycheck, decreasing hours may mean working part time and risk losing some benefits which come with full-time work such as 401(K) or healthcare. Yes, the poor household may be able to spend more quality time with the child by decreasing work hours, but because of decreased income, it may not be able to send the child to school at all, let alone to a prestigious school. As a result the poor household may prefer to work longer hours at the cost of fewer Family activities.

While a rich household faces the same tradeoff, the magnitude of the tradeoff may differ significantly. To put some numbers in the picture, a rich household earning one million dollars a year may have to give up, say, $100,000 worth of Work in favor of Family activities. This, however, may not register in any meaningful way. It may just mean not owning a boat. The household still has $900,000 annual income. In terms of our diagram, this will mean moving to a point above R_{F1} along the Family axis and moving to the left of the point R_{W1} on the Work axis while still remaining on the GEN_1 curve. For a poor household giving up, say, $10,000 from an annual income of $50,000 could be significant. For the poor household it could mean giving up a reliable mode of transportation to and back from work, which can further limit the poor household's opportunities.

How does the "choice" on the part of our poor household (if you can call it a choice) affect the next generation? That is, how does the choice on the part of the poor household to work longer hours and engage in fewer Family activities affect its child's wellbeing when she/he becomes an adult and joins the workforce as compared with that of the child of rich household? Recall that our rich household was able to increase Family activities without having to give up the ability to provide the basics of life, and then some.

Resources spent on children have consequences for the rest of their lives. Take the example getting a job. For the sake of simplicity assume that the employers are only looking at the degrees of the applicants. In the absence of other credible markers, all else constant, employers prefer to hire graduates of prestigious universities than those of less prestigious universities. A student graduating from, say, Harvard or any other Ivey League school, has a higher probability of getting a job and earning a larger salary as compared with his/her counterpart who is coming from a less prestigious school.

Why is that? The idea is that more prestigious universities have better quality professors and in turn better trained students. Take the example of universities hiring faculty members. (By virtue of being an academic, I am more familiar with this market). It is not any secret that universities pay a great deal of attention to the alma mater of the prospective employees. A student graduating from an elite school has a higher probability of getting a job at an elite university, and earning significantly more, than a student graduating from less prestigious school who is more likely to get a job at a less prestigious school, which pays a lot less. (The curious reader may want to look at an Ivey League university's faculty members' credentials. One will find that faculty members at Ivey League universities have invariably graduated from other Ivey League universities).

Someone from a less prestigious university may argue that his/her education is of equal quality as that of an Ivey Leaguer. This may be true at times. Objective measures, however, such as quality and number of journal publications, tell a different story. (More on "objective" measures shortly). Looking at the articles published in top-tier journals one finds that a significant majority of articles are by faculty members from prestigious universities. Now, the journal publication measure could very well be an artifact of a "catch-22." Risk-averse journal editors do not want to spend resources reviewing articles which have a lower probability of being of high quality because the authors (or their professors) do not have a track record of high-quality publications. In order to avoid mistakes, the editors become extra vigilant, which leads to a higher rejection rates, which further lowers the number of publications from authors from less prestigious universities in top journals, which further discourages the authors from less prestigious universities sending manuscripts to top journals, and so on.

A note about "objective" measures: There is some evidence that publication decisions made by editors are not exactly free of bias. Michael Shermer, in his book *The Mind of the Market*, takes up this point in greater detail and presents more examples of how in the publishing world success begets success.[38] A more recent example of this phenomenon is that of J. K. Rowling, the author of the hugely popular *Harry Potter* series. She wrote a book entitled *The Cuckoo's Calling*, under a pseudonym "Robert Galbraith." The book, however, had lackluster sales and began selling only after the true identity of the author was revealed.[39] J. K. Rowling wrote another book, *The Casual Vacancy*, under her own name. It sold over 1.3 million "hardcover" copies and was "No. 1 hardcover fiction title of 2012," even though the reviewers of the book were rather critical.[40] This issue, however, is beyond the scope of this book, and I will leave it at that.

Now back to spending resources on rearing children. Sending a child to a prestigious university, however, is rather costly. A poor household may not be able to afford it. Less prestigious universities compete on the basis of cost. Whereas a year of undergraduate education at an Ivey League may cost close to $50,000, sending a child to a less prestigious university may cost around $10,000 per year.[41] And this phenomenon perpetuates. It has consequences for intergenerational mobility. The resource gap between the rich and the poor expands with time. With time, the rich household has even higher resources for its child's education than does the poor household. This is what I have shown in Figures 6.3(a) and 6.3(b). While the production possibility curves of both the rich household and the poor households have moved to the right for the second generations—GEN$_2$—the production possibility curve of the rich household had moved by a greater magnitude, leading to a widening gap between the rich and the poor. The rich household's second generation's optimal points are represented by R$_{W2}$ on the Work axis and R$_{F2}$ on the Family axis. Analogously, for the poor household, P$_{W2}$ represents its optimal point on the Work axis and P$_{F2}$ on the Family axis.

The way I have drawn the production possibilities curves of the poor household, GEN$_2$ is to the right of GEN$_1$. That is, it shows that even the poor household's second generation is better off than its first generation. This, however, may not be the case. It is quite possible that the second generation will have fewer opportunities, and as a result poorer than the first generation. Indeed, depending upon one's socio-economic status, one may find that the production possibilities curve has shifted to the left.

What is the empirical evidence for this phenomenon? I turn to this question now.

6.3.2. Empirical Evidence of the Impact of Income Inequality on Income Mobility

I start by plotting median income, adjusted for inflation in 2011 constant dollars, from 1987 to 2011, data in Figure 6.4. Note that median income adjusted for inflation is lower now than it was during the 1990s. Median income in 2011 was $50,054. It was at that level during the mid-1990s.

Economists use Intergenerational Elasticity of Earning (IEE) to measure the link between the income of parents and the income of children. It is a measure of income mobility. More formally, IEE is defined as the percentage change in a child's adult earnings due to one percent change in his/her parents earnings. It ranges between zero and one. A value of zero indicates that parents' income does not matter at all—perfect income mobility—and a value of one indicates that parents' incomes are perfect predictors of their offsprings' earnings. Miles Corak provides measures IEE of various countries.[42] According to his estimates Italy, the United Kingdom, and United States have estimated IEEs around 0.5 (0.5, 0.5, and 0.47, respectively), and Denmark, Finland, and Norway have estimated IEEs around 0.16 (0.15, 0.17, and 0.18,

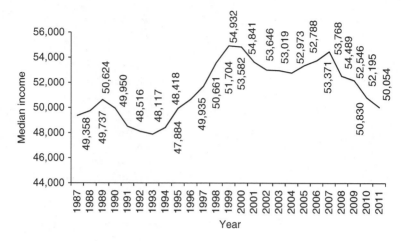

Figure 6.4   Median household income from 1987 to 2011 (in 2011 constant dollars)[43]
Source: The United States Census Bureau (www.census.gov).

respectively). Put another way, out of these countries, children born to poor parents in Italy, the United Kingdom, and the United States are the least likely to escape poverty, and children born to poor parents in Denmark, Finland, and Norway are the most likely to move up the income ladder. A curve which plots IEEs along the vertical axis and income inequality as measured by the Gini coefficient along the horizontal axis was nick-named "The Great Gatsby Curve" by Alan Krueger, now former chairman of the Council of Economic Advisors, in his address to the audience at Center for American Progress, on January 12, 2012, which I referenced above.[44]

I bring these examples to highlight the point made earlier: poverty is a multidimensional and nuanced concept, and income is just a starting point to estimate poverty. Furthermore, poverty has a tendency to persist over generations, unless steps are taken by governments which try to break the vicious cycle.

Looking at the IEE of the United States (0.47) and its place along the Great Gatsby Curve one may ask the question though: If the lack of intergenerational earnings mobility is as persistent as the data show, why hasn't there been more public outcry in the United States? An answer to this question may be found in the public perception of the state of intergenerational earnings mobility. Polls show that general public in the United States consistently overestimates the intergenerational earnings mobility. According to the World Values Survey,[45] less than 30 percent of Americans believe that they are stuck at the lower end of the income distribution.

6.4. Do Formal Social Safety Nets Affect Income Distribution and Poverty?

Have formal social safety nets been effective in reducing poverty and distributing income relatively more equally? In the income space, one straight forward way to answer this question is to look at the pre- and post-distributive policies Gini coefficients. If tax structure is progressive—high income earners pay higher taxes than low income earners—then before-tax Gini coefficient and after-tax Gini coefficient will serve as an indicator of the success or failure of formal social safety nets. In Figure 6.5, I plot before-tax and after-tax Gini coefficient values for 23 OECD countries for 2009.[46]

It is easy to see the difference between before-tax and after-tax Gini coefficient estimates: after-tax Gini coefficient estimates are lower than the before-tax estimates, pointing to the income inequality lowering effects of taxes.[47]

This should not be a surprising outcome of taxes, especially, as noted above, if taxes are levied in a progressive manner. The point to ponder, however, is whether redistributive policies and decreased income inequality lead to reduced poverty, not only along the income dimension but also along other dimensions alluded to above—"instrumental freedoms" á la Amartya

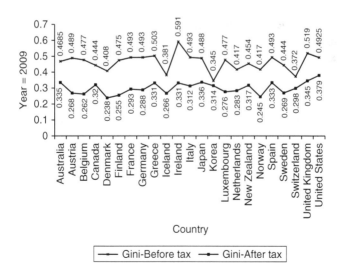

Figure 6.5   Before-tax and after-tax Gini coefficient estimates
Source: OECD income distribution database.

Sen,[48] intergenerational income mobility, increased educational opportunities, better living conditions, better health outcomes, and so on. The answer seems to be in affirmative.[49] Not only did progressive institutional arrangements which promoted income redistribution help the poor and indigent, such institutions also became the foundations of successful societies. One such example is the "Old Poor Laws (1601–1834)," also known as "Poor Laws." (I referred to Poor Laws earlier in Chapter 5).

Avner Greif and Murat Iyigun (2013)[50] argue that Poor Laws played a pivotal role in the Industrial Revolution and the modernization of England. The impact of these institutional arrangements showed up along at least two dimensions. Along one dimension Poor Laws helped create peaceful political and social environment. One damaging factor, at least as far as investment and in turn, economic growth, are concerned, is socio-political unrest.[51] Modernization and mechanization, while beneficial for the society as a whole, have destabilizing effects on those whose jobs are being replaced by technological changes. Poor Laws provided financial relief to those who lost their jobs to machines in uncertain economic times. This, in turn, avoided political and social unrest and promoted investment and economic growth.[52]

Another effect of the Poor Laws was to provide insurance against risky innovative adventures. Innovative activities, as discussed in greater detail in earlier chapters, are inherently risky and have uncertain outcomes. Risk-taking, however, is also a constitutive ingredient of such an activity. Poor Laws provided an insurance against the unsuccessful outcomes. Innovators assured of having at least the basic needs met even if an experiment resulted in failure, embarked on such endeavors. Successful outcomes led to financial riches and fame for the individual and deeper and wider pool of knowledge for the society as a whole and promoted growth.

Did Poor Laws create a "dependent" society and sacrifice efficiency at the altar of equity? Studies show that this was not the case.[53] The net effect of Poor Laws was a more prosperous society and economic growth which was widely shared.

The relationship between social insurance and economic growth is not unique to the Poor Laws of the seventeenth century and eighteenth century England. Elizabeth M. Caucutt et al. (2013)[54] use data for the US and other countries and find that formal means of "social insurance" and industrialization and urbanization go together. The reason, they argue, is the changing dynamics of economic and social structures. As industrialization takes hold, people move away from villages and agriculture to urban areas where manufacturing industry and the related service providers are the main, and perhaps the only, economic enterprises. This geographic movement results in the loss of familial safety nets—they rely less on land as a means of insurance in old age and the need for formal social safety nets arises. The presence of social insurance feeds into further industrialization, and so on.

A more recent example of how formal social safety nets may have helped the unfortunate and the economy as a whole comes from the aftermath of the Great Recession which started in 2007. Gabriel Chodorow-Reich et al. (2012)[55] look at the impact of American Recovery and Reinvestment Act (ARRA) of 2009. The ARRA provided aid to state governments through Medicaid reimbursement. The amount was about $88 billion. Their results led them to conclude that

> ...the ARRA transfers to states had an economically large and statistically robust positive effect on employment. Assuming that employment does not persist beyond the time during which it is funded, our preferred specification suggests that a marginal $100,000 in Medicaid transfers resulted in 3.8 net job-years (i.e., one job that lasts for one year) of total employment through June 2010, of which 3.2 are outside the government, health, and education sectors. (p.121)

While the poor and less fortunate obviously benefit from redistributive policies and progressive taxation which make income less unequal and decrease poverty, the question still remains: Why should the rich support such policies? I turn to this question next.

6.5. Income Distribution, Poverty, and the Haves and Have-Nots: Why Should the Haves Care?

Why should the "haves" care about the inequality of income distribution and the poverty levels of the "have-nots"? I will try to address this question first from purely "quantitative" point of view. That is, whether or not it is a good business strategy for the haves to care about the have-nots. Then I will turn to the other "softer" sides.

6.5.1. Why Should the Haves Care? The "Quantitative" Side

Let us put the emotional, the caring, and the empathizing parts of ourselves aside for a moment. Also assume that we, the readers, are rather well off and relatively free of financial constraints. We earn our living by producing widgets which are in great demand and we do not have any foreseeable threats from any competitors. All is well except that for us to sell our widgets, the buyers have to be able to buy them. If the buyers cannot afford to buy our ware, the quality of products and our monopoly position is not worth much. Our inventory will pile up and before long rust will set in. In this scenario increasing the aggregate demand is recommended. This is especially true during recessions when machinery and labor are sitting idle. That is, there is excess capacity.

Another way to put it is that from the point of view of the economy as a whole, one person's expenditure is another person's income, and vice versa. If I decrease my expenditure it will lead to the decrease in another person's income. While it may be prudent for an individual to decrease expenditure in uncertain times and save more, however, when everyone adopts the same strategy everyone's income decreases, without an increase in the aggregate saving. This is a lesson which every student of elementary economics learns during the first few of weeks of classes.

But who will pick up the slack and increase spending in times of recession? This is where government comes to rescue. An active fiscal policy (and monetary policy) is needed—a combination of increased government spending and lower taxes (and expansionary monetary policy) during recessions and a combination of decreased government spending and higher taxes (and contractionary monetary policy) during times of economic expansion beyond the "normal" or "potential" level of output. This solution is very much Keynesian in nature—to stimulate economic activity aggregate demand has to go up, and vice versa.

One may ask: wouldn't increases in government spending lead to increased deficit[56] (and debt, which is the sum of deficits minus surpluses) as a percentage of output? Or more accurately: is the financial condition of such a country sustainable? To answer this question, first note that this quantity has two parts: deficit (or debt) is in the numerator and output is in the denominator.[57]

Take the example of expansionary fiscal policy—a combination of increased government spending and decreases in taxes. All else constant, if the government does not step in and increases aggregate demand by increasing government spending, it may not have an increased deficit right now. However, because decreased aggregate demand will lead to a decline in output—the denominator—in the very near future, deficit (or debt) as a percentage of output will increase even further. If government engages in expansionary fiscal policy to spur aggregate demand which leads to an increase in output, as long as output—the denominator—increases more than the deficit (or debt)—the numerator—deficit (or debt) as a percentage of output will decrease. The opposite may be true if the government does not step in and picks up the slack. Such a situation may lead to even lower output and higher deficit (or debt) as a percentage of output.

Indeed, this is exactly what we observed in the United Kingdom in the aftermath of the 2007–2008 financial crisis and the Great Recession.[58] Under the stewardship of David Cameron, the United Kingdom's Prime Minister, Conservative government of the United Kingdom insisted on austerity and cut government spending sharply. This led to a second recession—the so-called "double-dip recession"—in the United Kingdom. The developed countries which did not adhere to such sever austerity, fared much better.[59] The tough economic conditions lingered on in the United Kingdom, so much so that there were fears of a third recession within a very short time period—the so-called "triple-dip recession." The country took a collective sigh of relief when a triple-dip recession was averted, at least for the time being.[60]

The situation was not much better in most of the Euro-area due to the strict guidelines regarding deficit and public debt.[61] Countries such as Spain (See Figure 6.6) which had budget surplus on the eve of the financial crisis ended up with huge deficits soon after the crisis hit. As economies shrank and output declined, deficit (or debt) as a percentage of output increased. Guidelines for the Euro-area countries dictated a reduction in government spending. This further led to declines in aggregate demand and output, further worsening the hardship of the residents of those economies.

Arguments such as this have developed a political hue and people have visceral reactions. The moment one mentions aggregate demand management, the political divisions become hard to overlook. Liberals tend to support expansionary fiscal policy more heavily weighted in increases in government spending. They argue that increases in government spending will not only

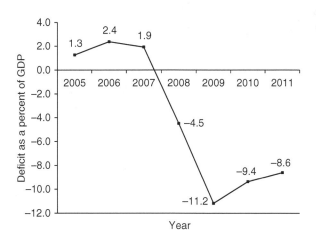

Figure 6.6 Spanish deficit as a percent of GDP[62]
Source: OECD website.

lead to increases in government purchases which will pick up the slack created due to individuals and firms pulling back, increased government spending on safety net programs, such as unemployment insurance, will lead to increased household income and increased consumption in turn.[63]

Conservatives favor expansionary fiscal policy heavily weighted towards lowered individual and corporate taxes. They tend to equate increases in government spending with increasing size of the government.[64] Conservatives support a smaller government and argue for lower taxes so that, on the one hand, profits increase and firms increase investment and hire more workers, and on the other hand household after-tax income increases, which leads to increased consumption. Note, however, that consumption, investment, and government spending, along with net exports, are all part of aggregate demand. The question is not whether or not to stimulate aggregate demand, the question is which component of aggregate demand, if affected, will have the most impact. The answer depends upon the state of the economy. During times of economic downturns, expansionary fiscal policy tilted heavily towards increased government spending seems to do the trick.[65] Why is that? A brief explanation seems in order.

6.5.1.1. Why does Government Spending Have a Bigger Punch during Recessions?

Recall that during a recession, output declines. A recession is usually defined as a time period when output declines over two consecutive quarters.[66] Alternatively, recession may also be defined as a time period when output is below potential level of output. Note that by "potential" we do not mean the maximum output which could be produced. Potential output is the output which would be produced if resources—machines, labor, buildings, et cetera—were working "normal hours." And by "normal hours" we mean that resources are working neither over-time nor part-time. More formally, it may be defined as "... the rate of output the economy would have if there were no nominal rigidities but all other (real) frictions and shocks remained unchanged."[67] The Congressional Budget Office defines potential output as follows:[68]

> Potential output—the trend growth in the productive capacity of the economy—is an estimate of the level of GDP [gross domestic product, a measure of an economy's total output] attainable when the economy is operating at a high rate of resource use. It is not a technical ceiling on output that cannot be exceeded. Rather, it is a measure of maximum *sustainable* output—the level of real GDP in a given year that is consistent with a stable rate of inflation. If actual output rises above its potential level, then constraints on capacity begin to bind and inflationary pressures build; if output falls below potential, then resources are lying idle and inflationary pressures abate. (Italics original)

This means that during recession at least some resources (machines, buildings, workers, raw materials) are sitting idle. If aggregate demand were to increase due to increase in government spending, output would increase without putting any upward pressure on wages and/or prices. If prices and/or wages were to increase with an increase in aggregate demand, the result may be different. This is an important point. I will provide more explanation shortly. First, why would wage and/or prices not increase during a recession if aggregate demand were to increase?

Take the example of a worker who is either out of job or is working part-time due to the fact that the economy is in a recession. Note that demand for inputs, be it workers, machines, buildings, or raw materials, is a derived demand. Firms do not hire workers for the sake of workers. Firms hire workers for what they can produce. If there is a demand for what a worker can produce, firms will hire the worker. Same goes for machines, buildings, and raw materials. If the economy is in a recession, output is declining. Firms are not able to sell their products, at least not as much as before the recession. Their inventories pile up and they decrease production. This means that the demand for the worker, in this example, also decreases. The employer may ask a worker to work part-time or just fire the worker. In such a situation, the worker will be happy to go back to work if he/she was unemployed, or work full-time if he/she was working part-time, without asking for a raise.

Similar logic holds for prices. With the onset of the recession firms cannot sell their products and inventories pile up. During recession, some of the machines and buildings are also sitting idle or under-used. That is, there is excess capacity. If the demand for the widgets which a manufacturer is producing were to increase, the manufacturer would clear the piled up inventory. Furthermore, firms will utilize the machines and buildings which are not being used to capacity, without any corresponding increase in the costs of production, except of course for the increase in the raw material used. This will keep prices from increasing.

What would happen if prices and/or wages were to increase? An upward pressure on wages/prices would trigger, under normal circumstances (more on this shortly), a reaction from the monetary authorities. The central bank of a country (the name of the central bank of the United State is the Federal Reserve System, or the Fed, for short) is the body which conducts monetary policy. That is, changes in money supply. It is mandated to maintain a stable price level. If prices are increasing rapidly, it will decrease money supply, thereby raising interest rates. Increases in interest rates will raise the borrowing costs of businesses as well as households. Businesses borrow, not only to build factories, but also to finance their payrolls. Households usually borrow to buy big-ticket items such as houses, cars, and appliances. This in turn will lead to a decrease in spending, both by business as well as households. This decline in spending will choke-off the pressure on prices and wages.

6.5.1.2. Liquidity Traps, Inflation, and Deflation

I used the term "under normal circumstances." By this I mean that the economy is not in a situation where the inflation rate—the percentage increase in price level—is below the central bank's target and the nominal interest rate is not up against the zero-lower bound. Note that nominal interest rate cannot be below zero. A negative nominal interest rate would mean that you are paying the borrowers to borrow. In such a situation, it would make sense not to lend at all, just keep your saving "under the mattress," so to speak. If an economy is in recession and the zero-lower bound has been hit, as it happened in recent history in Japan during the 1990s and in the United States in the aftermath of the financial crisis of 2008, a central bank runs out of its usual tools to conduct monetary policy. Technical term for such a situation is called "liquidity trap." There is a lot of "liquidity"—interest rates are very low—but the economy is "trapped" in a recession.

Notice that the purpose is to increase aggregate demand so that output may increase. And recall that components of aggregate demand include consumption demand, investment demand, government spending, and demand by foreigners, that is, net exports. The amount by which a given dollar increase in aggregate demand will lead to an increase in output is called multiplier. For instance, if a one dollar increase in government spending leads to an increase in output by, say, two dollars, we would say that the value of the government-spending multiplier is two. Same goes for the other components of aggregate demand. What do studies show about the estimated value of government spending multiplier during recessions? According to some of the most carefully done studies, estimates range between 1 and 1.5 during recession.[69] During liquidity traps, the estimates are higher still. Studies show that during liquidity traps, an increase in government expenditure packs an especially larger punch; each dollar spent by the government may lead to an increase in aggregate output as high as four dollars, or higher.[70]

The notion that a central bank would want to have a positive inflation rate may take some by surprise. Why would a central bank want to maintain inflation rate above a certain point? Isn't a zero inflation rate or better yet, a declining price level—a deflation—desirable? We hear all the time that prices are increasing. People romantically recall the times when they could buy a bottle of Coke for a nickel, or when the price of an average house was less than the price of an average, run of the mill, car would now carry. Let us spend a few paragraphs on this topic.

Since the Great Depression of the 1930s, economists have learned quite a lot about certain facets of the macroeconomy. We have learned that while a rapidly rising price level—inflation beyond a certain rate—is undesirable, a declining price level, as appealing as it may sound to some, is even worse. Central banks around the world set targets for inflation rate around 2–3 percent. Sometimes these targets are explicit, at other times these targets are implicit. For instance in the case of the United States, the Federal Reserve System did not declare an explicit inflation rate target. The financial crisis which started in 2008 brought a lot of changes. One of the changes is the open talk of the inflation rate target. The Federal Reserve System deems an annual inflation rate of 2 percent consistent with its mandates.[71]

Why would a declining price level be detrimental to the economy? Imagine that you could buy a chair today for, say, $100. You have been noticing that the prices of chairs are declining. If you waited a week, you may be able to buy the same chair for $80. Unless you really need the chair right now, it would make sense to wait. Assume that next week the price does indeed decline to $80. Again, unless you are badly in need of the chair, it would make sense to wait even longer. Perhaps if you waited yet another week, the price would be $60. Notice, however, that you are not the only one who is thinking in these terms. Other chair buyers are also keeping an eye on the prices. While it makes sense to wait at an individual level, if everyone else used the same reasoning, the chair manufacturers will not be able to sell their chairs, at least not all the chairs produced. And if they cannot sell their chairs, they would not need workers to build those chairs. They will fire some of the workers or ask them to work fewer hours, or perhaps some combination of the two. Workers, who have either lost their jobs or who have fewer hours to work, will cut down on their purchases. The firms which produce what these workers buy will also have to lay off some workers or ask them to work fewer hours, or some combination of the two. Now multiplier is working in the reverse. These events can spell disaster for the economy as a whole. Recall the discussion with regard to gross domestic product (GDP). It was noted that in an economy as a whole, one person's income is someone else's expenditure, and vice versa. This is just an application of that fact. If I cut my spending, someone else's income is lowered by the same amount, and vice versa.

Another negative side effect of a declining price level is the increasing debt burden for the borrowers. When we borrow (or lend) we borrow in nominal terms. That is, we borrow certain amount of, say, dollars. We promise to repay the amount borrowed, plus the interest. Let us continue the example of the $100-dollar chair. You borrowed $100 to buy the chair. Now assume that after a certain period of time when you are supposed to repay the debt, along with the interest, the prices of chairs have declined to $50 per chair. For simplicity, let us ignore the interest payment for the moment. This means that in real terms your debt burdened has doubled: you borrowed one chair but you have to return two chairs. Another way to put it is that in the case of declining prices, wealth has been transferred from the borrower to the lender. (The reverse will happen if prices were increasing, especially rapidly; wealth will be transferred from the lender to the borrower. When prices are increasing at a modest pace, the interest payments account for the change in prices.) Households whose debt burden has increased they feel poorer and will further cut their expenditure. This may be because they cannot afford to buy or because they are being careful. This will further decrease aggregate demand. Also, some households who have debt and can repay their debts right away, in order to avoid higher debt burdens may do so. The flip side of this is that these households are spending less on consumption. This further decreases aggregate demand. Again, because in an economy as a whole, one person's income is someone else's expenditure, when everyone is cutting down on expenditure, everyone's income is decreasing. The economy goes into a downward spiral. This is where the role of government expenditure comes in. Government can increase its expenditure to pick of the slack.

Now, this does not mean that economy will never recover without government intervention. Eventually, houses need repairs, firms need new machines as old ones have either rusted due to sitting idle or worn out due to the regular use, and so on. When houses need fixing or firms need new machines, et cetera, expenditure increases and multiplier does what it is supposed to do. Economy recovers. But this may take a very long time. In the meantime a lot of people will suffer unnecessarily. This suffering could be avoided by government intervention. "Would an increase in government expenditure not lead to an increased federal debt and deficit?" one may ask. The short answer is: "yes," it would. However, the increased debt will be relatively small compared to the benefits it would yield. Once output increases, government revenue will also increase as households' incomes go up. And as households get jobs, government expenditure on unemployment and other formal social safety nets will decrease. Both will lead to a decline in government deficit and debt.

6.5.1.3. The Impact of Tax Cuts on the Economy: Predictions of the Economic Theory

Change in government expenditure is one part of fiscal policy; the other part is change in taxes. To stimulate the economy government may also cut taxes. The impact of tax cuts has a behavioral component which works along several dimensions.[72] The results on output may differ depending upon whether or not tax cuts are perceived to be permanent or temporary. Results on output may also depend upon whether or not the inter-temporal substitution effect is larger than the wealth effect (more on inter-temporal substitution effect and wealth effect shortly). The theoretical discussion here (and later in Chapter 7), of how a given tax change may affect various economic aggregates, is not in any way meant to be exhaustive. Here I outline the basic impact of a tax change. Curious reader is referred to Alan J. Auerbach and Laurence J. Kotlikoff (1987)[73] for an in-depth analysis. The purpose of providing this brief overview is to set the stage for empirical evidence which follows.

Broadly speaking, tax cuts may be divided into two categories: tax cuts on labor income and tax cuts on non-labor income. The latter income is usually referred to as "capital income." It may come from the interest on saving. Tax cuts may also be temporary or they may be permanent. By "temporary" I mean that, taking the example of labor income, taxes are expected to go up within my working life-time. If they go up after I have retired, for me, they are permanent. By the same token, temporary tax cuts on capital income would mean that taxes will go up on such income before I die. If they went up after I had died, for me they are permanent. The behavior of economic agents will be different under a temporary tax cut than under a permanent tax cut.

If the tax cuts on labor income are presumed to be temporary, economic agents may make inter-temporal substitutions. That is, they may opt to work more now and earn higher labor income when taxes on labor income are lower and give up leisure. It makes sense. Right now, their after-tax income is high because tax is low. This means that the opportunity cost of leisure is high. They have to give up more if they take an hour break than they would if they took an hour break in the future when taxes on labor income would be higher and disposable income will be low. This also has consequences for output. If workers are working more, all else constant, output will increase.

This has implications for saving by workers. All else constant, this means that their saving *rate* will be high. If they kept their consumption the same, the *proportion* of income saved will be high. This is not the end of the story, however. When an economic agent's income increases, she/he feels wealthy, which leads to higher consumption. This is the so-called "wealth effect" or "income effect" of income change. The wealth effect and inter-temporal substitution effect work in the opposite directions. The wealth effect leads to increased consumption and lower saving, and the inter-temporal substitution effect leads to higher saving and lower consumption.

Let us now turn to temporary taxes on capital income. If taxes on capital income decrease temporarily, all else constant, saving may decrease. This is because economic agents expect the taxes on capital income to increase in the future, they would rather consume more than save and pay taxes on capital income.

What happens when tax cuts end? First, let us look at the impact of ending tax cuts on labor income. Now that tax cuts on labor income have ended, disposable income has gone down, and labor supply will go down as well. Economic agents would rather take an hour break than work because leisure is cheaper. How about saving when tax cuts on capital income end? Saving may also decline. This is because capital income has higher taxes than before. It makes sense to consume rather than save. The impact on output, once tax cuts have ended, is negative, whether it is the labor income or the capital income. Decreased labor supply leads to decreased output, all else constant. And decreased savings lead to lower capital stock and the resultant lower output.

Now let us turn to tax cuts which are presumed to be permanent. First, let us see the possible impact on saving. If tax cuts on labor income are of permanent nature, then there should not be any inter-temporal substitution effect. My disposable labor income is expected to be higher forever. Given that economic agents want to smooth their consumption, saving will decrease and consumption will increase, now and later. What about permanent tax cuts on capital income? In this situation, on the one hand it makes sense to save more and decrease consumption. This is substitution effect. On the other hand, however, since an economic agent can maintain a certain level of wealth while increasing consumption, saving may go down. This is the wealth effect. Whether saving will increase or decrease due to cutting taxes permanently on capital income will depend upon which effect dominate: the wealth effect or the substitution effect.

How would the output be affected under permanent tax cuts? As we just saw, with a permanent tax cut on labor income, saving may decrease. This will lead to a decline in capital stock and a resulting decline in output. If the permanent tax cut is on capital income, and substitution effect dominates, saving may increase, leading to an increase in capital stock and a resultant increase in output. If the wealth effect of permanent tax cuts on capital income dominates, saving may decrease, leading to a lower capital stock and lower output.

6.5.1.4. The Impact of Tax Cuts on the Economy: Empirical Evidence

This is what economic theory tells us. What do empirical studies show? Alan J. Auerbach (2002)[74] looked at the possible impact of the Economic Growth and Tax Relief Reconciliation Act, commonly known as the "Bush tax cuts." Under this act, significant tax cuts were enacted by the US Congress during 2001. His simulation results showed that the impact on output in the short run was positive. In the long run, however, output declined. With regard to the impact of tax cuts on government revenue, the simulation results of the Auerbach (2002) study showed that government revenues also declined.

The question arises though, "If the results of tax cuts are so unfavorable in the long run, why is there so much support for such a measure, as opposed to increased government spending?" Opinion surveys, conducted properly, can be revelatory. Larry M. Bartels (2006)[75] analyzed survey data. It turns out that general populace is extremely un-informed about tax policies and their impacts. Information, to the extent that it exists, is incorrect. Bartels finds that respondents' answers point to ideological predispositions. Information or lack thereof, seems to have relatively little to do with the formation of opinions. People have a visceral reaction to taxes. Whether or not they are the beneficiaries of tax cuts, they prefer tax cuts to tax increases by a large margin. One such example is the repeal of estate tax, or "death tax," as the opponents of the estate tax labeled it. He writes:

> ... among those with family incomes of less than $50,000 who want more spending on government programs *and* said income inequality has increased *and* said that is a bad thing *and* said that government policy contributes to income inequality *and* said that rich people pay less than they should in federal income taxes—the 11 percent of the sample with the strongest conceivable set of reasons to support continuation of the estate tax—64 percent favored repeal. (p.410, italics original)

When it comes to issues for which there is a strong support among the body politic, elected officials rarely take the opinions of general public into consideration. They tend to support the views of their "core supporters." Bartels (2006) cites the example of minimum wage. While there is strong support for increasing minimum wage among public, policy preferences of elected officials are directed by "the ideological convictions of political elites."(p.417).

6.5.2. Why Should the Haves Care? The "Softer" Side

So far I have addressed the question of "why should the haves care?" purely from the "quantitative" point of view. That is, is it a good business strategy to increase aggregate demand? If I am producing widgets and want to sell them, I need buyers. A depressed aggregate demand does not help. And as long as the marginal cost of producing the widgets is less than the marginal revenue, it makes sense to incur that marginal cost. It makes sense even if the marginal cost is in the form of increased taxes to pay for the increased government spending. Now I turn to the "softer" side of this issue.

Lester Thurow (1971)[76] argues that we care about, not only our own incomes, but the incomes of others as well. Our neighbors' wellbeing affects our wellbeing. Seeing an indigent on the street arouses feelings of pity. Indeed, relying on the arousal of such feelings, charities soliciting donations show pictures of children with potbellies and cleft lips and pallets. Perhaps to avoid these depressing feelings companies in the business of pleasure cruises ward off areas of islands and make every effort to keep poverty out of sight—only the happier parts of life are on display.

We could build walls around our neighborhoods to ward off unpleasantness. We, however, live in a social environment. Contact with other humans is not only inevitable it is a necessity. An alternative to building walls maybe alleviation of poverty. As Thurow (1971) argued " . . . individuals may simply want to live in societies with particular income distribution and economic power." And that " . . . the individual is simply exercising an aesthetic taste for equality or inequality similar in nature to a taste for paintings."(p.327). Using the language of economics, our utility functions are interdependent. "When the income distribution appears in individual utility functions, income transfers take on a different characteristic than when they are generated by either of the other two motives" (p.328). (The other two motives Thurow (1971) mentions are (1) " . . . incomes of other individuals may appear in their own utility functions. To maximize their own utility they may find it necessary to redistribute their income to some other person." And that (2) "Individuals may also receive utility from the process of giving gifts (charity).") "*The income distribution is a pure public good.*" (p.328, italics original), Thurow (1971) argued.

If that is the case then redistribution of income may be utility enhancing in and of itself. And this is exactly what Alberto Alesina et al. (2004)[77] find. While there are differences between Europeans and Americans and also along the ideological and socio-economic lines, inequality does seem to reduce utility and make us less happy. If living happily is one of the motives of acquiring wealth, then reducing inequality and poverty by giving some of our acquisitions away may help bring additional joy.

6.6. Chapter Summary

I started this chapter by discussing income distribution and poverty. We looked at how developed countries rank along poverty's various dimensions. We saw that poverty may persist over generations in the absence poverty-alleviating governmental policies. We saw that during times of recession an increased government spending provides a better chance of recovery than tax cuts, and that increasing government spending during times of recession may not lead to an increased debt-to-GDP ratio in the long run.

I presented arguments about why the haves should care about the have-nots. We saw that formal social safety nets, indeed, decrease income inequality, which may be beneficial not only for the have-nots, but also for the haves. In Chapter 7, I turn to issues related to financing of social safety nets with taxes. I discuss whether or not increasing taxes to finance social safety nets has any impact on economic growth.

Appendix

Table 6.A Variable definitions and data sources

Variable Name	Definition	Source
Average Disposable Income	Average equivalised household disposable income in households with children (0–17-year-olds), USD PPP thousands, circa 2005. Income data is average family income for children aged 0–17 years. Data is for various years between 2003 and 2005. It is drawn from national household panel surveys of all OECD countries. Data is converted to common USD using OECD purchasing power parity exchange rates, and equivalised using the square root of the family size." Educational Deprivation: "Percentage of children reporting less than four educational possessions aged 15 yrs: 2006.	OECD Income Distribution database, developed for OECD (2008b), Growing Unequal – Income Distribution and Poverty in OECD Countries, mid-1980s to mid-2000s.
Children in Poor Homes	Children in poor households (50% of median income), 2005. The child poverty measure used is the proportion of households with children living on an equivalised income below 50% of the national median income for the year 2005. Children are defined as those aged 0–17 years. All OECD countries are included.	OECD Income Distribution database, developed for OECD (2008b), Growing Unequal – Income Distribution and Poverty in OECD Countries, mid-1980s to mid-2000s.
Educational Deprivation	Percentage of children reporting less than four educational possessions aged 15 yrs: 2006. Educational deprivation data are derived from PISA 2006 (OECD/PISA, 2008). PISA asks questions about the possession of eight items, including a desk to study; a quiet place to work, a computer for schoolwork, educational software, an internet connection, a calculator, a dictionary, and school textbooks. The proportion of children reporting less than four of these educational items is used (less than four items best represented results for cut-off points at three, four, five and six items). PISA collection processes employ standardised questionnaires, translation, and monitoring procedures, to ensure high standards of comparability.	OECD Programme for International Student Assessment database 2006 (OECD/PISA, 2008).

Overcrowding	Percentage of children living in overcrowding homes as a proportion of all children (2006). Overcrowding is assessed though questions on "number of rooms available to the household" for European countries from the Survey on Income and Living Conditions (EU-SILC) conducted in 2006; on the "number of bedrooms" in Australia; on whether the household "cannot afford more than one bedroom" or "cannot afford to have a bedroom separate from eating room" in Japan; and on the "number of rooms with kitchen and without bath" in the United States. Overcrowding is deemed to prevail when the number of household members exceeds the number of rooms (i.e. a family of four is considered as living in an overcrowded accommodation when there are only three rooms – excluding kitchen and bath but including a living room). Data is for various years from 2003 to 2006. The Japanese survey is an unofficial and experimental survey designed by the National Institute of Population and Social Security Research, with a nationally representative sample limited to around 2 000 households and around 6 000 persons aged 20 years and above. Canada, Korea, Switzerland, and Turkey are missing.	Data for 22 EU countries are taken from EU-SILC (2006). Data for Australia are taken from the survey Household Income and Labour Dynamics in Australia (HILDA) 2005. Data for Japan are from the Shakai Seikatsu Chousa (Survey of Living Conditions) 2003. Data for the United States are taken from the Survey of Income and Program Participation (SIPP) 2003. Aggregate data for Mexico was provided by the Mexican Delegation to the OECD.
Poor Environmental Conditions	Percentage of children living in homes with poor environmental conditions as a proportion of all children (2006). Local environmental conditions are assessed through questions on whether the household's accommodation "has noise from neighbours or outside" or has "any pollution, grime or other environmental problem caused by traffic or industry" for European countries; whether there is "vandalism in the area", "grime in the area" or "traffic noise from outside" for Australia; whether "noises from neighbours can be heard" for Japan; and whether there is "street noise or heavy street traffic", "trash, litter, or garbage in the street", "rundown or abandoned houses or buildings" or "odors, smoke, or gas fumes" for the United States. Data is for various years from 2003 to 2006. Canada, Korea, Mexico, New Zealand, Switzerland, and Turkey are missing.	Data for 21 EU countries are taken from EU-SILC (2006). Data for Australia are taken from the survey Household Income and Labour Dynamics in Australia (HILDA) 2005. Data for Japan are from the Shakai Seikatsu Chousa (Survey of Living Conditions) 2003. Data for the United States are taken from the Survey of Income and Program Participation (SIPP) 2003.

Table 6.A (Continued)

Variable Name	Definition	Source
Average Mean Literacy Score	Average mean PISA literacy score, 2006. Mean literacy performance is the average of mathematics, reading and science literacy scores. Data is for 15-year-old students.	OECD Programme for International Student Assessment database 2006 (OECD/PISA, 2008).
Literacy Inequality	Ratio of 90th to 10th percentile score in mean PISA literacy achievement. The measure is of country inequality in scores, averaged across the three literacy dimensions. The measure of inequality used is the ratio of the score at the 90th percentile to that at the 10th percentile. Data is for 15-year-old students.	OECD Programme for International Student Assessment database 2006 (OECD/PISA, 2008).
Youth NEET Rates	Percentage of the 15–19 population not in education and unemployed: 2005. Data records children not in education and not in employment or training. The data cover those aged 15 to 19 years of age in 2006. Data for Mexico is from 2004 and data for Turkey is from 2005. Data for Japan is for the population aged 15 to 24 years. Education and training participation rates are self reported. Surveys and administrative sources may record the age and activity of the respondent at different times of the year. Double counting of youth in a number of different programmes may occur. Data for Iceland and Korea are missing from this comparison.	OECD Education at a Glance, 2008

Source: OECD website (http://stats.oecd.org/Index.aspx?DataSetCode=CWB) (Accessed: June 22, 2013).

CHAPTER 7

Financing of Formal Social Safety Nets

I have argued in this book that as economies grow beyond a certain point, informal social safety nets do not suffice, and just as a legal tender is needed for a smoothly functioning financial system, formal social safety nets, financed by taxes, are needed for economies to grow beyond a certain level. It is only natural, then, that whenever one talks about government providing social safety nets, one has to answer at least two important, and related, questions. First, how this provision will affect government expenditure? And second, how is the government going to finance social safety nets? The discussion of the provision of government-provided social safety nets is intimately related to the state of government finances. By a government's financial status I mean government revenues versus government expenditure situation. After all, if government is going to provide social safety nets, it will have to raise revenue to support such an endeavor. And since the main source of government revenue is taxes, it will need enough tax revenue to support increased expenditure due to its decision to provide social safety nets. In this chapter, along with discussion about government finances, I will also present research that looks at the impact of taxes on various aggregate economic measures including saving, investment, output growth, and income distribution. Before we go any further, however, let us look at the current economic conditions of the United States and compare these conditions with other developed countries.

7.1. Current Economic Realities

A lot has been written about increasing national deficits and debts since the onset of the Great Recession of 2007–2009. If history is any guide, still more will be written for years to come. This economic calamity brought to the fore not only the need for formal safety nets, but also the debate over deficits and debt. One argument extended against the provision of formal social safety nets by the government is that such a plan will lead to increased deficits and debt. So before I start, a few definitions will be instructive.

Building on the discussion of deficit and debt in Chapter 6, deficit will occur if government revenue is larger than government expenditure per time period, usually per annum. A situation in which government revenue is greater than government expenditure is called surplus.[1] Debt is the accumulated deficits minus surpluses. Generally, deficits are an artifact of recessions. When an economy goes into a recession, government revenues decrease and government expenditures increase. There are two main reasons. One, as an economy enters into a recession, households' incomes decrease, which leads to a decline in the taxes that households pay. This leads to a decrease in government revenue. Second, during recessions, some households will become unemployed and apply for unemployment benefits. (For the sake of simplicity I am using "unemployment benefit" as an umbrella term for all government formal social safety net expenditure—unemployment insurance benefits; Supplemental Nutritional Support Program (SNAP), formerly known as "food stamps"; Medicaid; etc.) This will lead to an increase in government expenditure. Deficit that results from the economic downturns is called cyclical deficit.

When an economy is on a positive trajectory, that is, when output is increasing and households have jobs, incomes increase. As their incomes increase, their tax bills also increase, and so does the government revenue. Of course, during recoveries tax bills of firms also increase, leading to further increase in government revenue. Not only that, as households find jobs, they get off of unemployment benefits. This leads to a decline in government expenditure. These two phenomena represent the normal functioning of fiscal policy—the policy related to government revenue and expenditure. And indeed, this is exactly what fiscal policy is supposed to do. It is supposed to have a moderating effect in the economy. As we saw in Chapter 6, government expenditure takes up some of the gap in aggregate demand created by decreased household expenditure due to decreased incomes, a decrease in investment demand, and a decrease in a country's output bought by the rest of the world. Recall that aggregate demand is the sum of consumption demand, investment demand, government expenditure, and whatever a country exports to the rest of the world. And when economy recovers and households have high enough incomes and as a result firms have high enough demand for their widgets, aggregate demand does not need support from the government. Furthermore, as household incomes increase, taxes paid by households also increase, leading to an increase in government revenue.

Both these events—an increase in government expenditure during recessions and a pullback during recoveries—have a moderating impact on economic activity. Economists use the term "automatic stabilizers" to represent

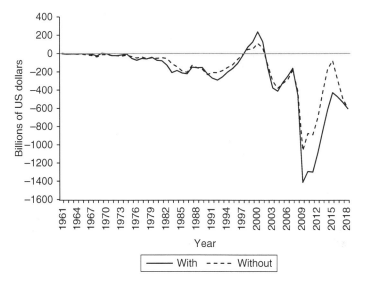

Figure 7.1 Deficit or surplus, with and without automatic stabilizers[2]
Note: Data from 2013 to 2018 are projected estimates.
Source: US Congressional Budget Office (www.cbo.gov).

this phenomenon. Indeed, the purpose of fiscal policy (or monetary policy) is to reduce the severity of business cycles—that is, reduce the peaks and trough of short-run ups and down in economic activity. In Figure 7.1, I plot deficit and surplus data with (solid line) and without (broken line) automatic stabilizers from 1969 to 2018. Data from 2013 to 2018 are projected estimates. Note that deficits and surplus will be lower if automatic stabilizers did not do their jobs or did not exist. The result, however, will be accentuated business cycles.

Another type of deficit is the so called "structural" deficit. This refers to a situation in which government expenditure is greater than government revenue even when economy is not in recession. That is, fiscal policy is "structured" in such a way that deficits take place even when economy is operating at a normal rate. That is, output is at potential level. We encountered the concept of "potential output" in Chapter 6. Recall that potential output does not mean the maximum output that an economy can produce. Rather it is the level of output that an economy can produce over the long run, without putting an upward pressure on prices. In the short run, output may rise above or fall below this potential level of output. Structural deficits are over and above the deficits that occur during recessions, that is, the cyclical deficits.

Taxes are one way to finance increased government expenditure. A government, of course, may also borrow to finance its expenditure, at least in the short run. *Ordinarily*, however, when a government borrows, it may run the risk of putting an upward pressure of interest rates. This is because, given the amount of funds available to be borrowed, government is competing with private borrowers—firms, households, etc. Increases in interest rates raise borrowing costs. This means that households borrowing to finance big-ticket items—houses, cars, appliances, furniture, and so on—may avoid or delay their purchases. Firms may also find that certain projects are no longer profitable to pursue. Both these activities will result in a decreased aggregate demand, which, in turn, will depress economic activity. Indeed, as we saw in chapters 2 and 6, the Federal Reserve System (or the "Fed" for short)— the US central bank—steers the economy in a certain direction by affecting interest rates. When the Fed considers that the economy is producing below its potential output, it may choose to lower interest rates, thus lowering the borrowing costs. On the other hand, when the Fed deems the output level to be above potential output, it may raise interest rates, and as a result raising the borrowing costs.

(Recall that the Fed affects interest rates by changing money supply.[3] The Fed does not dictate the lenders to charge a particular interest rate on loans. Rather it sets a target interest rate and changes the money supply such that the target is met.)

Another artifact of increased interest rates is that it may further worsen a government's financial situation. Increased interest rates mean increased borrowing costs for the government as well. This makes borrowing more expensive and limits a government's ability to affect economic activity through increased government expenditure. In the absence of such a constraint, if an economy is slowing down, government can borrow and increase government expenditure. As we saw above and in Chapter 6, during recessions government can increase its expenditure and fill in the gap left by households, firms, and the foreign sector. If, however, government is unable to increase expenditure (or in some cases unwilling to increase expenditure as a matter of policy) the economy may stay in recession a lot longer than it has to. This would mean that peoples' incomes will be lower for an extended period of time.

Increased government-borrowing costs may also extremely limit a government's ability to respond during natural disasters. Say, a hurricane hits a town and destroys the town's infrastructure and its residents' lives. The federal government may need to step in and provide support and help rebuild. The higher costs of borrowing may pose a veritable constraint to the government's ability to provide help.

I italicized the word "ordinarily" a few paragraphs ago. This is because in situations when liquidity traps exist (see Chapter 6), this expected upward pressure on interest rates is minimal or non-existent. Indeed, in the aftermath of the Great Recession, when the United States entered liquidity trap, the US government could borrow at historic low interest rates. So much so that starting in early 2011 and going all the way well into the fourth quarter of 2013, for certain loans (for instance, five-year inflation-indexed constant maturity securities, and ten-year inflation-indexed constant maturity securities),[4] people were willing to charge the US government a negative interest rate: They were *paying* the US government to borrow from them.

What further complicates the situation is that government's tax revenues are tied to economic agents' incomes. All else constant, the longer an economy stays in recession, the lower the incomes of economic agents, and the lower the government tax revenue. Government, in other words, has to perform a balancing act: It will have to weigh the costs and benefits of borrowing. The costs of increasing borrowing are possible increases in interest rates and benefits of borrowing are increased output due to increase in government expenditure. The point I am trying to make is that whether borrowing by government is a "good" thing or a "bad" thing depends upon the state of the economy. While an individual may prefer being debt free, from an economic point of view, for a government there is no virtue in being absolutely debt free. A cutback by the government may, indeed, end up worsening the financial situation of the government. In Chapter 6, I cited the example of Spain (see Figure 6.6). On the eve of the financial crisis, Spain was running a surplus. However, the effort to cut back government expenditure led to a sharp increase in government-budget deficit.

7.1.1. Budget Deficits, Budget Surpluses, and Formal Social Safety Nets

As I mentioned in the beginning of this chapter, the provision of government-financed formal social safety nets and government finances have a close relationship. It is instructive to take a look at the social expenditure of various countries and their governments' financial statuses. Since objections raised against providing formal social safety nets by the government rest, at least partly, on the idea that such expenditures will invariably lead to increased government-budget deficits, it also makes sense to explore how different countries fare along these dimensions, that is, see whether or not countries that have relatively generous government-provided formal social safety nets also have higher budget deficits.

The other major objection is, of course, that if governments want to provide formal social safety nets, they will have to increase tax rates to meet the increased expenditure needs. And increased tax rates may have a detrimental impact on economic growth. I will address this question after I have presented data for social expenditure and budget deficits.

We saw in Chapter 1, Figure 1.1, that over time public social expenditure,[5] as a percentage of gross domestic product (GDP), has been increasing. In Figure 1.1, I plotted annual data for Australia, France, Japan, the United States, the aggregate data for 21 countries of the European Union, and the aggregate data for 34 Organization for Economic Co-operation and Development (OECD) member countries from 1960 to 2012. These aggregates were labeled in Figure 1.1 as EU-21 and OECD-34, respectively. Here I present quinquennial social expenditure data as a percentage of GDP for 23 OECD countries individually, from 1980 to 2005. These data are plotted in Figure 7.2.[6]

A couple of points need highlighting. One, while there is variation over time, there is also variation from country to country.[7] Second, as we saw in Figure 1.1, over time social expenditure as a percentage of GDP has been increasing.[8] Note that the solid line representing the year 2005 for most countries tends to lie above various "broken" lines, which represent earlier years.

By way of focusing rather narrowly and for the ease of exposition, in Figure 7.3, I plot data for the year 2007 across 34 OECD member countries.[9] The reason for picking 2007 as the year for a narrower focus is to see the picture just prior to the onset of the financial crisis of 2007–2008, and the Great Recession of 2007–2009.[10] Once the Great Recession hit, different policies were adopted by different countries, which led to different outcomes. As I discussed in Chapter 6, and recounted the example of Spain above,

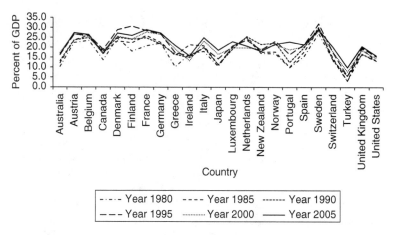

Figure 7.2 Total public social expenditure as a percentage of GDP (quinquennial data from 1985 to 2005)[11]

Source: OECD social expenditure database.

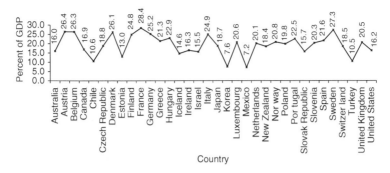

Figure 7.3 Total public social expenditure as a percentage of GDP (2007)[12]
Source: OECD social expenditure database

countries that opted for cutting government spending, that is, "austerity," ended up with even higher deficit to GDP ratios. The reason: Austerity led to a decline in GDP, the denominator in the deficit to GDP ratio, far more than it decreased the numerator. For elucidatory purposes, in Figure 7.3, I also show data labels (for instance, 16.2 for the United States, 20.5 for the United Kingdom, and so on) for each country. I did not show data labels in Figure 7.2 for fear of cluttering the diagram and rendering it unreadable.

For the year 2007 (Figure 7.3), the country with the highest percentage of GDP dedicated to social expenditure is France (28.4 percent), and the country that dedicates the lowest percentage of GDP on social expenditure is Mexico (7.2 percent). The mean percentage expenditure for these 34 countries is 19.2 percent (and the median is 19.95 percent), with a standard deviation of about 5.5 percent.

Now let us look at the deficit to GDP ratios of eight industrialized Western countries that have relatively similar living standards but have different policies toward public social expenditure. These countries are Canada, Denmark, France, Norway, the Netherlands, Sweden, the United Kingdom, and the United States. I have selected these countries to represent a cross section of countries that have relatively more generous welfare spending—France (28.4 percent), Denmark (26.1 percent), the Netherlands (20.1 percent), Norway (20.8 percent), and Sweden (27.3 percent)—and compare these countries to those that have relatively less generous welfare spending— Canada (16.9 percent), the United Kingdom (20.5 percent), and the United States (16.2 percent). Figure 7.4 plots these data.

While the curves in the figure are admittedly hard to read, I show these data to make a point: Except for Norway, which has a surplus for almost

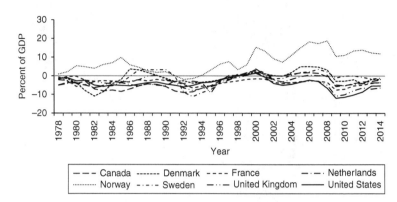

Figure 7.4 Deficit/surplus as percent of GDP from 1978 to 2014[13]

Note: Negative numbers represent deficits and positive numbers represent surpluses. Data for 2013 and 2014 are forecasts).

Source: OECD website.

Table 7.1 Average deficit/surplus as a percent of GDP from 1978 to 2014

County	Years	Mean
Canada	37	−3.37
Denmark	37	−1.11
France	37	−3.33
Netherlands	37	−3.12
Norway	37	7.56
Sweden	37	−1.37
United Kingdom	37	−3.82
United States	37	−4.18

Note: Negative numbers represent deficits and positive numbers represent surpluses. Data for 2013 and 2014 are forecasts.

Source: OECD website[14].

the entire time period (except for 1992 and 1993), the rest of the countries' deficit to GDP ratios move rather closely. In Table 7.1, I provide the averages of the eight countries whose deficit/surplus to GDP ratios are plotted over the 1978–2014 period (37 years).

Note again that, except for Norway, every country included in the table on average ran a deficit over this time period. The mean of the deficit-to-GDP ratios of all eight countries is −1.59, with a standard deviation of about 3.86. If we exclude Norway, an obvious outlier, from the analysis, the mean of the deficit-to-GDP ratios of the remaining seven countries over this time period is −2.9, with a standard deviation of about 1.19.

In this "back-of-the-envelope" analysis we do not find that countries that have generous formal social safety nets also run deficits. That is, if the contention that generosity of government-provided formal social safety nets translates into higher deficit to GDP ratios were true, then we would see that countries with generous formal social safety nets would also have higher deficit-to-GDP ratios. This analysis, however, does not point to this tendency. Even if we did see this correlation, it would not necessarily mean that generosity of formal social safety nets is the reason for higher deficits. Deficits could arise from a number of other reasons, and generosity of formal social safety nets could just be one contributing factor. It could also be the case that a third factor is affecting the expenditure on formal social safety nets and deficits. For instance, as discussed earlier, when countries go through economic downturns, government revenues decrease and government expenditures increase. This will lead to an increase in budget deficits. And deficit may increase even if the level of government expenditure stayed the same. This is because, as mentioned earlier, deficit is the difference between government revenue and government expenditure. And since government revenue has decreased due to lower tax receipts, deficit will increase.

Another reason may be structural deficits. Recall that structural deficit is the deficit that exists even when an economy is operating at full employment and output is at potential level. For instance, in the case of the United States (and Canada), the "baby-boom" generation—individuals born between the late 1940s and the early 1960s—is starting to retire. This has led to an increase in government expenditure, on the one hand, and a decrease in government revenue, on the other. Why is that? As the baby-boom generation is retiring, it is relying more on government-provided services such as Medicare and social security benefits. This translates into increased government expenditure. At the same time, since they are retiring, their incomes are declining and so are their tax bills—a decline in government revenue. Combine the two and you have a deficit. And this will happen even if the economy is not in a recession or the tax rates remain unchanged.

So far we have primarily looked only at the numerators in the deficit-to-GDP ratio, and in social expenditure-to-GDP ratio. In both ratios, the denominator is GDP. Just looking at the correlation between deficit/surplus and social expenditure makes the rather simplistic assumption that such redistributive policies that tend to equalize incomes across the body politic do not affect GDP. For a complete picture we have to see what impact, if any, these policies may have on GDP. In Chapter 4, I presented my own research in which we saw that formal social safety nets (with a five-year lag) have a positive impact on innovative activities. Inequality of income, on the other hand, has a negative impact on innovation (with a five-year lag). In Chapter 4, the empirical evidence presented also showed that taxes (with a five-year lag) have a positive impact on innovative activities. Given that innovation leads to higher economic growth, it implies that formal social safety nets have positive impact on output.

As we also saw in chapters 5 and 6, research shows that redistributive policies have a statistically significant impact on GDP. Just by way of recalling, in chapters 5 and 6, I presented research on the negative correlation between inequality and economic growth, which works, among other channels, through investment.[15] As increasing inequality engenders political unrest, investment declines, and in turn economic growth falters. If indeed GDP declines with increased inequality, in an effort to decrease the deficit when a country cuts back on social expenditure, it may end up worsening the situation. It may end up lowering GDP and retarding economic growth. I repeated this rather lengthy discussion to make the point that focusing only on current deficits is perhaps misguided. In doing so, we are ignoring the positive impact of an increased government expenditure on GDP.

One way to avoid increases in deficits and debts is to increase government revenue by increasing tax rates. The concern, however, is that an increase in taxes will harm economic growth, thereby hurting GDP, the denominator in deficit-to-GDP ratio and in the social expenditure-to-GDP ratio. Recall that this is a major concern when it comes to providing formal social safety nets financed by taxes. It is argued that since an increase in tax rates will lower the after-tax income, the incentive to earn an extra dollar may decrease, leading to lower overall economic activity and lower economic growth. I turn to this point now.

7.2. Financing Formal Social Safety Nets with Taxes

I start the discussion in this sub-section by providing a very brief overview of what economic theory has to say about the possible effects of tax increases on the economy. This is a continuation of discussion from Chapter 6, Section 6.4.1.3.

Public finance is a broad field with a rich scholarly tradition. It goes without saying that I am not doing justice to the topic by trying to squeeze the discussion in a few paragraphs. My excuse for this abridgement, however, is that a more detailed theoretical discussion of which particular economic activity to tax (for example, levy tax on potatoes or on dishwashers; if potatoes then levy tax on growing potatoes or on buying potatoes, etc.), by how much, and for how long (that is, should tax increases be temporary or permanent), whether the supply and demand curves of the activity in question are linear or non-linear, where we are on a given curve, and who bears the tax burden (producer or buyer) and by how much, is beyond the scope of this book. This is because the main argument presented in this book is that as economies grow, informal social safety nets prove insufficient and indeed serve as constraints on further growth. Formal social safety nets financed by taxes are needed for an economy to grow beyond a certain point. If we accept the argument that the marginal social benefit of formal social safety nets may be higher than the marginal social cost, then the question of how to raise taxes to finance formal social safety nets, while no doubt important, is a secondary question. So here I present the broader theoretical contours of public finance and the findings of recent empirical research about how taxes have impacted various economic aggregates. For a deeper understanding of the theoretical aspects of public finance, I refer the curious reader to the studies cited as a starting point.

It is not hard to imagine, nor is it a matter of any significant debate, that if a government wants to widen and deepen formal social safety nets, and wants to finance the extra expenditure with taxes, it will have to increase taxes. For instance, research estimates show that the implementation of the Affordable Care Act[16] will result in an increase in the "marginal tax rates" (tax on the additional dollar earned) of about 5 percent.[17] This expected increase in taxes and the possible negative impact on economy creates opposition to the idea of provision of goods and services by government. At times the opposition to the provision of goods and services by the government is so severe that talks between the opposing parties break down for extended periods of time. For instance, the disagreement over the Affordable Care Act led to the US government shutdown for 16 days during October 2013.[18]

Note, by the way, that "marginal" tax rate refers to the portion of the last dollar earned paid in taxes. Marginal tax rate may differ (and as we shall see below that it does differ) depending upon whether income is coming from, say, wages and salaries versus income coming from interest on saving. A related concept of tax rate is called "average" tax rate. It refers to the portion of overall income paid in taxes. Average tax rate on a given group of earners (say, individuals earning between $100,000 and $200,000, and so on) helps us understand the total tax burden borne by that group.

Generally speaking when one talks about income tax rates, one is often referring to the overall income, regardless of the source of income. As we know, income, of course, can come from several sources. It could come in the form of wages, interest, profit, capital gains, and so on. It is quite possible that the behaviors of these economic agents are characteristically different from one another; the reaction to a given tax change of someone earning wage income by supplying labor may be different from the reaction of someone earning interest income by supplying savings, and so on. Not only that, as we saw in Chapter 6 while discussing how tax cuts may affect output, the impact on output of cutting taxes also depends upon whether or not tax cuts are considered temporary or permanent. It is important, then, to see how changes in tax rates on income from a given activity will change the behavior of participants in that activity.[19] The combined effects of these changes on various activities help us ascertain the impact of a given tax change on the overall economy.

7.2.1. *Difference in Responsiveness to Tax Changes: A Few (More) Theoretical Considerations*

It is quite possible that an activity, say, Activity A, is relatively less responsive to tax changes as compared with, say, Activity B. Economists use tax elasticity to represent this phenomenon.[20] Elasticity, in general, means the responsiveness of one variable to the changes in another variable.[21] In our example of Activity A versus Activity B, if Activity A responds relatively less to a given tax change, as compared with Activity B, then Activity A will be considered less tax elastic than Activity B. Now the question is: Which activity should be taxed, Activity A or Activity B, and by how much?

Before we answer this question, however, we need to know the purpose of levying the tax. Is the goal of tax imposition to correct market externalities and curb a given activity, say, decreasing the use of gasoline,[22] or is the purpose to raise maximum revenue while having the minimum negative impact on the economy? Since in this book I am advocating providing formal social safety nets financed by taxes, I will focus on the revenue generation purpose of taxes. Note that the total tax revenue is just the amount of tax per "unit" of the activity times the "units" of that activity. So let us assume, then, that the purpose of levying a tax is to raise revenue so that a given expenditure can be supported while keeping the possible negative impact of tax at the minimum. For simplicity let us assume that we are not concerned with the question of who bears the tax burden (the buyer or the seller), and that both activities—Activity A and Activity B—if they change by the same magnitude, have the same impact on the economy. Activity A, however, has lower tax elasticity as compared with Activity B. That is, if tax of a certain amount is levied on Activity A, it will be affected less than Activity B by the same amount of tax. In that case, all else constant, taxing Activity A will be a better choice. This is because it will generate the maximum revenue with relatively lower negative impact on the economy. So breaking down the overall economic activity into its major components and looking at the impact of taxes on each of these constituents, then, can be insightful.

In Chapter 6 we saw that the impact of tax changes on private saving will depend upon whether or not tax changes are permanent or temporary, and whether or not tax changes are geared toward labor income or capital income. Note, however, that national saving is the sum of public saving and private saving. Public saving is government revenue minus government expenditure, and private saving is saving by households and firms. Let us look at the possible impact of tax on public saving—government revenue minus government expenditure. (By the way, "public saving" is just another term used for surplus or deficit. Surplus is positive public saving and deficit is negative public saving.) For instance, a reduction in taxes, all else constant, may have two opposing effects, depending upon how economy reacts to tax changes. A lower tax rate may lead to increased economic growth and higher incomes of economic agents. This means higher tax revenue for the government even if the tax *rate* is low. On the other hand, if a lower tax rate does not enhance economic growth and does not lead to increased incomes of economic agents, then, keeping the government expenditure constant, this will result in lower public saving.

Why do we care about having higher saving anyway? The argument is that if an economy has a higher saving rate, and assuming, of course, that the financial system is doing its job of connecting savers with borrowers who have productive uses for the funds, it will lead to higher investment, which in turn will lead to higher GDP. Why is that? Well, a higher level of saving, and hence funds to be borrowed, will lead to lower interest rates and lower borrowing costs. And as the standard economic theory dictates, lower borrowing costs will make more investment projects profitable, leading to higher investment, which will increase the productive capacity, which, in turn, will increase GDP, and so on. An increased level of saving, however, does not directly and automatically translate into higher investment and higher output. Indeed, it can happen that when everyone tries to save more, it can lead to lower GDP, without any effect on overall saving.

This phenomenon has been given the name of "Paradox of the Thrift." While principles-level students in macroeconomics classes are taught and tested on this topic, it is often omitted from policy debates. Here is how it works. Since at the level of the overall economy, one person's expenditure is someone else's income, if the first person, in order to save more, cuts down on spending, the person who is selling the first person his/her ware loses his/her income. While it may be prudent to save more at an individual level, if enough individuals in an economy cut down on expenditure, the output decreases, without any increase in saving. For investors to invest in various projects that may increase output, there has to be a demand for the goods and services that those investments will produce, a key link that often does not get the attention it deserves.

Let me now turn briefly to tax on capital gains. If an individual holds an asset, be it a financial asset like a share of stock or a bond, or real estate like a house or an office building, its price when sold may be different from when it was purchased.[23] The difference between the purchase price and the sale price, if positive, is called capital gain. That is, if the individual bought the asset at a lower price than what the individuals sold it for, it is called capital gain. If the difference is negative, it is called capital loss. How should the income from capital gain be treated during tax time has been the topic of discussion among policy makers and economists alike? This is because the after-tax return from such an investment is expected to influence the level of investment in an economy. All else constant, a high tax rate means a lower after-tax return, and vice versa. On the other hand, as Thomas Hungerford (2012)[24] points out:

> For risk-averse investors, the capital gains tax could act as insurance for risky investments by reducing the losses as well as the gains—it decreases the variability of investment returns. Consequently, a rise in the capital gains top [tax] rate could increase investment because of reduced risk. (p.6)

As noted earlier, real GDP, that is, GDP corrected for inflation, is expected to increase if investment increases. Why? The reason is that investment increases the productive capacity of a country and influences the economic activity in numerous ways. An increase in the quantity and quality of tools allows workers to produce goods and services in larger quantity and of better quality. Take the example of increasing investment in infrastructure, that is, building new roads, bridges, telecommunication networks, and so on. All else constant, the more roads, bridges, and telecommunication networks there are, the more connected are the various geographic areas, and more goods and services can be transported back and forth. But why the increased ability to transport goods and services will lead to increased real GDP? Recall from Chapter 2, increasing population size allows individuals to specialize in activities in which they have a comparative advantage, that is, in activities in which they have lower opportunity cost. Increased connectivity is akin to increasing population size and hence increasing the "extent of market," which in turn allows specialization and growth.

And this is just one avenue through which investment may increase output. In Chapter 3 I provided extensive discussion about the positive impact of investment in research and development (R&D) and education. Investments in R&D and education lead to technological improvements, that is, increases in the pool of knowledge. Increased knowledge allows us to produce more and better goods and services. Producing "more" goods and services, by the way, does not necessarily have to lead to conspicuous consumption at the cost of environmental degradation. Human ability to produce more food due to our increased pool of knowledge has helped feed billions across the globe. It is the increased pool of knowledge about human body and the environment that has allowed us to understand which foods are healthier and how to produce them in an environmentally friendly way. These increases in knowledge have helped us develop healthier life styles and live longer and productive lives, at least so far. As we saw in Chapter 3, increased production activities have also led to environmental degradation. Whether we use this knowledge about the environment and its connection to human wellbeing, and life on the planet in general, so that coming generations are able to survive and live healthy and productive lives, is a different question.

Economists use the concept of factor productivity. Productivity of a factor of production is the output per unit of that factor of production. For instance, labor productivity is defined as output divided by labor input, either number of workers or number of hours worked, depending upon the availability of data. A related concept is "multifactor productivity." Multifactor productivity is output divided by a combination of inputs—capital, labor, and so on.[25] Productivity can increase due to a number of reasons. Increased labor skills through formal education or on-the-job training can make workers more productive. Increased R&D investment can lead to the development of new and better tools, which allow workers to increase quantity as well as quality of the products and services. Increases in competition can also lead to increased productivity, and so can entrepreneurial efforts. Tax structure in an economy can affect most, if not all, of these factors leading to changes in productivity. Indeed, one argument in favor of lowering capital gains tax is that a decrease in tax will enhance productivity growth through increased investment and promoting entrepreneurship.

What does the empirical evidence say about the effects of tax changes on these economic aggregates? I turn to this question next.

7.2.2. Taxes and the Economy: Empirical Evidence

At what point a household and/or a firm will decide that earning an extra dollar is not worth it? Would an increase from any level of taxes and of any amount lead to the same conclusion or is there a "tipping" point? Furthermore, is there a difference in the impact of increased taxes on labor income versus interest income—that is, income earned from the interest on savings? As we saw earlier in Chapter 6, taxes on interest income have a different impact than taxes on labor income. It also matters whether tax changes are expected to be temporary or permanent. Does the level of income matter? That is, say, if tax is raised by 1 percent on an income level of one million or ten million or hundred million per year and a tax increase of 1 percent on income level of 50,000, would the impact on incentives be the same? Do increases in taxes have the same impact as decreases in taxes, only with a negative sign, or do economic agents view tax increases differently than tax decreases? If taxes do bring behavioral changes, are these effects a short-run phenomenon or the effects persist over longer periods of time? These are important and interesting questions that have kept economists in the area of public finance busy for decades. Because the impact of tax changes on economic activity depends upon, to a great extent, human behavior, so far we have not been able to state conclusively that tax increases have always, for instance, lowered output, and tax decreases have always increased output.

Let us look at some data. Let us start with the contention that higher taxes will lead to lower GDP growth rates. During the 1940s and 1950s tax rates were much higher than they are now: Top marginal tax rate during the 1940s and 1950s was over 90 percent, and today it is 35 percent. Similar trend is found in capital gains tax: During the 1950s and 1960s, top capital gains tax was 25 percent; it increased to 35 percent during the 1970s, and it is 15 percent today.[26] Have declining tax rates led to higher growth rates of GDP? Not exactly. In Table 7.2, I present average growth rates of real GDP per decade.

Perhaps at the risk of belaboring the point, looking at the graph, of the real GDP growth rate data, will be enlightening. In Figure 7.5 I plot these data. The "broken" line represents percentage change in real GDP from one year to the next, and the "solid" lines represent the average growth rates per

Table 7.2 Average growth rate of US real GDP per decade

Decade	Average growth rate (%)
1930s	1.33
1940s	6.03
1950s	4.25
1960s	4.53
1970s	3.24
1980s	3.15
1990s	3.23
2000s	1.83
2010–2012	2.40

Source: Bureau of Economic Analysis (www.bea.gov).

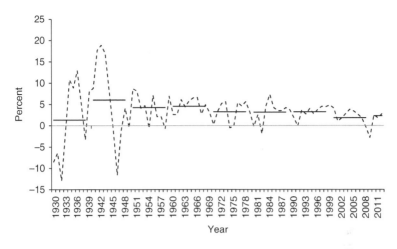

Figure 7.5 Growth rate of real GDP in the United States

Source: Bureau of Economic Analysis (www.bea.gov).

decade—1930s, 1940s, 1950s, and so on (see Table 7.2). Plotted data in Figure 7.5 also help us visualize the year-to-year variations.

We do not see any indication that lowering marginal income tax rate or lowering the capital gains tax rate has a positive impact on the economy, as measured by the growth rate of real GDP. Indeed, evidence to the contrary seems to be there. To make a more accurate statement about the relationship between tax rates and economic growth, however, one needs to take into account, along with the variation (variation in the growth rate of real GDP was a lot higher during the 1930 and 1940 than during the 1950s all the way to present), other factors that may have impacted the economy. Thomas Hungerford (2012)[27] does just that. His analysis does not show any statistically significant relationship between tax rates and the growth rate of real GDP.

Hungerford (2012) also looked at the impact of tax changes on saving, investment, productivity growth, and income distribution. His results led him to the conclusion that top marginal tax rate reductions have "little association with saving, investment, or productivity growth." As he notes, his results are consistent with the broader literature. What did change, due to tax changes, was the distribution of income. Thomas Hungerford uses two definitions of the wealthy: the top 0.1 percent income earners and the top 0.01 percent income earners. Under both definitions, top tax rate reduction led to concentration of income at the top end of the income distribution. Again, he is not alone in reaching this conclusion. As I showed in chapters 5 and 6, while discussing the causes of income inequality and the impact of taxes in reducing income inequality, his results are consistent with the broader literature.

Another point I mentioned above was about the impact of tax changes on labor supply. Do increases in tax rates lead economic agents to lower their supply of labor? Studies show that there is rather small effect, if at all, of changes in tax rate on the supply of labor. This is true of both men and women.[28]

Now, be it the talk of lowering marginal tax rates to increase economic growth, or raising tax rates to strengthen formal social safety nets and lower income inequality, the discussion invariably leads to increasing taxes on the rich of the society, however one defines being "rich." This is an important group to study the impact of tax changes. After all, the rich segments of the society are the ones who have the resources that can be taxed. It is often argued that if taxes are lowered on the high earners, it will affect their incentives positively and the society, as a whole, will benefit from the fruits of their labor. When the rich produce more goods and services due to increased incentives, they will hire more workers, whose incomes will increase, and so on. If taxes are raised on the high earners, their behaviors may change to the point where they may stop producing goods and services to the detriment of the society as a whole. The marginal tax rate reductions during the 1980s and then increases during the 1990s provide a "natural experiment" of the contention that raising tax rates will lower people's incentive to earn the extra dollar.

Indeed, this was the argument for the lowering of marginal tax rates during the 1980s and the 2000s. During the 1990s when marginal tax rates were increased, the opponents of tax increases based their warnings on this argument. In this regard, from a philosophical point of view, perhaps the most influential author has been Ayn Rand.[29] Representative Paul Ryan, who was the Republican vice-presidential candidate during the 2012 US presidential elections, spoke at the Atlas Society meeting—a gathering of Rand's admirers—on February 2, 2005. He mentioned that *Atlas Shrugged* and *The Fountainhead* were required readings for his "interns" and "staffs."[30]

Do the rich show a particular negative reaction to tax increases? Austan Goolsbee (2000)[31] looked at the impact of marginal tax rate changes on the incomes of high earners. Goolsbee's results showed that while there was a significant decline in the incomes of high earners in the short run, in the long run, however, the impact of tax increases was negligible. He shows that almost all the decline in incomes, however, was shift in timing and the change in the type of compensation (that is, wages, salaries, and bonuses versus stock options[32]). Perhaps not surprisingly, executives, in anticipation of tax changes, picked the compensation year and the type of compensation that lowered their tax payments. That is, when they had the option to choose between salary and stock options, they chose the type that lowered their tax bill. If they had chosen to be compensated with stocks options, they "exercised the stock option" when the tax obligations were the lowest. His estimates of the long-run "elasticity of taxable income"—the responsiveness of incomes to tax changes in the long run—range between zero and 0.4. Furthermore, "executives with relatively lower incomes, and more conventional forms of taxable compensation such as salary and bonus, show little responsiveness to tax changes" (p.352).

Why do the predictions of basic economic theory not hold up, at least not hold up as well? This is a very important question, and equally hard, if not even harder, to answer. At its very core, we are talking about the functioning of human brain. What motivates people to engage in a certain activity and what deters them. I do not pretend to have a definitive answer. But just because the predictions of a theory do not hold up in the light of empirical evidence does not mean that we should say that the reality is different than what it is. Perhaps a simpler answer is that the hypothesis that purports to provide ontological depiction is flawed, and should be rejected on the basis of empirical evidence.

Could it also be that we are making the focus of engaging in economic activities unnecessarily narrow by postulating that one engages in economic activities only to accumulate material wealth? Could it be that we engage in commerce, along with financial reasons, for social as well as personal reasons, and that this engagement is a source of satisfaction, in and of itself, and that the fears of free riding are overblown, as argued by Amartya Sen?[33] (More on this shortly.) Indeed, research on "happiness" by Alberto Alesina et al. (2004),[34] shows that being unemployed does lower our happiness. If happiness is the objective, then it would make sense to seek employment and stay employed. Could it also be that the relationship between happiness and financial wealth and what this accumulated wealth can buy is not linear? That is, a given increase in income does not increase our happiness by the same "amount" regardless of our financial status.

None of this precludes the fact that we need to be rewarded for our endeavors. It is just that we have to broaden our definition of "reward." By arguing, however, that the reward can come only in the form of financial wealth, we are putting unnecessary constraints on our understanding. One of these forms of reward may be living in a relatively less unequal society, as argued by Lester Thurow.[35] How else can one explain the existence of non-profit organizations and charities? (Here, of course, I am referring to charities and other non-profit organizations that genuinely provide a social good, and are not set up just to take advantage of tax benefits. I will return to charities for the provision of social safety nets shortly.) After all, as I suggested in Chapter 6, seeing signs of rampant poverty do tend to dampen our pleasure. I hypothesized that perhaps one reason pleasure cruise companies ward off islands or build their own islands is to keep life's unpleasantness out of sight.

Indeed, research shows that while there are differences between countries with regard to the negative correlation between inequality and happiness, this negative correlation is very much present. One such paper is by Alberto Alesina et al. (2004), which I cited above and in Chapter 6. With regard to the differences in social attitudes toward inequality and the correlation between inequality and happiness, Alesina et al. compared Europe and the United States. They write:

> There is no clear ideological divide in the US concerning the effect of inequality on happiness. In contrast, those who define themselves leftist show a strong distaste for inequality in Europe, while those who define themselves rightists are unaffected by it. The breakdown of rich versus poor also shows some differences between Europe and the US. In Europe, the happiness of the poor is strongly negatively affected by inequality, while the effect on the rich is smaller in size and statistically insignificant. In the US, one finds the opposite pattern, namely that the group whose happiness seems to be most adversely affected by inequality is the rich. A striking result is that the US poor seem totally unaffected by inequality. Any significance of the inequality coefficient in the US population is mainly driven by the rich. (p.2011)

7.2.3. Issues of Free Riding

Let me now turn to the issues of free riders. Recall that free riders are those who benefit from a given activity without making the required contribution. If there are non-economic considerations such as self-respect, for engaging in matters economic, and there is stigma associated with being unemployed, as argued by Amartya Sen (1999), or that being unemployed lowers our happiness, as the research by Alesina et al. (2004) shows, then the fears of a formal social safety net turning "into a hammock that lulls able-bodied people to lives of dependency and complacency, that drains them of their will and their incentive to make the most of their lives," as Representative Paul Ryan suggested in 2012 while discussing reforms in the welfare system,[36] certainly seem exaggerated. As Amartya Sen (1999) argued, convincingly in my opinion, that

> [t]he argument for social support in expanding people's freedom can, therefore, be seen as an argument for individual responsibility, not against it. The linkage between freedom and responsibility works both ways. Without the substantive freedom and capability to do something, a person cannot be responsible for

doing it. But actually having the freedom and capability to do something does impose on the person the duty to consider whether to do it or not, and this does involve individual responsibility. In this sense, freedom is both necessary and sufficient for responsibility. (p.284)

Realizing the beneficial effects of expanded government-supported formal social safety nets, if a country decides to implement such a plan then it will, of course, be wise to make sure that free riding is at least minimized, if not completely eliminated. Just because the fears of Cadillac-driving "welfare queens" clogging the streets are exaggerated does not mean that free riding does not exist. It would, indeed, hardly be considered a deep insight that there remains a positive probability of people taking advantage of the system. For social safety nets to perform their intended functions, free riding has to be minimized, if not completely eliminated. The question to be answered is: How do we make sure that the safety net functions as intended and is not misused, and who is better suited to carry out the function of minimizing free riding?

A key to avoiding free riding is to make sure that everyone who is currently benefiting or expected to benefit in the future, from the activity in question, makes his/her contribution. Either that or deny benefits to those who have not contributed their share. As I will show shortly using the example of health insurance, in a situation like social safety nets, it is relatively easier to adopt the former approach than the latter. Denying help to someone, who has fallen on hard time, because he/she has not made a contribution raises a number of moral and ethical issues. At the same time if everyone does not make his or her contribution, the system falls apart. And here is where the government's authority and its ability to levy taxes come in. A government can mandate that everyone, depending upon income level, makes the required contribution, and collect those contributions through taxes.

Take the example of healthcare insurance provision by private firms. One reason for the higher premiums is that while hospitals are obligated to treat whoever enters their premises, hospitals cannot make their decisions about providing treatments based on the individual's ability to pay, either by virtue of having a health insurance or out of pocket. If, however, the patient does not or cannot pay, the hospitals are left with the unpaid bill. A way out of this dilemma, for the hospitals, is to charge higher fees to everyone, so that they can compensate for those who do not or cannot pay. (Note that the increased price of treatments means that the quantity demanded of treatments will decrease, all else remaining constant. That is, fewer treatments will be sought. This avoidance to seek treatment of minor illness may lead to a major illness down the road, further burdening healthcare system and complicating the healthcare infrastructure.)

While those who are paying out of pocket end up writing larger checks, those who are covered by insurance, their insurance companies are stuck with the excess fees. To cover these excess costs, insurance companies have to raise the premiums their members pay. Added is another wrinkle to the situation by the fact that (most) insurance companies are for-profit entities. One way to increase profits is to raise revenues by raising premiums, and the other is to lower costs. While the former option leads to increased prices of services rendered for the customers, leading to a decline in quantity demanded, the latter leads to increased profits without any loss of customers. (Which option, or which combination of the two options, will be chosen depends upon the demand elasticity.) At the risk of omitting some crucial details, assume that the insurance company choses the cost-lowering option. If the insurance company opts for lowering costs then one way to lower costs is to insure only those who are the least likely to seek any treatment. That is, insure only the healthy ones and leave out the ones with "pre-existing conditions." Another way to lower costs may be to deny the payment of certain treatments. In this example, individuals who either cannot pay or do not pay for their hospital visits are free riding. The Affordable Care Act dealt with the free-rider problem by mandating that everyone in the country must obtain insurance. (It also mandated that the insurance companies insure everyone, even those with "pre-existing conditions.")

So far I have argued that government can provide formal social safety nets and finance the expenditure by levying taxes. One may ask: Why can't non-profit organizations—secular as well as religious—provide these services, perhaps more efficiently, and government can provide grants and subsidies to meet the financial needs? Why does government have to be the sole provider? I turn to this point now.

7.3. Non-Profit Organizations and the Provision of Social Safety Nets

Non-profit organizations play a major role, not only in the United States, but all over the world. Note that while all charities are non-profit organizations, not all non-profit organizations are charities: Charities, both secular as well as religious (also known as faith-based organizations), are a subset of the non-profit organizations. An example of a non-profit organization, which is not a charity, is the National Football League (NFL) in the United States.[37]

Before we go any further, let us look at some figures about the non-profit organizations. According to a report by the Urban Institute, titled "The Nonprofit Sector in Brief: Public Charities, Giving, and Volunteering,"[38] the non-profit landscape has expanded considerably over the years. The data reported here come from this report.

There were 1.58 million non-profit organizations registered with the Internal Revenue Service (IRS) in 2011, "an increase of 21.5 percent since 2001." While the total number of non-profit organizations is not known with precision, it is almost certainly larger than 1.58 million. There are a couple of reasons behind this assertion. One, non-profit organizations with revenues less than $5,000 per year are not required to register with the IRS. And second, "religious congregations are not required to register with the IRS, although" according to the report, "many do."

All "reporting nonprofits"[39] had a total of $4.63 trillion in assets during 2011. Their revenue in 2011 was $2.1 trillion and their expenses totalled to $1.99 trillion. The report notes that during the 2001–2011 period, the non-profit sector's revenues and assets grew by "about 35 percent after adjusting for inflation."[40] Over this period the expenditures of non-profit organizations grew by 40.6 percent, the report notes.

As noted above, charities are a subset of non-profit organizations. Such organizations fall under the IRS Code 501(c)(3).[41] These organizations enjoy a tax-exempt status and donations made to such organizations are tax detectable. The IRS website notes that[42]

> [t]he exempt purposes set forth in section 501(c)(3) are charitable, religious, educational, scientific, literary, testing for public safety, fostering national or international amateur sports competition, and preventing cruelty to children or animals. The term *charitable* is used in its generally accepted legal sense and includes relief of the poor, the distressed, or the underprivileged; advancement of religion; advancement of education or science; erecting or maintaining public buildings, monuments, or works; lessening the burdens of government; lessening neighborhood tensions; eliminating prejudice and discrimination; defending human and civil rights secured by law; and combating community deterioration and juvenile delinquency.
>
> (Italics original)

According to the Urban Institute's report, during 2011 about 1 million out of the 1.58 million of the total non-profit organizations were categorized as charitable organizations. While registered non-profits grew from 2001 to 2011 by about 21.5 percent, charitable organizations grew by about 34.3 percent. As for the financial situation of public charities, during 2011, they reported $1.59 trillion in revenues and $1.50 trillion in expenses. Public charities' assets during 2011 were $2.83 trillion—about 61 percent of the total non-profit sector's assets. About one-half of the revenue of public charities came from "fees for services and goods from private sources," such as "tuition payments" and "hospital patient revenues." The remaining revenue is divided between government sources (34.5 percent)—Medicaid and Medicare payments about 25 percent, grants about 9.5 percent. The remaining, about 12.6 percent, came from "private charitable giving." The report also notes that about 32.7 percent of the total non-profit sector's revenues come from government contracts and grants (p.3).

As I mentioned earlier, non-profit organizations provide invaluable services to their local communities. Examples of help extended, not only in times of natural disasters but also in times of peace, abound. Above, I quoted from the IRS website the type of organizations that fall under the "charitable" category of the non-profit sector, and the services they provide; arguably this is a very short list of the extensive services provided by the overall non-profit sector. Looking at the revenues, expenditures, and assets, one may argue that the non-profit sector is large enough to provide social safety nets to the needy, and that relying on the government to provide social safety nets will lead to further governmental intrusion in people's lives.

First on the question of whether or not the non-profit sector can meet the needs of a society, given its size. I do not know of any study that has estimated how big, relative to the size of the economy, an entity has to be to provide social safety nets in a country. It may very well be that with a few adjustments the non-profit sector can meet the challenge. We do know, however, from the examples of natural disasters such as hurricanes, earthquakes, and floods in recent history, that charities, as benevolent as they were, could not meet the needs. In the United States, the examples of Hurricane Katrina in 2005 and Hurricane Sandy in 2012 come to mind. The devastation was of such magnitude that, indeed, even state governments could not do the job and they had to rely on the federal government for help.

On the question of governmental intrusion in people's lives, as noted above, about one-third of the revenues of the non-profit sector already come from government grants and contract. And then there is the tax-exempt status of the non-profit sector. Whether the government intervenes directly or through the non-profit sector, it is already very much involved in people's lives. So, in my view, this point is rather moot.

What about the question of efficiency? Can the case not be made that public charities can provide social safety nets more efficiently than the government? Indeed, in the United States and perhaps in other countries as well, there is a sense of romantic belonging to charity organizations. When the topic of US tax reform gained popularity, and suggestions came to get rid of charitable deductions from the tax code, a very well-respected economist and one of the recipients of the Nobel Prize in 2013, Robert Schiller, argued against the suggestions to remove charitable deductions from the tax code.[43] It may very well be the case, except that we do not have access to the data, especially data of religious organizations, to conduct efficiency studies. I go into a lot more detail on this issue in the next chapter. Since religious organizations (or faith-based organizations) are a major part of the non-profit sector, I devote a complete chapter, Chapter 8, to the role of religion and religious organizations in the delivery of social services and the provision of social safety nets.

Then there are other constraints of informal social safety nets, which I detailed in Chapter 2. Recall that safety nets provided by the non-profit sector fall under informal social safety nets. As I discussed in Chapter 2, informal social safety nets, casual or organized, are perhaps better suited to monitor their members, and provide safety nets in an efficient manner, if the members stayed in the vicinity. The fact that their services are not portable across geographic areas makes them unsuitable for the modern economy. Also, while the issues of efficient delivery and monitoring to avoid free riding are of great import, the issue of anonymity to preserve self-respect cannot be overlooked. As I discussed in Chapter 2, informal social safety nets, casual or organized, may have to sacrifice anonymity and hence self-respect of the recipients to gain efficiency.

What if a country develops a non-profit sector that is large enough to encompass the entire country, has pockets deep enough to render support even in the most catastrophic of events, and hires individuals who do not know the recipients on a personal level so that anonymity is preserved? Note that in this case we are only changing the name of the government. It is, in effect, what government in a democratic society is.

7.4. Chapter Summary

The provision of formal social safety nets financed by taxes raises two major objections. One, such expenditure on the part of the government will lead to an increased deficit as a percentage of GDP. I showed in this chapter that we do not find any evidence that countries that provide relatively generous formal social safety nets have significantly higher deficits. Such an argument perhaps also ignores the beneficial effects of formal social safety nets on GDP, the denominator in the deficit-to-GDP ratio. The second argument against the provision of tax-financed formal social safety nets is that raising taxes to pay for the expenditure will lower economic growth. As I showed in this chapter, we do not have an empirical evidence of statistically significant negative effects of tax increases on GDP and other economic aggregates. I also argued that in a modern economy the non-profit sector, in spite of its size, is not suited to undertake the provision of social safety nets. Not only that, once we turn to the non-profit sector, the issues of anonymity and the possible loss of self-respect and dignity of the recipient surface.

The non-profit sector includes secular as well as religious organizations, and in the United States, people hold religious organizations in an especially high regard. I devote the next chapter to looking at the roles of religious organizations and their ability to provide social safety nets in a dynamic society such as the United States.

CHAPTER 8

Faith-Based Organizations and the Provision of Informal Social Safety Nets

In this chapter I argue that the provision of social safety nets by faith-based organizations (FBOs) is not a good idea. I argue that because there is significant discrimination on the part of the faithful toward those who either practice a different religion or do not strictly adhere to the tenets, or do not practice religion at all, religious organizations are not suitable for such a purpose. I also argue that the provision of social safety nets through FBOs may not be a good idea on efficiency basis either. For one to measure the efficiency of an organization, one needs data. Since FBOs do not provide data about their financial undertakings, we cannot take it on "faith" that FBOs are more efficient in the delivery of social safety nets as compared with the government.

8.1. The Religious Landscape in the United States and Around the World

Before I discuss why the provision of informal social safety nets by religious organizations may not be a good idea, it is instructive to look at some data about the religious landscape. I start with presenting data in Table 8.1, on religious affiliation in the world as well as in the United States. The first column in the table lists the name of the religion, while the second and third columns present the number of adherents and their percentages worldwide, respectively. The fourth and fifth columns present the number of adherents and their percentage for the United States, respectively. These data pertain to 2010.

Both worldwide as well as in the United States, Christianity has the largest number of followers. In terms of percentage, Christians constitute

Table 8.1 Worldwide and US religious affiliations

[1]	[2]	[3]	[4]	[5]
Religion	Worldwide		United States	
	Numbers	Percent	Numbers	Percent
Buddhists	487,540,000	7.1	3,570,000	1.2
Christians	2,173,180,000	31.5	243,060,000	78.3
Folk Religionists	405,120,000	5.9	630,000	0.2
Hindu	1,033,080,000	15.0	1,790,000	0.6
Jews	13,850,000	0.2	5,690,000	1.8
Muslims	1,598,510,000	23.2	2,770,000	0.9
Other Religions	58,110,000	0.8	1,900,000	0.6
Unaffiliated	1,126,500,000	16.3	50,980,000	16.4
Total Population	6,895,890,000	100	310,390,000	100

Source: Pew-Templeton Global Religious Futures Project.[1]

about 31.5 percent of the total population worldwide. In the United States, Christians constitute about 78.3 percent of the population. Worldwide, Muslims make up the second biggest religious group, about 23.2 percent, followed by the "Unaffiliated," about 16.3 percent. In the United States, "Unaffiliated" is the second largest group, about 16.4 percent.

According to this dataset, in the United States, Protestants are the largest subgroup among Christians. They number around 115,550,000. They constitute about 64 percent of the total Christian population of the United States. Catholics are the second largest Christian subgroup, about 75,380,000 adherents, that is, about 31 percent of the total Christian population. Orthodox Christians are about 1,820,000, less than 1 percent of the total Christian population. The remaining 10,310,000 fall under "Other Christians." They are about 4.2 percent of the total Christian population in the United States.

Who falls under the "Unaffiliated" category? According to the data source, "The religiously unaffiliated include atheists, agnostics and people who do not identify with any particular religion in surveys."[2] With regard to their geographic distribution,[3]

> The religiously unaffiliated are heavily concentrated in Asia and the Pacific, where more than three-quarters (76%) of the world's unaffiliated population resides. The remainder is in Europe (12%), North America (5%), Latin America and the Caribbean (4%), sub-Saharan Africa (2%) and the Middle East and North Africa (less than 1%).

Of the 232 countries and territories included in the Global Religious Futures project, there are six countries where the religiously unaffiliated make up a majority of the population: the Czech Republic (76% are religiously unaffiliated), North Korea (71%), Estonia (60%), Japan (57%), Hong Kong (56%) and China (52%).

Notice that both, worldwide as well as in the United States, the "Unaffiliated," while a minority as compared with their religious counterparts, are a large minority.

Just as a clarificatory remark, North America includes Bermuda, Canada, Greenland, St. Pierre and Miquelon, and the United States.[4] The geographic distribution of the Unaffiliated within North American is as follows. (The percentage of religiously "Unaffiliated" population is given in parentheses.): Bermuda (19.4 percent), Canada (23.7 percent), Greenland (2.5 percent), St. Pierre and Miquelon (3.8 percent), and the United States (16.4 percent).

8.2. A Brief History of Faith-Based Organizations in the United States

In the United States, the history of FBOs providing social services goes back at least to the founding of the nation. Overtime, FBOs have gained more notoriety and fame. In recent history, under President Clinton, the 104th Congress in 1996 passed the Personal Responsibility and Work Opportunity Reconciliation Act and the Charitable Choice provision (Public Law 104–193),[5] and President George W. Bush established the Faith-Based and Community Initiative in 2002.[6] The initiative allowed government agencies to "contract directly with pervasively sectarian organizations—churches, mosques, and synagogues . . . —without imposing restrictions on displays of religious symbols or other religious activities," write Richard M. Clerkin and Kirsten A. Gronbjerg (2007, p.115).[7] The Faith-Based and Community Initiative became the Whitehouse Office of Faith-Based and Neighborhood Partnerships, under President Barack Obama in 2009.[8] On August 7, 2013, the US Department of State launched the Office of Faith-Based Community Initiatives.[9]

As Anna Amirkhnyan, Hyun Kim, and Kristina Lambright (2009, p.491)[10] note, FBOs started relying on public funding with the 1967 amendment to the Social Security Act. Once FBOs started relying and getting access to public funding, the reliance and access kept on increasing. It created a symbiotic relationship between the patriarchs (to my knowledge, even now there are hardly any matriarchs) of the FBOs and politicians. This is how it worked. Access to a larger pool of funds allowed the FBOs to wield greater influence on a larger number of individuals. As a result, the patriarchs of these FBOs gained more clout among general public. This increased public clout drew the attention of more politicians who needed their votes, who in return provided more funding, and so on. Over time these patriarchs would have enormous influence over public policy (more on this point shortly).

Examples of this symbiosis abound, on both sides of the isle. They surface especially around election time. During the 2000 Republican primaries, then Governor George W. Bush was the favored candidate by the religious right. Senator John McCain of Arizona, who was also competing for the Republican nomination, in a speech on February 28, 2000, tried to show his independence from the religious right. Here is a part of his speech.[11]

> The political tactics of division and slander are not our values, they are ... They are corrupting influences on religion and politics, and those who practice them in the name of religion or in the name of the Republican Party or in the name of America shame our faith, our party and our country. Neither party should be defined by pandering to the outer reaches of American politics and the agents of intolerance, whether they be Louis Farrakhan or Al Sharpton on the left, or Pat Robertson or Jerry Falwell on the right.

This strategy, however, did not work for McCain. He lost to George W. Bush, who would win a larger share of the religious right vote. Six years later in 2006, when Senator McCain was preparing for another run, political calculus dictated mending fences. He would be the commencement speaker at the Liberty University on Saturday, May 13, 2006.[12] It bears mentioning that Dr. Jerry Falwell, Sr. was the founder of Liberty University.[13] In an interview with Dr. Falwell, *The Washington Post* asked if their reconciliation would help Mr. McCain in his political ambitions. Dr. Falwell answered, "I don't think there's any question about that. There are 80 million evangelicals in this country. My intent was to say that John McCain and I are friends, that I respect him and that there are no problems with yesterday."[14]

During the 2008 presidential election campaign after then Senator Barack Obama became the Democratic candidate and Senator John McCain won the Republican nomination, they both appeared at a forum held at the Saddleback Church run by Pastor Rick Warren.[15] When Mr. Obama won the 2008 presidential election, Pastor Rick Warren would deliver the invocation on the inauguration. The negative views about gays and same-sex marriage held by Pastor Rick Warren were public knowledge.[16] That President Obama would invite Pastor Warren to deliver the invocation was unnerving for a majority of the Obama supporters who favored same-sex marriage and supported gay rights. The dictates of the political calculus, however, won again. Indeed, Mr. Obama himself, first state Senator, then US Senator and presidential hopeful, has been often quoted as saying that his views on same-sex marriage were "evolving."[17] Cynics, skeptics, and critics took Mr. Obama's views on same-sex marriage to be a matter of political expediency. Curiously, fierce supporters of Mr. Obama who also supported same-sex marriage took comfort in this opacity. I guess accepting that one has been taken for a ride is hard. President Obama openly supported same-sex marriage only during 2013.[18]

This increased political power and financial riches for the FBOs, however, came at a price: Their operations came under increasing public scrutiny. Not only were there questions about blurring the line between "church and state" by civil libertarian societies such as Americans United for Separation of Church and State,[19] the economic value of FBOs also became a research topic. To measure the efficacy of FBOs, one may compare the services provided by FBOs with similar services provided by their secular counterparts. I turn to this question now.

8.3. The Performance of FBOs versus Secular Organizations

I have argued throughout this book that informal social safety nets do not meet the demands of a modern society. Some may still argue, however, that informal social safety nets provide a valuable service, perhaps, at a "personal" level. That is, informal social safety nets may serve a niche population, which formal social safety nets cannot reach. It may be that support from informal safety nets is accessible more quickly than their formal counterparts because of the lack of bureaucratic delays. It is likely that individuals working in an informal organization are better acquainted with the neighborhood and know the needy personally. It is also possible that, along with financial support, a kind word from a familiar face just may do the trick.

Fair enough! If this is the case, then, the next question is: Which organized informal social safety nets serve these needs better? If the society has to spend resources in the form of subsidies or tax breaks to charities (more on this point later), which kind of charity uses the resources in a more efficient manner, a secular organization or a religious one? This comparison may help us decide which of the two, FBOs or the secular organizations, serve the purpose of providing social services better.

First, let us see why might there be any difference between services provided by FBOs versus secular organizations? Perhaps the difference may arise from the management (and employees) because in the former case individuals are "God fearing." This may lead them to do a better job of service provision. After all, for believers, the appeasement of some superhuman deity—Yahweh, God/god/gods, Rama, Allah, or a group of deities, too numerous to list here—and the threat of damnation are pretty good motivating factors. Members of a secular organization may not feel this pull. Indeed, some may even be non-believers. In fact there is a higher probability of someone belonging to a secular charity of being a non-believer, or at least an agnostic, if not outright atheist. This is because for a believer, all else constant, it would make sense to give to an FBO as opposed to a secular organization where there might be non-believers. And as we saw from the 2007 *USA Today/Gallup* poll results presented in Chapter 5, Table 5.1, atheists is the least favored group.

As a side note, readers curious about the various names that have been used for various deities throughout the recorded human history may find *The Evolution of God* by Robert Wright (2009)[20] a good source. The reader is, however, cautioned about the "use-mention" error, which, in the words of the philosopher Daniel Dennett, refers to "confusing a phenomenon with either the name of the phenomenon or the concept of the phenomenon."[21] In Robert Wright's case, he confuses the evolution of the *concept* of God with the evolution of God.

Going back to the efficiency question, what is the evidence? To my knowledge economics literature on FBOs, in general, and the efficiency of FBOs, in particular, is rather limited. It's not that there aren't enough economists interested in the subject; there are plenty of professors and graduate students who are looking for fertile topics. It's the dearth of publically available data that keeps this topic relatively under-studied. Not all FBOs are required to make all of their data available; recall from Chapter 1, many religious organizations are exempt from filing Form 990, which allows public to get information about the organization.

The lack of available data is a problem not only for academic economists but for government agencies as well, whose job is to monitor how public funds are used. In Chapter 1, I referred to a report by the Government Accountability Office (GOA).[22] Since the introduction of Faith-Based and Community Initiative in 2001, various government agencies are involved in implementing the initiative. According to the GOA's report, since "fiscal year 2002" these government agencies have "spent more than $24 million on administrative activities." And "Since 2001, federal agencies have awarded over $500 million through new grant programs to provide training and technical assistance to faith-based and community organizations and to increase the participation of these organizations in providing federally funded social services." According to the GOA's report:

> [I]t is unclear whether the data reported on grants awarded to FBOs provide policymakers with a sound basis to assess the progress of agencies in meeting the initiative's long-term goal of greater participation of faith-based and

community organizations. Moreover, little information is available to assess progress toward another long-term goal of improving participant outcomes because outcome-based evaluations for many pilot programs have not begun. Also, OMB [Office of Management and Budget] faces other challenges in measuring and reporting on agencies' progress in meeting the long-term goals of the initiative.

So caution is in order. What we can glean, however, from the available economics literature in the area is that the results do not bode well for FBOs. First, as it turns out, FBOs are no more efficient in their resource use than their secular counterparts. Anna Amirkhnyan, Hyun Kim, and Kristina Lambright (2009)[23] looked at the non-profit nursing home industry. They used a nationwide panel data (that is, data spanning across states and over time) of 11,877 nursing homes. Some of the nursing homes were affiliated with a church, whereas others were not; all were, however, non-profit. Their findings suggest that church-affiliated nursing homes did not provide any better care than the secular ones.

Amirkhnyan, Kim, and Lambright (2009) also looked at the accessibility of nursing home services by the "impoverished," that is, "Medicaid-funded residents." They asked the question whether or not the "impoverished" could get nursing home services provided by FBO-run facilities more easily as compared with their secular counterparts. The authors write:

We also fail to find consistent evidence of faith-based status affecting the level of access for impoverished, Medicaid-funded residents. Accessibility of faith-based nursing homes is indeed significantly lower in our OLS [Ordinary Least Squares, an estimation technique] model examining the effect of faith-based status on the share of countywide Medicaid recipients. Overall, however, our findings fail to confirm the assumption that FBOs perform relatively better than secular nonprofit organizations, at least in the case of the nursing home industry. (p.504)

The authors mention that their results do not support the findings of earlier literature, which looked at the quality of nursing home services provided by FBOs. The authors argue that their study is superior to the previous literature on this topic, both in methodology as well as in data.

Another researcher, Laura A. Reese (2004),[24] looked at the performance of FBOs in the promotion of economic development in urban areas. Her results led her to conclude that

faith-based development efforts may not be a viable alternative to government programs at this time and are not prevalent enough to significantly enhance government efforts. Furthermore, financing and administering faith-based development activities raises several concerns; for example, many FBOs do not create nonprofit entities, making it difficult to maintain a sacred and secular separation and oversee the use of public funds. (p.50)

The point about FBOs' inability to separate the "sacred" from the "secular" was also raised in the GOA's report to which I referred earlier.[25]

While officials in all 26 FBOs that we visited said that they understood that federal funds cannot be used for inherently religious activities, a few FBOs described activities that appeared to violate this safeguard. Four of the 13 FBOs that provided voluntary religious activities did not separate in time or location some religious activities from federally funded program services.

How well suited are FBOs in providing social safety nets? Most of the research shows that FBOs do not seem to have the technical and managerial skills or the financial resources needed for the provision of such services.[26] This is the case even after various government agencies have spent over $500 million since 2001 on "training and technical assistance" to FBOs, according to the GOA report cited above.

Recall from Chapter 1 that a subset of FBOs is congregations associated with a particular place of worship—a church, a synagogue, a temple, a mosque, and so on. One may argue that since this subset of FBOs operates at a neighborhood level, it may have a better level of familiarity with the needy, and hence may be able to provide social services in a more efficient manner. These efficiencies may arise from the lack of bureaucracies. Perhaps these smaller FBOs are better at providing services to the disadvantaged in the area. What does the research show? Clerkin and Gronbjerg (2007)[27] compared the performance of "HS-Congregations," "HS-FBOs," and "HS-Seculars," where "HS" stands for "human service." That is, organizations in each category—congregations, FBOs, and secular organizations—provide human services. The authors distinguished between a "congregation" and an "FBO" based on the size of the management. In their sample the median number of full-time employees in a congregation was one, and the median number of full-time employees in an FBO was five (Table 1, p.119 of the study). Their results led them to conclude that

HS-Congregations were less likely than HS-FBOs or HS-Seculars to target services based on income (16 percent versus 41 percent and 30 percent) and racial or ethnic status (13 percent versus 35 percent and 18 percent). HS-Congregations were more likely to target by gender (61 percent, most likely related to men's and women's groups and bible study), youth (85 percent, perhaps related to youth groups), and—not surprisingly—people of a particular faith (66 percent) than HS-FBOs and especially HS-Seculars. We conclude that HS-Congregations are more likely to target on the basis of programs related to worship than human services. (p.121)

Caution, again, is in order: the Clerkin and Gronbjerg (2007) study uses survey dataset only from Indiana. As such the results may not be applicable on a wider scale. This brings us back to the question of the availability of data. If FBOs want to avoid public suspicion, as suggested earlier, perhaps it will be better if they made their data public.

8.4. Transparency and the FBOs

Transparency on the part of FBOs and making their data available are needed not only to estimate efficiencies, or lack thereof, of FBOs and to recommend solutions if problems are found, but also to build trust. Indeed, lack of transparency may be one main reason that "a few bad apples" end up ruining the whole crate. It is arguably the case that individuals who take advantage of an institution have some reasonable expectation of not being caught. Examples abound, among the votary as well as the secular. Here I briefly mention three arenas: religious, political, and sports.

In the religious arena, it is highly unlikely that priests[28] and rabbis[29] who "sexually abused" children would have done so if they did not have reasonable expectation that they would not get caught. And even if they did get caught, they would be protected by their higher-ups. Indeed, as more information is coming out, it has become abundantly clear that there was concerted effort to protect the perpetrators at the expense of children. Not only that, as the news of "child abuse" were becoming public, the higher-ups took steps to protect their financial assets.[30] In 2007 Cardinal Timothy Dolan was archbishop of Milwaukee. (At the time of this writing, he is archbishop of New York.) According to the reports, he sought permission from the Vatican to transfer Church's financial assets to an account where they were safe from the victims of priest sex-abuse. He wrote in a letter to the Vatican that "I foresee an improved protection of these funds from any legal claim and liability." He was granted the permission and he "moved nearly $57 million into a cemetery trust fund to protect the assets from victims of clergy sexual abuse who were demanding compensation."

I have put "sexually abused" in quotation marks because the late Christopher Hitchens forcefully argued that it is "child rape," plain and simple.[31] And I agree. Another point that needs mentioning is that it would be a mistake to think that these rapes are taking place only in the church or the synagogue, and that other places of worship, mosques, temples, etc., or for that matter secular arenas, are immune to such practices. It is a matter of exerting power over the powerless, and not a matter of a particular religion or religion in general being especially susceptible to such practices. Indeed, the "sexual abuses" that took place at Penn State happened on the campus of a state university—a secular arena. And the perpetrator, Jerry Sandusky, a defensive coordinator at the time, who engaged in such practices over a 15-year period, was not a clergy.[32] As such, I will conjecture that the reason we have not heard about other religions' child rape practices is that they haven't come to light yet, or at least they are not a matter of wide public knowledge yet. The question arises though that if such practices exist in other religions, why haven't they come to light? One answer may be that individuals aware of the existence of such practices are afraid of the ardent followers of that religion. And, indeed, these fears are well founded. I will expand on this point shortly.

Lack of transparency and the expectation of not getting caught show their effects in politics as well, be it the private lives or the public lives of politicians. Politicians, just as non-politicians, admit only when they are confronted with undeniable proofs. In public lives, it seems like a weekly event when politicians are caught taking bribes in explicit or implicit forms. I pointed to the examples of the Illinois governor Rod Blagojevich and the former House Majority Whip Tom DeLay earlier in the book. In private lives, on the Democrat side, former president Bill Clinton; former governor of New York, Elliot Spitzer; and former US representative from New York, Anthony Weiner, are just a few examples. One finds similar stories of illicit affairs on the Republican side as well. Max Blumenthal, in his book *The Republican Gamorrah*,[33] provides details of politicians' fall from grace after their affairs became public.

Similarly, lack of transparency and the expectation of not getting caught have plagued sports, college sports as well as professional sports. In recent history, use of banned substances by athletes has come to the fore. Examples include the cyclist and seven times winner of Tour de France, Lance Armstrong,[34] who lost, along with his titles, multimillion-dollar endorsements; the Olympian Marion Jones,[35] who also lost her title and went to prison; and numerous professional baseball players[36] who suffered similar fates, among many other sports too numerous to list here.

Going back to FBOs, absence of reliable dataset prohibits a broad statistical analysis. Are there any other aspects of FBOs that are public and bode well for FBOs and silence the critics? Since we lack reliable data, one way out is to find a suitable proxy and ascertain the impact of FBOs on society through proxy. One commonality among all FBOs is, of course, faith in some super-human deity. For the ease of exposition, let us call that super-human deity, or group of deities, "God." By definition all FBOs belong to one religion or another, or in the case of "inter-faith" FBOs, to a number of religions. That is, the one constant or a binding force is religion among all FBOs. Observance of basic human rights can serve as a proxy for social services. In the absence of reliable data, one can see how has the relationship between religion and human rights been over the years and ascertain the relationship between FBOs and social services?

8.5. Religion and Human Rights[37]

Some readers may argue that I am presenting only the unflattering picture of religion while leaving out all the humane activities in which religions have over the centuries participated. This is true, and I will address this issue shortly. First, let us take a peek into the record of religion in the area of human rights. I will focus on the three main religions of the world—Judaism, Christianity, and Islam. I will start by quoting from the Bible (the Old Testament and the New Testament) and the Koran. I do this because religious authorities invariably refer to the sacred texts—the Bible (the Old Testament and the New Testament) and the Koran. It is instructive, then, to look at the actual verses to which religious authorities refer.

The record of religion on human rights leaves a lot to be desired. This should not come as a surprise though; the main focus of any religion is the service of the deity. If any good comes toward humans, it is incidental. It is not the mainstay. Take the example of the Judeo-Christian religions, that is, Judaism, Christianity, and Islam. The patriarch of these religions, Abraham, is ordered to sacrifice his son to show his devotion to God.

According to *Genesis* 22.2, God commands Abraham to "Take your son, your only son, whom you love—Isaac—and go to the region of Moriah. Sacrifice him there as a burnt offering on a mountain I will show you."[38] It was only after God was assured of Abraham's devotion and faith that angels intervened on behalf of God and Isaac's life was spared. A ram was sacrificed instead.[39]

Similar account of Abraham sacrificing his son to appease God appears in the Koran.[40]

When the boy was old enough to work with his father, Abraham said, "My son, I have seen myself sacrificing you in a dream. What do you think?" He said, "Father, do as you are commanded and, God willing, you will find me steadfast." (37.102)

One difference in details is the son who was offered as sacrifice. According to the Bible, it was Isaac, whereas according to the Muslim tradition, it was Ishmael. (The name is often spelled as "Ismail" in English translations of the Koran, the holy book of Islam.[41] "Isaac" is spelled as "Ishaq." The Koran is written in Arabic, and these differences in spelling result from an effort to phonetically spell Arabic words.)

In 1969 Pope Paul VI issued an encyclical—"Humanae Vitae"—in which he answered questions related to birth control—"REGULATION OF BIRTH"—as it was mentioned in the title.[42] In this encyclical the Pope categorically banned the use of "artificial" contraceptives. The reason? God's commands supersede any human concern. The Pope mentioned that often policymakers rationalize the use of contraceptives on the basis of resource constraints, both at the national level and at the household level.

> [T]here is the rapid increase in population which has made many fear that world population is going to grow faster than available resources, with the consequence that many families and developing countries would be faced with greater hardships. This can easily induce public authorities to be tempted to take even harsher measures to avert this danger.

> There is also the fact that not only working and housing conditions but the greater demands made both in the economic and educational field pose a living situation in which it is frequently difficult these days to provide properly for a large family.

He, however, ruled that those were not legitimate reasons for using "artificial methods" of contraception. The Pope did allow sex though, within the bounds of traditional marriage between a man and a woman, during the periods when the woman is "infertile."

> If therefore there are well-grounded reasons for spacing births, arising from the physical or psychological condition of husband or wife, or from external circumstances, the Church teaches that married people may then take advantage of the natural cycles immanent in the reproductive system and engage in marital intercourse only during those times that are infertile, thus controlling birth in a way which does not in the least offend the moral principles which We have just explained.

To address the possible confusion of the laity with regard to banning contraceptives while allowing sex during "infertile period," the Pope wrote:

> Neither the Church nor her doctrine is inconsistent when she considers it lawful for married people to take advantage of the infertile period but condemns

as always unlawful the use of means which directly prevent conception, even when the reasons given for the later practice may appear to be upright and serious. In reality, these two cases are completely different. In the former the married couple rightly use a faculty provided them by nature. In the later they obstruct the natural development of the generative process. It cannot be denied that in each case the married couple, for acceptable reasons, are both perfectly clear in their intention to avoid children and wish to make sure that none will result. But it is equally true that it is exclusively in the former case that husband and wife are ready to abstain from intercourse during the fertile period as often as for reasonable motives the birth of another child is not desirable. And when the infertile period recurs, they use their married intimacy to express their mutual love and safeguard their fidelity toward one another. In doing this they certainly give proof of a true and authentic love.

In this encyclical he also clarified the roles of various constituents in addressing this issue. With regard to doctors and nurses, who may have to tend to such matters, the encyclical dictated:

Likewise we hold in the highest esteem those doctors and members of the nursing profession who, in the exercise of their calling, *endeavor to fulfill the demands of their Christian vocation before any merely human interest.* Let them therefore continue constant in their resolution always to support those lines of action which accord with faith and with right reason. And let them strive to win agreement and support for these policies among their professional colleagues. Moreover, they should regard it as an essential part of their skill to make themselves fully proficient in this difficult field of medical knowledge. For then, when married couples ask for their advice, they may be in a position to give them right counsel and to point them in the proper direction. Married couples have a right to expect this much from them.

(Italics mine)

The emphasis is again on the appeasement of God, and human rights are merely incidental.

In the Muslim tradition, the practice of sacrificing animals to appease God continues till today. At the conclusion of the Muslim pilgrimage to Mecca, the *Hajj*,[43] the faithful kill sacrificial animals. It is practiced not only by those who perform the pilgrimage, but also by devout Muslims all across the globe. The list of sacrificial animals has increased to include, along with rams, lambs, goats, camels, cows, and bulls; exceptions are, of course, animals belonging to the *Suidae* species (that is, swine, pigs, boars, hogs, etc.).

Another Abrahamic sacrificial tradition, which has survived, is circumcision of male children. Male circumcision is "the surgical removal of some, or all, of the foreskin (or prepuce) from the penis."[44] In Genesis, God orders Abraham to go through this ritual as follows.[45]

> This is my covenant with you and your descendants after you, the covenant you are to keep: Every male among you shall be circumcised. You are to undergo circumcision, and it will be the sign of the covenant between me and you. For the generations to come every male among you who is eight days old must be circumcised, including those born in your household or bought with money from a foreigner—those who are not your offspring.
>
> (Genesis 17: 10–12)

Male children born, mostly, to Jewish and Muslim parents are put through this ritual. Indeed, it is a required element of the Jewish and Muslim faiths. According to some estimates, circumcision is performed on about 55 percent of male infants born in the United States each year.[46] In Europe the estimate is about 10 percent.

A further extension of this practice carried out by the ultra-Orthodox Jews is *metzitzah b'peh*, "a technique for orally suctioning a circumcision wound."[47] Former New York mayor Michael Bloomberg had instituted a policy that required written consent of parents before a *mohel*, the person performing the circumcision, could perform *metzitzah b'peh*. Concerns have been raised about the health risks of such practice. It is argued that sexually transmitted diseases, such as herpes, are very likely to be passed on to the child when the *mohel* orally "cleanses" the recently circumcised penis of the baby. During the summer of 2013, candidates seeking the mayoral office were asked by the ultra-Orthodox Jewish community their views about the practice and whether or not they would continue to require the written consent. Except for one candidate, Christine Quinn, all other hopefuls defended the practice of *metzitzah b'peh* on religious grounds. They promised either to repeal the written consent requirement or at least have a debate about the issue.[48]

Recently, the debate over the risks and health benefits associated with male circumcision has been revived by the publication of a study in *Pediatrics*, a journal of the American Academy of Pediatrics.[49] According to this study, "Specific benefits from male circumcision were identified for the prevention of urinary tract infections, acquisition of HIV, transmission of some sexually transmitted infections, and penile cancer." The authors of the study also noted that "[m]ale circumcision does not appear to adversely affect penile sexual function/sensitivity or sexual satisfaction."[50] The debate, however, is far from settled. A New York-based non-profit organization, Intact America, came out strongly against the study's recommendation of circumcision of male infants.[51]

I mentioned above that the main focus of any religion is the appeasement of God, and that any benefit that may come to humans is incidental. Whenever there is a clash between God and humans, the faithful take the side of God. I will present a few examples of recent history, a couple of decades, in support of this statement. Why take examples only from recent history? Did the sacrifice of humans at the altar of deities stopped between, say, Abraham's desire to slay his son or the Mayan rituals of sacrificing humans,[52] and now? Not at all! Indeed, the faithful in an effort to appease God at the cost of human suffering have a remarkable tendency to continue their practices, in one form or another, unabated. While the forms of sacrifices have changed, the spirit endures. I refer the curious reader to *The God Delusion* by Richard Dawkins,[53] and *God Is Not Great* by Christopher Hitchens,[54] for detailed accounts of the faithful's persistence in inflicting pain on fellow humans to appease God.

One reason I focus on recent history is that these episodes are relatively fresh in our memories, and as a result, more relatable. While the tortures, and the resulting pain, that were inflicted upon those who did not abide by the Christian doctrine during the Catholic Church's Inquisitions[55] were real, they tend not to have the same impact as events that are more recent in time. Memories tend to fade. This is perhaps a survival mechanism developed by the human brain to avoid constant torture by the reminders of bad times. While a historical perspective is extremely important and indeed vital for a deeper understanding, I want to highlight the point that the state of the present-day religion is not any better suited to the protection of humans and human rights than that of the centuries past. The atrocities committed by the faithful span over millennia and encompass the globe.

Galileo Galilei was persecuted and put in prison in the early 1600s for questioning the geo-centric views held by the Catholic Church. In early 1989, Iran's Ayatollah Khomeini issued a decree (a *fatwa*) against the novelist Salman Rushdie for writing *The Satanic Verses*,[56] and asked Muslims all over the world to kill the author for committing blasphemy against Muhammad, the founder of Islam. And of course who can forget the attacks on September 11, 2001, by the *Al-Qaeda* on the World Trade Center in New York?[57] These attacks have changed the social and political landscape, not only in the United States, but world over, for the foreseeable future. The fate that befell the Danish cartoonist for depicting Muhammad in cartoons remains fresh in people's memories.[58] In Pakistan, an 11-year old (14, according to some accounts[59]) Christian girl was accused of burning pages of the Koran, and was arrested, *The Guardian* reported on August 19, 2012.[60] Burning the Koran is considered blasphemy and it carries a death penalty according to the Pakistani laws. On October 9, 2012, Malala Yousafzai, a 15-year-old girl (14, according to some accounts) was shot in the head by the Pakistani Taliban in Swat Valley, Pakistan.[61] Her crime? She advocated education for girls. She would survive the attack and address the United Nations on July 12, 2013—her 16th birthday.[62] The list goes on.

As I write these pages, *The New York Times* reports in its Sunday, August 25, 2013, edition that a former physician, Dr. Narendra Dabholkar, was murdered in Pune, India.[63] What was his crime? He revealed frauds perpetrated by gurus, holy men, fortunetellers, sorcerers, and "mystical entrepreneurs," who had accumulated fortunes by scamming the innocent villagers. He wanted to instill scientific thinking among people. According to the reports, he would go to villages and replicate the "miracles" (lying on a "bed of nails," setting "coconuts on fire," et cetera) performed by the holy men, thus revealing the frauds.

Curiously, similar activities are performed by the likes of Anthony "Tony" Robbins and Donald Trump, and many others. For instance, according to Tony Robbins's website he would hold a weekend-long event, from November 7 to November 10, 2013, which would include "Firewalk Experience."[64] This event is called "Unleash the Power Within" and it was held in "New York Area." An all-inclusive ticket for one "Seating in Front Section (Close to Tony!)" was advertised for $2,695. This was, of course, one of the many events that were on his schedule for the remainder of 2013. Others included "Date With Destiny Leadership" (Australia, August 21–28, 2013), "Date With Destiny" (Australia, August 23–28, 2013), "Life & Wealth Mastery" (Canary Islands, September 15–23, 2013), "Wealth Mastery Leadership" (Canary Islands, September 19–23, 2013), "Life & Wealth Mastery" (Fiji, September 27–October 4, 2013), "Leadership Academy" (San Diego, October 3–6, 2013), "Business Mastery" (London, October 19–22, 2013), "Life & Wealth Mastery" (Fiji, November 15–22, 2013), "Date With Destiny Leadership" (Palm Springs, December 6–8, 2013), and "Date With Destiny" (Palm Springs, December 8–13, 2013).[65]

A busy man, indeed!

By the way, he also has a special program for special people. It is called "Anthony Robbins Platinum Partnership."[66] If you join him in this "partnership,"

[y]ou and your Platinum Partners will receive exclusive invitations to up to four incredible adventures per year. Tony and Sage Robbins will join you on selected trips as you learn, network, and play in such diverse locations as a private palazzo in Venice, the cascading beaches of Bora Bora, a private session on top of the Great Wall of China, 100 mph boat races in South Beach, a private invitation to Scotland's exclusive Skibo Castle, and riding camels through the Great Pyramids of Egypt.

New York Attorney General Eric Schneiderman filed a lawsuit against Donald Trump, seeking a "restitution of at least $40 million," for operating an "investment school" in which students were promised that they would learn the secrets of real estate investment.[67] A three-day seminar would cost $1,495. However, a "Trump Elite" package that included "personal mentorship" from Mr. Trump himself would cost $35,000 per course. Some seminar participants who were promised a picture with the man himself had to settle for a picture next to a "cardboard cutout."[68] According to the lawsuit, over 5,000 individuals all over the United States were coerced into taking courses in the "Trump University."

Going back to my reasons for bringing examples from recent history, it is the topic of discussion at hand. That is, why FBOs may not be suitable to provide social safety nets in modern societies. Since my primary focus is the provision social safety nets in the United States, I will bring examples from the United States to support my argument. I will look at two recent events. One, the Affordable Care Act, nicknamed "Obamacare." The other example is that of same-sex marriage. In my opinion these two recent events reveal the drawbacks of using FBOs for the provision of social safety nets.

8.5.1. *Affordable Care Act and Its Provisions*

On March 23, 2010, President Barack Obama signed the Affordable Care Act (ACA) into law.[69] Some of the main features of the ACA included ending the practices of insurance companies to deny healthcare insurance coverage to those with pre-existing conditions. That is, if someone already had some chronic illness, insurance companies reserved the right to, and did, deny insurance coverage. The insurance companies would also deny coverage and even cancel insurance if it turned out that there was a reasonable chance that a given ailment could be the result of a condition that existed prior to signing the contract, even if the patient could not have known about the connection. Indeed, insurance companies reserved the right to collect the bills they had already paid, and they did. In other words, if an individual had made a mistake in filling out the application unbeknown to the individual, she/he could be denied coverage and her/his insurance would be canceled. Given that health insurance contracts are rather lengthy and complicated, it is not an uncommon occurrence. The ACA dealt with the problem in two ways. First, it mandated that the applications and contracts be simple and readable by a layperson. Second, if someone happened to make a mistake on the application, she/he could not be dropped because of this mistake.

Another common practice of the healthcare insurance industry is to put a limit on the amount that will be reimbursed for a treatment during a given time period. So if someone had a chronic disease, say, some form of cancer, which would require expensive treatment, the insurance company would put a limit on how much it will pay during a given time period. This means that the patient has two options. One, pay out of pocket, and two, stop the treatment. The ACA ended the limits on healthcare provided.[70]

One feature of the ACA was the provision of "free preventive care."[71] These services included "blood pressure and cholesterol tests, mammograms, colonoscopies, and more." One set of these preventive services provided specifically to women, free of charge, was contraceptives.[72] Under the ACA, employers (above certain size) were required to provide health insurance to their employees and the insurance plans were required to cover these preventive services. While these preventive services listed 22 items, the most attention was given to the provision of contraceptives. A whole host of religious organizations including churches, and church-run facilities, such as schools, universities, and other agencies, which provide social services and hire employees who may not belong to their particular religion or do not adhere to the dictates, objected to the idea of providing contraceptives to their employees on religious grounds.

In their opposition to this provision, various religions and religious sects presented a united front; Roman Catholics joined Lutherans, Baptists, and Jews. Testifying in front of the House Committee on Oversight and Government Reform, they all argued that such a mandate was contrary to their religious beliefs, and that the government by forcing them to provide contraceptives to their employees infringed on their religious freedoms.[73] They argued that using birth control was equivalent to abortion, even though that equation was factually wrong. And medical experts pointed out this fact. The medical community's advice, however, was not considered relevant on this issue.[74] Rather curiously, those who testified in the first two rounds in the hearings were all men. Women, religious or otherwise, were missing.[75] The strangeness of the situation was not lost on Representative Carolyn B. Maloney, a Democrat from New York. She asked, "Where are the women? It's outrageous that the Republicans would not allow a single individual representing the tens of millions of women who want and need insurance coverage for basic preventive health care services, including family planning." Perhaps not surprisingly, since the clergymen were making factually incorrect statements about the abortive capabilities of contraceptives, another group missing from the testimony was medical experts.

In an attempt to calm the situation the Obama administration offered a compromise. It suggested a solution according to which religious institutions may not get involved directly in the provision of contraceptives, and that the insurance companies will provide these services on their own. The

Catholic bishops rejected the idea. They responded that since the Church was paying for the insurance premium, effectively the Church was providing the services. John H. Garvey, president of the Catholic University of America, said that there was "no real difference" between the policy that required religious organizations to provide contraceptive and shifting the provision to the insurance providers. Similar sentiments were expressed by the rabbi, Meir Soloveichik of Yeshiva University and Congregation Kehilath Jeshurun in New York City. He argued that "[r]eligious organizations would still be obligated to provide employees with an insurance policy that facilitates acts violating the organization's religious tenets." (They were right on this point; there isn't any difference between an organization providing the contraceptive and the insurance company providing the contraceptive for which the organization pays.)

On May 21, 2012, the Catholic Church filed a law suit "in 12 federal courts" across the country.[76] Cardinal Timothy Dolan of the New York archdiocese issued a statement in which he said, "We have tried negotiations with the administration and legislation with the Congress—and we'll keep at it— but there's still no fix." By the way, this is the same Cardinal Timothy Dolan we encountered earlier in this chapter. If you recall, Cardinal Dolan, now archbishop of New York, was archbishop of Milwaukee in 2007. To make sure that the victims of child-sex abuse did not get their hand on the Church's assets, he transferred "nearly $57 million into a cemetery trust fund."[77]

Not all the faithful Catholic were against the provision of preventive services, including contraceptives, to women. An influential conference of Catholic nuns—the Leadership Conference of Women Religious—supported the ACA and challenged the Church's opposition to the law.[78] The conference had also challenged the Catholic Church's "teaching on homosexuality and male-only priesthood." The Vatican, however, did not approve of the conference's stance. An investigative report issued by the Vatican's Congregation for the Doctrine of the Faith noted that the conference was involved in propagating "radical feminist themes incompatible with the Catholic faith." The Vatican's investigative report also made another point. According to this *New York Times* article, the group of nuns belonging to the Leadership Conference of Women Religious was "focusing its work too much on poverty and economic injustice, while keeping 'silent' on abortion and same-sex marriage."[79] One would expect that speaking out about "poverty and economic injustice" would be encouraged since such activism would help promote human rights. That is, of course, if human rights were the mainstay.

The ACA and its provisions related to women's health brought out previously suppressed, or perhaps not so suppressed, sentiments to the surface.

Anyone who spoke in favor of its provisions became a target of the opponents. This was especially so if the supporter happened to be a female. Ms. Sandra Fluke, at the time a law student at Georgetown University, was castigated for speaking out about women's health issues. She spoke in favor of providing contraceptives to women. In February 2012, she testified before the House Democrats about the contraceptive coverage in Georgetown University's health insurance plan. Rush Limbaugh, an extremely influential, if not the most influential,[80] Conservative radio talk-show host called Ms. Fluke a "slut" and a "prostitute."[81] Mr. Limbaugh talked ad nauseam, for three days, on his talk show "The Rush Limbaugh Show" about Ms. Fluke's personal life, suggesting that she was so promiscuous that she needed taxpayer help to afford contraceptives. She was later nominated by the *Time* magazine as a candidate for the Person of the Year 2012.[82] She would also speak at the 2012 Democratic National Convention.[83]

8.5.2. Same-Sex Marriage

The issue of same-sex marriage and the related debates highlight yet another area where deities' demands trump human rights. Again, it should not come as a surprise. According to the Bible, homosexuality is an "abomination." For instance, in Leviticus 18:22, God commands "Thou shalt not lie with mankind, as with womankind: it is abomination."[84] There are several references to "sodomites" and how God punished them for their "un-natural" acts in the Bible.[85] According to the Bible, certain individuals will not go to heaven. Among them are "effeminate."[86]

> Know ye not that the unrighteous shall not inherit the kingdom of God? Be not deceived: neither fornicators, nor idolaters, nor adulterers, nor effeminate, nor abusers of themselves with mankind, Nor thieves, nor covetous, nor drunkards, nor revilers, nor extortioners, shall inherit the kingdom of God.
>
> (1 Corinthians 6: 9–10)

And the acts of women who dress as men and men who dress as women are also considered abominations.[87]

> The woman shall not wear that which pertaineth unto a man, neither shall a man put on a woman's garment: for all that do so are abomination unto the LORD thy God.
>
> (Deuteronomy 22: 5)

In a similar fashion, according to the Koran, God has declared homosexuality a sin and has condemned homosexuals.

We sent Lot and he said to his people, "How can you practise this outrage? No one in the world has outdone you in this. You lust after men rather than women! You transgress all bounds!"

(7: 80–82)[88]

"Must you, unlike [other] people, lust after males and abandon the wives that God has created for you? You are exceeding all bounds," but they replied, "Lot! If you do not stop this, you will be driven away." So he said, "I loathe what you do: Lord, save me and my family from what they are doing."

(26: 165–169)[89]

We also sent Lot to his people. He said to them, "How can you commit this outrage with your eyes wide open? How can you lust after men instead of women? What fools you are!"

(27: 54–55)[90]

And Lot: when He said to his people, "You practise outrageous acts that no people before you have ever committed. How can you lust after men, waylay travellers, and commit evil in your gatherings?" the only answer his people gave was, "Bring God's punishment down on us, if what you say is true." So he prayed, "My Lord, help me against these people who spread corruption."

(29: 28–29)[91]

On February 26, 2012, Frank Rich of the *New York* magazine wrote an article recalling the legalization of same-sex marriage in New York State.[92] The Marriage Equality Act was passed in New York State on June 24, 2011. He is right in saying that while the path to gay civil rights has been smoother than "the other civil-rights battles in America," gays are far from fully accepted and members of society. As Frank Rich in his *New York* magazine article reminded us, Liberal politicians have much blame to share with the Conservative politicians. It was none other than President Bill Clinton, a Democrat, who signed the Defense of Marriage Act (DOMA) in 1996.[93] Frank Rich writes, "While 'don't ask, don't tell' can be rationalized (by some) as a bungled rookie effort at compromise during his early months in office, DOMA is indefensible." On top of that, he had the support from the Democrats in the Congress. Vice President Joe Biden, who was a senator at the time, was one of the senators who cast "YAE" votes; only 14 senators, all Democrats, voted against DOMA.[94] It took until June 26, 2013, before DOMA was ruled unconstitutional by the United States Supreme Court.[95]

While it may seem like a daily occurrence that one politician or another would revisit his or her political calculus and come forth in favor of same-sex marriage, significant hurdles remain. It was only in May 2013 that a gay man was killed in Greenwich Village, New York City,[96] of all places. According to the Police Commissioner Raymond W. Kelly, as compared with the last year, there had been an uptick in hate crimes against gays in New York City, "22 compared with 13 during the same period last year," the article reported. While things are bad in metropolises, they are worse in smaller towns, especially in the Southern states.

One group of individuals that has been discriminated against throughout the US history is African Americans. And as strange as it may sound, they are among the ones who opposed, and still do, same-sex marriage. In California, Proposition 8, which banned same-sex marriage, was on the ballot in 2008.[97] "Catholics, evangelical Christians, conservative black and Latino pastors, and myriad smaller ethnic groups with strong religious ties" joined Mormons in door-to-door campaign to convince voters that same-sex marriage was a threat to hetero-sex marriage. And while sentiments among the general public and among African Americans are changing and they are becoming more accepting of same-sex relations, African Americans are still one of the largest groups that opposes such shift.[98]

Going back to the religion-based persecution of lesbian, gay, bisexual, and transgender individuals, perhaps relying on the verses of the Bible (1 Corinthians 6:9–10; Deuteronomy 22:5, cited above), which prohibited men wearing "dresses" and women wearing "pants," Pastor Sean Harris of the Berean Baptist Church in Fayetteville, North Carolina,[99] ordered his congregation to "crack" the "limp wrist" of their "girlish" son. He said, "Dads, the second you see that son dropping the limp wrist, you walk over there and crack that wrist. Man up. Give them a good punch. OK?"[100] With regard to their daughters' wardrobe choices, Pastor Harris said to dads, "[W]hen your daughter starts acting too butch, you rein her in." He went on, and asked dads to tell their daughters that they were going to "wear a dress," and that they were going to "look pretty."[101] Later, upon reflection, or perhaps forced by the public outcry, he had the following to say about his remarks:[102]

> If I had to say it again, I would say it differently, no doubt. Those weren't planned words, but what I do stand by is that the word of God makes it clear that effeminate behavior is ungodly. I'm not going to compromise on that.

Another pastor, in North Carolina (again!), Pastor Charles Worley of the Providence Road Baptist Church in Maiden, North Carolina,[103] addressing his congregation suggested a solution to the "gay problem."[104]

> I figured a way out—a way to get rid of all the lesbians and queers. But I couldn't get it passed through Congress. Build a great big large fence, 150 or 100 miles long. Put all the lesbians in there. Fly over and drop some food. Do the same thing with the queers and the homosexuals. Have that fence

electrified so they can't get out. Feed 'em, and—And you know what? In a few years they'll die out. You know why? They can't reproduce.

Pope Francis has been hailed for his modesty and his love for the poor and the indigent. An article by Howard Chua-Eoan, which appeared in July 29, 2013, issue of the *Time* magazine, was entitled "A Pope for the poor."[105] Breaking with the tradition he opted for simple Papal regalia instead of an ostentatious garb—no handmade red leather shoes for this successor of St. Peter. Visiting Brazil on his first trip as the Pope, he mingled with the laity, without any regard for his personal security. On his flight back to the Vatican he chatted with the reporters and answered their questions in a courteous and frank manner, an act so uncommon that reporters and others accompanying the Pope were taken by surprise.[106]

He answered questions about homosexuality and ordination of women, among others. With regard to women, while he sought a bigger and more prominent role in the Church, becoming priest was not up for discussion. He said that Pope John Paul II had put the matter to rest. When it came to the topic of homosexuality, his remarks, "If someone is gay and he searches for the Lord and has good will, who am I to judge?" hit the news media instantaneously. Apparently even using the word "gay" in public was such a break from the past[107] that some even wondered if he would change the Church's stance on this issue. His predecessor, Pope Benedict XVI, had declared homosexuality an "intrinsic moral evil," and considered homosexuals being "intrinsically disordered." These hopes, however, were short lived. The Vatican was quick to point out that that was just a change in "tone" and not in content. The Church still considered the practice of homosexuality a sin and forbade the members of the laity from engaging in such a practice.

Some in the ecclesiastic community were thankful for even this change in tone. Gene Robinson, the first openly gay bishop elected in the Episcopal Church, wrote an article in the *Time* magazine August 12, 2013, issue.[108] In that article, while being critical of the Catholic Church's stance on homosexuality, he noted that even the change in tone was an encouraging sign. In Robinson's assessment, due to the Pope's tone, other Christian denominations were reassessing their policies toward homosexuals. "Even evangelicals understand that changing their stance on this issue may be key to attracting young people, whether gay or straight, to the church and keeping them," he noted. And here is where a skeptical mind wonders whether this reassessment of policies toward homosexuals is the result of dwindling ranks. After all, religions, and various denominations within each religion, do need to maintain a certain level of adherents to stay relevant. The religious market place is not immune to the forces of competition.

I provided this lengthy discussion to make the point that human rights are not, at the risk of repeating, religion's mainstay; whatever human rights exist or are observed are incidental. The main purpose of religion, any religion, is to appease the deity. Whenever there is clash between human needs and the needs of the deity, the deity wins.

Some may argue that religions, through FBOs, do provide a number of social services. Just look at the number of hospitals run by religious organizations, the number of schools and colleges that provide education to billions of people around the world, the number of charity organizations that help victims of natural disasters across the globe, and so on. Indeed, this is what Robert Shiller, an economist and a Nobel laureate, whom we met in Chapter 7, argued. True, they do provide a number of vital services. There are, however, at least two issues in this counter-argument. One, FBOs provide only those services that do not conflict with their doctrines. (I will have more to say about this point shortly.) And second, since we do not know the exact social opportunity cost (that is, what society has to pay to get these services through FBOs) of the provision of these services, we cannot determine whether or not these services provided by FBOs are worth it. Recall that FBOs get significant tax breaks. However, the amount of tax breaks is not available to the public.

Ryan T. Cragun, Stephanie Yeager, and Desmond Vega estimated the tax subsidies enjoyed by FBOs. The result of this research was a report titled: *How Secular Humanists (and Everyone Else) Subsidize Religion in the United States.*[109] It was published by the Council for Secular Humanism. According to this research report, taxpayers subsidize FBOs to the tune of over $71 billion per year (Table 1 of the report). These are very conservative estimates though. The authors did not include, among other items, "[l]ocal income and property tax subsidies" and "[d]onor tax exempt subsidies" due to lack of data. The actual amount of subsidies is almost certainly higher. Now, it may very well be the case that FBOs are, indeed, the most efficient way to provide these services, and the sum of $71 billion is well worth it. But, as I argued earlier, until we have the data, we cannot be sure. Perhaps by opening their ledgers, FBOs will help their cause.

8.5.3. "But This Is Not the True Religion"

Let us go back to the treatment of issues and/or individuals who fall afoul of the religious dictums. Indeed, as we saw that whenever any member of the ecclesiastic society diverges from the doctrine, she/he becomes a target for the institutional authorities. Remember the Catholic nuns—The Leadership Conference of Women Religious—who questioned the Catholic Church's stance on homosexuality and all-male priesthood? They were investigated by the Vatican and asked to tamper down their efforts in the areas of poverty and healthcare. We also saw that in opposition to the provisions of ACA the Catholic Church was joined by other Christian denominations and the faithful belonging to other religions who are often competitors in the religious marketplace.

And then, of course, there was the case of Cardinal Dolan. He transferred millions from one account to another, lest the "child-sex abuse" victims got their hands on the money. It is notable that he made this transfer with the blessings from the Vatican. As I said before, this should not come as a surprise though. The main purpose of any religion is to serve the deity. The service of human beings is incidental. Whenever there is clash between human needs and the needs of the deity, the deity wins. The faithful are ordered by the clergy that they are supposed to come down hard on their sons and daughters if they find any sign of deviation from the tenets of the religion. Even putting those who express their natural tendencies in sexual matters contrary to the teachings of the religious texts behind electrified fences is advised.

Some may argue that those who sacrifice humans at the altar of the deity are not followers of the "true" religion. They are imposters who are "using" religion to advance their own agenda. I find this argument rather curious. Here is why? For one to judge whether or not a religious practice is the true practice as intended, one has to have an objective measure, against which a given practice can be evaluated. Since we do not have any such objective measure, we cannot say that person A's practice is the true practice and person B's is not. What about the religious texts—the Bible, the Koran, the Gita, and so on? As many scholars over the years have shown, there are numerous interpretations and contradictions.[110]

Some may further argue that interpretations that lead to trampling human rights—ban on gay marriage, denial of contraception, and so on— are extreme. Moderate interpretations do not lead to such conclusions. Again, for one to determine which interpretation is "moderate" and which interpretation is "extreme" and which interpretation goes too far in the execution of the tenets of faith, one needs an objective measure. In the absence of objective guideposts we cannot declare one interpretation too extreme and the other moderate, and thus, the "right" interpretation. For instance, if a deity is pleased by the offering of one virgin as sacrifice, why would offering two virgins be too much? Who gets to determine offering two virgins leads to divine dyspepsia, and how does one determine this?

Self-proclaimed moderates among the faithful have tried to square this circle. One such example is an explanation by Reza Aslan, especially with regard to Islam. In the aftermath of the September 11, 2001, attacks, in the prologue of his book entitled *No god but God*[111] (pp.xviii–xix), Aslan writes, "After all, religion is, by definition, interpretation; and by definition, all interpretations are valid. However, some interpretations are more reasonable than others." In order to discern which interpretation is a "reasonable" interpretation and which interpretation is not, he goes on to say that "scholars [of religion] form a reasonable interpretation of a particular religious tradition . . . by merging that religion's myths with what can be known about the spiritual and political landscape in which those myths arose." He defines "myth" as "stories of the supernatural." He also distinguishes between "truth" and "fact." He argues that stories told in religious texts (that is, myths) tell us the "truths" about the supernatural, and "have little to do with historical facts." He argues that questioning the factual natures of Moses parting the Red Sea, or Jesus raising the dead, or God speaking through Muhammad, "is to ask totally irrelevant questions. The only question that matters with regard to a religion and its mythology is 'What do these stories mean?' "

I find his explanation about the "reasonableness" of interpretations, and that myths should be looked at in the context of the time and space in which they arose, rather unconvincing. Here is why? First, if one accepts that a given myth (religious story) had relevance in a given time and space, one gives up any claim to its applicability for all eternity. One has to entertain at least the idea that it may not be applicable. However, as the examples I cited above in the cases of ACA, same-sex marriage, and male circumcision, to name just a few, the eternal applicability and infallibility of the lessons of religious texts is what guided the actions of the faithful. For the faithful, these entities, which "by definition" (borrowing Aslan's phraseology) are divine—God— and divinely ordained—prophet, et cetera—and have sacred proclamations, are meant to be taken on faith. Questioning them is sacrilege. In the realm of reason, however, all entities are "by definition" (again, borrowing Aslan's phraseology) human, and their proclamations up for questions. Nothing, "by definition" (borrowing Aslan's phraseology yet again) is sacred.

Secondly, and more importantly, the moment one accepts that there is a supernatural deity of any kind, and that there was someone who had contact with that supernatural deity, one has left the territory of reason, and has entered the faithland. Calling one interpretation more reasonable than the other is a distinction without difference. I do not think it is a matter of degree.

Furthermore, as I argued and provided evidence above, because claims made in religious texts have implications for human rights, all questions asked about such claims, even about Moses parting the Red Sea, or Jesus raising the dead, or God speaking through Muhammad's lips, are legitimate and relevant questions. Apologists,[112] try as they might, cannot hide behind the false dichotomy of what they "mean" and what they "said."

Now, as promised, I come to the question of why I am only using verses that present a less flattering picture of religion. The reason: These are the verses that are used to justify persecution of fellow humans. This objection would be valid if the faithful were not justifying their persecution of other humans on these grounds. As it stands, this is not a valid objection.

So far I have made the case that FBOs are an inferior mode of delivering social services and providing social safety nets. What about secular organization? Studies, small in number as they are on the topic, do show that secular organizations are relatively better at providing these services as compared with their religious counterparts. Secular organizations run into the problems detailed in Chapter 2: namely, lack of depth of resources, geographic portability, measurability, and anonymity. For these reasons secular organizations are also not up to the task in a modern economy. The solution, again, is government-provided tax-financed social safety nets.

8.6. Chapter Summary

I have argued in this chapter that religious organizations are not a suitable candidate for the provision of social safety nets. The reasons I have mentioned include, first and foremost, their lackluster record on human right. Their primary purpose for existence is to serve God, and not fellow humans. Another reason why religious organizations may not be suitable for the provision of social safety nets is their lack of transparency. This paucity of information prevents one to gauge their efficiency in the provision of human services.

In the next and final chapter, Chapter 9, I make a few concluding remarks.

CHAPTER 9

Concluding Remarks

Just as there is no pride in adhering to the ideas that have been proven wrong, there is no wisdom in maintaining institutions that do not meet the needs of changing ontological realities. In this spirit I have proposed in this book that formal social safety nets should be provided by the government and financed by taxes. Given that a society needs social safety nets, the question is how to provide these safety nets in a manner that not only preserves human dignity but also serves the intended purpose in the most efficient manner possible. I have argued in this book that informal social safety nets, organized or casual, serve their purpose up to a point. And in the United States, as in any other country, they did. As populations increase and economies grow, in order to take advantage of expanded set of possibilities, individuals leave their families and friends. Informal social safety nets no longer remain viable. Going beyond a certain point on the economic growth and development trajectories requires the role of government. I have argued that, as an example, we should look to the modern-day monetary system and compare it with the barter system. Barter system served its purpose when economies were small and there were only a few trades. In a modern economy with its almost unimaginable complexity, barter system stops being viable; a well-functioning monetary system and a legal tender are needed. Along the same lines, formal social safety nets financed by taxes are needed in today's societies.

To strengthen my argument I presented empirical evidence of how formal social safety nets may help increase innovation—arguably one of the main determinants of economic growth. The empirical evidence I presented in Chapter 4 is based on the analysis of data from 19 Organization for Economic Co-operation and Development member countries. These countries vary in depths and breadths of formal social safety nets and the data span over two decades. The results point to the positive impact of formal social safety nets on innovation. The results of my empirical study as well as of those cited in the book also show that taxes may not be as detrimental to economic growth as some may proclaim them to be. In the empirical evidence I presented in Chapter 4, taxes, lagged five years, in fact have a positive impact on innovative activities. Income inequality, on the other hand, has a negative impact.

I do not propose that every country should have the same depth and breadth of formal social safety nets. The extent of formal social safety nets may very well depend upon socioeconomic and cultural factors. Countries differ along a number of dimensions. Indeed, as Amartya Sen in his book *Development as Freedom*,[1] comparing the "social ethics" of the United States with those of the Western European countries, noted that while in the United States, society may have a higher tolerance for poverty, Americans would "find the double-digit levels of unemployment, common in Europe, to be quite intolerable" (p.95). While each society has to figure its own answers as to what level of poverty or unemployment level it can tolerate, the range of choices, however, is rather narrow. The range of choices does not include a complete absence of formal safety nets, nor does it include 100 percent coverage. The choice between the two is a false choice. While some income inequality may provide incentives to prosper, poverty and income inequality beyond certain levels breed hopelessness and despair. Rampant poverty and income inequality limit income mobility.

I have also argued in this book that providing informal social safety nets by non-profit organizations, secular as well as religious, is also not an option. Not only do these organizations lack resources, the issues of human dignity and self-respect cannot be overlooked either. The very reason—the possibility of having an intimate knowledge of the community—which may make (a local branch of) a non-profit organization reach out quickly—makes it very likely that the recipients' dignity will be endangered. This is true even if these non-profit organizations had the resources and the nationwide network needed to undertake such an enterprise.

Because religion and religious organizations hold a special place in the social, economic, and political landscape in the United States, I devoted a complete chapter to the issue of faith-based organizations (FBOs) providing informal social safety nets. Comparing the secular non-profit organizations with the religious ones (that is, FBOs), I presented research that points to the lackluster performance of FBOs. The research, though limited, showed that FBOs are relatively inefficient in providing human services as compared with their secular counterparts. It is important to note that the reason for the dearth of research in the case of FBOs is the lack of data. Data are needed to make efficiency comparisons. I suggested that if FBOs want to contest these findings, perhaps opening their books and making their financial data available would be helpful.

I also discussed at length why FBOs may not be suitable for the provision of informal social safety nets even if they were relatively more efficient than their secular or governmental counterparts. I argued that because of the poor record of religion on human rights, FBOs are especially ill-suited. Given that in any religion, humans take a back seat to the divine, and whenever the rights of humans collide with the divine wishes, the deity wins, and since we are talking about helping fellow humans in need, who are quite likely to fall afoul of the divine dictum due to varied belief systems or lack thereof, any given FBO is bound to refuse help. Disobeying the deity, of course, is not an option for the faithful. For this reason, in any scenario where there is even a possibility of such a collision, FBOs stop being viable. Some religiously inclined readers may take offence to this line of reasoning. This, however, is not my intention. In support of my argument I have quoted not only the religious texts but also the interpretations provided by those very religious authorities who have raised objections in various situations. Recent cases in point are the Affordable Care Act's provisions regarding contraceptives and the same-sex marriage issue, among others.

I understand that talking about the increasing role of government in day-to-day lives of individuals is a contentious topic in the United States. Given the divided social and political landscapes of the day, it tends to flare up tempers. Recent revelations about the US government spying on American citizens and foreign citizens, and politicians make this proposal still harder to swallow. The flawed role-out of the Affordable Healthcare plan in the fall of 2013 does not help this case either. My hope, however, is that the readers look beyond the very immediate, and objectively evaluate the arguments presented in this book.

Notes

Chapter 1

1. During June 2013, the unemployment rate was 7.6 percent. (Source: www.bls. gov) (Accessed: July 11, 2013).
2. www.bls.gov (Accessed: July 11, 2013).
3. These are seasonally adjusted data. Without seasonal adjustment the peak was 41.4 weeks reached during April of 2011. (www.bls.gov) (Accessed: July 11, 2013).
4. http://www.doleta.gov.
5. http://www.doleta.gov/etainfo/mission.cfm.
6. George F. Zook, "The President's Commission on Higher Education," *Bulletin of the American Association of University Professors* 33, no. 1 (Spring 1947), 10–28.
7. Ibid.
8. Amartya Sen, *Development as Freedom* (Westminster, MD: Alfred A. Knopf Incorporated, 1999).
9. Ibid., Chapter 3, for extensive discussion on the utilitarian, libertarian, and Rawlsian theories of social justice.
10. http://www.washingtonpost.com/wp-srv/politics/2012-presidential-debates/ republican-primary-debate-september-12-2011/ (Accessed: July 10, 2013).
11. http://www.washingtonpost.com/wp-srv/politics/2012-presidential-debates/ republican-primary-debate-september-12-2011/ (Accessed: July 10, 2013).
12. http://timeline.stlouisfed.org/index.cfm?p=timeline (Accessed: July 14, 2013).
13. Michael Lewis, *The Big Short: Inside the Doomsday Machine* (New York: W. W. Norton and Company, Inc., 2011); Carmen M. Reinhart and Kenneth Rogogg, *This Time is Different: Eight Centuries of Financial Folly* (Princeton, NJ: Princeton University Press, 2009).
14. http://askafreemason.org (Accessed: July 14, 2013).
15. http://www.elks.org (Accessed: July 14, 2013).
16. http://www.scouting.org (Accessed: July 14, 2013).
17. http://www.girlscouts.org (Accessed: July 14, 2013).
18. http://www.kiwanis.org (Accessed: July 14, 2013).
19. http://www.ymca.org/about-us.html (Accessed: August 10, 2013).
20. http://www.ywca.org/site/c.cuIRJ7NTKrLaG/b.7515891/k.C524/History.htm (Accessed: August 10, 2013).

21. http://www.salvationarmyusa.org/usn/www_usn_2.nsf/vw-dynamic-arrays/
52372817A7D7EBD28525743500535DA8?openDocument&charset=utf-8
(Accessed: August 10, 2013).

22. Steven B. Stritt, "Estimating the Value of the Social Services Provided by
Faith-Based Organizations in the United States," *Nonprofit and Voluntary Sector
Quarterly* 37, no. 4 (December 2008), 730–742. doi: http://nvs.sagepub.com/
archive/.

23. http://www.catholiccharitiesusa.org/ (Accessed: August 10, 2013).

24. http://www.ymca.org/about-us.html (Accessed: August 10, 2013).

25. http://www.ywca.org/site/c.cuIRJ7NTKrLaG/b.7515891/k.C524/History.htm
(Accessed: August 10, 2013).

26. http://www.salvationarmyusa.org/usn/www_usn_2.nsf/vw-dynamic-arrays/5237
2817A7D7EBD28525743500535DA8?openDocument&charset=utf-8
(Accessed: August 10, 2013).

27. I searched for "interfaith" charities on the Charity Navigator Website (charity-
navigator.org). It showed 34 such charities which are registered with the Internal
Revenue Service (IRS). (Accessed: August 10, 2013).

28. http://www.irs.gov/pub/irs-pdf/i990.pdf (Accessed: August 10, 2013).

29. "Faith-Based and Community Initiative: Improvements in Monitoring Grantees
and Measuring Performance Could Enhance Accountability (GAO-06-
616, June 19, 2006)" http://www.gao.gov/products/GAO-06-616 (Accessed:
August 15, 2013).

30. See, for instance, the membership requirements of The Benevolent and Protective
Order of Elks of the United States of America. (https://www.elks.org) (Accessed:
July 14, 2013).

31. For instance, the Elks offer help with school expenditure to the children of a
deceased member. http://www.elks.org (Accessed: July 14, 2013).

32. http://www.fns.usda.gov/snap (Accessed: July 14, 2013).

33. While Freemasonry, the Elks, Kiwanis, and other such orders have branches
spread out in different cities, as mentioned earlier, their help extended even to
the members is limited.

34. GDP is a measure of aggregate output or income of a country. It is defined as
the market value of all the goods and services produced in an economy in a given
time period. See, for instance (http://bea.gov/glossary/glossary.cfm?letter=G), for
a definition.

35. http://www.oecd.org/social/soc/socialexpendituredatabasesocx.htm
(Accessed: July 14, 2013).

36. Alberto Alesina, Edward Glaeser and Bruce Sacerdote, "Why Doesn't the
US have a European-Style Welfare System?" *NBER Working Papers* 8524
(2001).

37. Elhanan Helpman, *The Mystery of Economic Growth* (Cambridge, MA: Harvard
University Press, 2004).

38. Joseph E. Stiglitz, *The Price of Inequality: How Today's Divided Society Endangers our Future* (New York: W. W. Norton and Company Inc., 2012); Miles

Corak, *How to Slide Down the "Great Gatsby Curve": Inequality, Life Chances, and Public Policy in the United States* (Washington, DC: Center for American Progress, December 2012).

39. Robert J. Barro, "Inequality and Growth in a Panel of Countries," *Journal of Economic Growth* 5, no. 1 (2000), 5–32; Alberto Alesina and Roberto Perotti, "Income Distribution, Political Instability, and Investment," *European Economic Review* 40, no. 6 (June 1996), 1203–1228. doi:DOI: 10.1016/0014-2921(95)00030-5. http://www.sciencedirect.com/science/article/B6V64-3VW8NB4-1/2/86ba47e246e3c7d026640bc39b637c9b.

40. W. Adema and M. Ladaique, *How Expensive is the Welfare State?: Gross and Net Indicators in the OECD Social Expenditure Database (SOCX)* (Paris, France: OECD Publishing, [2009]); Willem Adema, Pauline Fron and Maxime Ladaique, *Is the European Welfare State really More Expensive?* (Paris, France: Organisation for Economic Co-operation and Development, 2011). doi:10.1787/5kg2d2d4pbf0-en. http://www.oecd-ilibrary.org/; jsessionid=1vsj805459pn3.x-oecd-live-01content/workingpaper/5kg2d2d4 pbf0-en.

Chapter 2

1. See the credit list that rolls on seemingly forever after a movie ends.

2. For more information see, http://www.federalreserve.gov/faqs/currency_15197.htm (Accessed: July 14, 2013). See also http://www.treasury.gov/resource-center/faqs/Currency/Pages/legal-tender.aspx (Accessed: November 2, 2013).

3. http://lexicon.ft.com/Term?term=monetary-system (Accessed: July 24, 2013).

4. http://dictionary.cambridge.org/us/dictionary/british/monetary-system (Accessed: July 24, 2013).

5. United States Code, 2010 Edition; Title 31—Money and Finance; Subtitle IV—Money; Chapter 51—Coins and Currency; Subchapter I—Monetary System; Sec. 5103—Legal tender (http://www.gpo.gov/fdsys/pkg/USCODE-2010-title31/html/USCODE-2010-title31-subtitleIV-chap51-subchapI-sec5103.htm) (Accessed: July 24, 2013).

6. http://www.bostonfed.org/education/pubs/coincurr.pdf (Accessed: December 1, 2013).

7. http://www.federalreserveeducation.org/about-the-fed/history/ (Accessed: December 1, 2013).

8. Edwin M. Truman, *The International Monetary System and Global Imbalances* (Washington, D.C.: The Peterson Institute of International Economics, 2010).

9. http://www.washingtonpost.com/world/europe/the-rise-of-the-bitcoin-virtual-gold-or-cyber-bubble/2013/04/04/8be37506-9d34-11e2-9219-51eb8387e8f1_story.html?wpisrc=emailtoafriend. See also, "Bitcoin: A Primer" (http://chicagofed.org/digital_assets/publications/chicago_fed_letter/2013/cfldecember2013_317.pdf) (Accessed: November 19, 2013).

10. http://www.philadelphiafed.org/publications/economic-education/ben-franklin-and-paper-money-economy.pdf (Accessed: December 1, 2013).

11. Source: http://markets.on.nytimes.com/research/markets/currencies/currencies. asp (Accessed: July 30, 2012). Note that I have mentioned not only the date but also the time. The reason is that exchange rates change rather rapidly.

12. http://www.census.gov/foreign-trade/balance/c4120.html (Accessed: July 30, 2012).

13. United States Code, 2010 Edition; Title 31—Money and Finance; Subtitle IV—Money; Chapter 51—Coins and Currency; Subchapter I—Monetary System; Sec. 5103—Legal tender (http://www.gpo.gov/fdsys/pkg/USCODE-2010-title31/pdf/USCODE-2010-title31-subtitleIV-chap51-subchapI.pdf) (Accessed: July 24, 2013).

14. Paul Seabright, *The Company of Strangers: A Natural History of Economic Life* (Princeton, NJ: Princeton University Press, 2010).

15. See, for instance, Frank and Bernanke, *Principles of Macroeconomics* (New York, NY: McGraw-Hill/Irwin, 2008), 262.

16. Milton Friedman, *The Island of Stone Money*, E-91-3 ed. (California: Stanford University, The Hoover Institution, 1991).

17. R. A. Radford, "The Economic Organisation of a P.O.W. Camp," *Economica* 12, no. 48 (November 1945), 189–201.

18. Yaroslav Trofimov, "Shrinking Dollar Meets its Match in Dolphin Teeth; Solomon Islands Prize Commodity Over Cash; Closing in for the Kill," *The Wall Street Journal* (2008), A.1.

19. On December 2, 2013, the average price of regular unleaded gas was $3.272 per gallon. http://research.stlouisfed.org/fred2/series/GASREGW?cid=32217 (Accessed: December 8, 2013).

20. See Chapter 14. L. Ball, *Money, Banking, and Financial Markets*, 2nd ed. (New York: Worth Publishers, 2012).

21. http://www.federalreserveeducation.org/about-the-fed/history/   (Accessed: December 1, 2013).

22. *Encyclopedia Britannica Online Academic Edition*. Encyclopedia Britannica Inc., (Accessed: August 03, 2012).

23. Smith, Adam. 1776 (2010). *An Inquiry into the Nature and Causes of the Wealth of Nations*, edited by Edwin Cannan. Chicago, IL, USA: University of Chicago Press.

24. Seabright, *The Company of Strangers*; Daron Acemoglu and James A. Robinson, *Why Nations Fail: The Origins of Power, Prosperity, and Poverty* (New York: Crown Publishers, 2012).

25. www.britannica.com.

26. http://www.census.gov/main/www/popclock.html.

27. http://www.census.gov/prod/2004pubs/wp-02.pdf. According to this report, 65 percent of 60 years or older population lived in less-developed countries in 2010.

28. A qualification is needed: In July 2013 the North Carolina legislature approved a cut in state-unemployment benefits, and due to certain technical reasons,

federal benefits were also cut. (http://www.nytimes.com/2013/07/02/us/north-carolinas-deep-cut-to-jobless-benefits-takes-effect-amid-protests.html) (Accessed: July 13, 2013).

29. John Rawls, *A Theory of Justice* (Cambridge, MA: Harvard University Press, 1973); Amartya Sen, *Development as Freedom* (Westminster, MD: Alfred A. Knopf Incorporated, 1999).

30. For concerns related to the validity of "qualitative" data see discussion and references cited in Alberto Alesina, Rafael Di Tella and Robert MacCulloch, "Inequality and Happines: Are Europeans and Americans Different?" *Journal of Public Economics* 88, no. 9–10 (2004), 2009–2042.

31. Data source: http://www3.norc.org/GSS+Website/.

32. Author's calculations. Data source: http://www.census.gov/hhes/migration/data/acs/state-to-state.html.

Chapter 3

1. http://www.nytimes.com/2013/06/20/health/study-finds-sharp-drop-in-hpv-infections-in-girls.html?pagewanted=all (Accessed: July 20, 2013).

2. http://pediatrics.aappublications.org/content/early/2013/03/12/peds.2012-2384.abstract (Accessed: July 20, 2013).

3. Source: http://unstats.un.org/unsd/nationalaccount/sna.asp (Accessed: May 28, 2013).

4. Source: http://unstats.un.org/unsd/nationalaccount/docs/SNA2008.pdf; ISBN: 978–92–1–161522–7 (Accessed: May 28, 2013).

5. Joel Mokyr, "The Intellectual Origins of Modern Economic Growth," *The Journal of Economic History* 65, no. 2 (June 2005), 285–351.

6. http://bea.gov/about/mission.htm (Accessed: May 14, 2013).

7. http://bea.gov/newsreleases/national/gdp/gdpnewsrelease.htm (Accessed: May 14, 2013).

8. Joseph E. Stiglitz, Amartya Sen and Jean-Paul Fitoussi, *Mismeasuring our Lives: Why GDP Doesn'T Add Up* (New York: The New Press, 2010).

9. Ibid.

10. Amartya Sen, *Development as Freedom* (Westminster, MD: Alfred A. Knopf Incorporated, 1999); Amartya Sen, "Poor, Relatively Speaking," *Oxford Economic Papers* 35, no. 2 (July 1983), 153–169.

11. Sudhir Anand and Martin Ravallion, "Human Development in Poor Countries: On the Role of Private Incomes and Public Services," *The Journal of Economic Perspectives* 7, no. 1 (Winter 1993), 133–150.

12. Elhanan Helpman, *The Mystery of Economic Growth* (Cambridge, MA: Harvard University Press, 2004).

13. Jakob Madsen, James Ang and Rajabrata Banerjee, "Four Centuries of British Economic Growth: The Roles of Technology and Population," *Journal of Economic Growth* 15, no. 4 (December 2010), 263–290. doi:10.1007/s10887-010-9057-7.

14. Mokyr, "The Intellectual Origins of Modern Economic Growth," 285–351.

15. Klein Jürgen, "Francis Bacon," *The Stanford Encyclopedia of Philosophy* (Winter 2012 edition), Edward N. Zalta, ed., (http://plato.stanford.edu/archives/win2012/entries/francis-bacon) Accessed: May 17, 2013.

16. See also, Angus Maddison, "Shares of the Rich and the Rest in the World Economy: Income Divergence between Nations, 1820–2030," *Asian Economic Policy Review* 3, no. 1 (June 2008), 67–82. doi:http://www3.interscience.wiley.com/journal/118501086/home.

17. Robert M. Solow, "A Contribution to the Theory of Economic Growth," *The Quarterly Journal of Economics* 70, no. 1 (February 1956), 65–94.

18. See www.bea.gov for definitions.

19. One such advancement is the introduction in May 2013 of a computer by Google that one can use as eyeglasses. The company calls it "Google Glass." http://www.nytimes.com/2013/05/07/technology/personaltech/google-glass-picks-up-early-signal-keep-out.html?pagewanted=all (Accessed: July 20, 2013).

20. M. Alfo, G. Trovato and R. J. Waldmann, "Testing for Country Heterogeneity in Growth Models using a Finite Mixture Approach," *Journal of Applied Econometrics*, 23, no. 4 (2008), 487–514; Mohammad Ashraf and Khan A. Mohabbat, "Output Convergence and the Role of Research and Development," *Annals of Economics and Finance* 11, no. 1 (2010), 35–71; Nazrul Islam, "What Have We Learnt from the Convergence Debate?" *Journal of Economic Surveys* 17, no. 3 (July 2003), 309–362. doi:http://www.blackwellpublishing.com/journal.asp?ref=0950-0804.

21. Richard Dawkins, *The Ancestor's Tale: A Pilgrimage to the Dawn of Evolution* (New York: Houghton Mifflin Company, 2004).

22. Marshall Alfred, *Principles of Economics* (1920). (Book IV, Chapter IX, p.25). Macmillan and Co. Ltd., Library of Economics and Liberty. Retrieved May 18, 2013 from the World Wide Web: http://www.econlib.org/library/Marshall/marP.html.

23. Kenneth J. Arrow, "The Economic Implications of Learning by Doing," *The Review of Economic Studies* 29, no. 3 (June 1962), 155–173.

24. Paul M. Romer, "Growth Based on Increasing Returns due to Specialization," *The American Economic Review* 77, no. 2, Papers and Proceedings of the 99th Annual Meeting of the American Economic Association (May 1987), 56–62.

25. Philippe Aghion and Peter Howitt, *Endogenous Growth Theory* (Cambridge, MA: The MIT Press, 1998).

26. See Ibid., Chapter 1.

27. Source: InfoBrief, NSF 12–309, March 2012. (http://www.nsf.gov/statistics/infbrief/nsf12309/nsf12309.pdf).

28. Ibid.

29. OECD, "Gross Domestic Expenditure on R&D," *Science and Technology: Key Tables from OECD*, no. 1 (2012). doi: 10.1787/rdxp-table-2012-1-en.

30. http://www.oecd-ilibrary.org/science-and-technology/gross-domestic-expenditure-on-r-d-2012_rdxp-table-2012-1-en (Accessed: January 23, 2014).

31. Petra Moser, "Patents and Innovation: Evidence from Economic History," *Journal of Economic Perspectives* 27, no. 1 (2013), 23–44.
32. Ibid.
33. www.oecd.org/sti/outlook.
34. "Manhattan Project." *Encyclopædia Britannica*. *Encyclopædia Britannica Online Academic Edition*. Encyclopædia Britannica Inc., 2013. Web. May 21, 2013. http://0-www.britannica.com.uncclc.coast.uncwil.edu/EBchecked/topic/362098/Manhattan-Project.
35. "Internet." *Encyclopædia Britannica*. *Encyclopædia Britannica Online Academic Edition*. Encyclopædia Britannica Inc., 2013. Web. May 21, 2013. http://0-www.britannica.com.uncclc.coast.uncwil.edu/EBchecked/topic/291494/Internet.
36. David T. Coe and Elhanan Helpman, "International R&D Spillovers," *European Economic Review* 39, no. 5 (May 1995), 859–887. doi:DOI: 10.1016/0014-2921(94)00100-E. http://www.sciencedirect.com/science/article/B6V64-3YRSMDP-16/2/284085b19eb1258bb9c372cf767051c5; Marios Zachariadis, "R&D, Innovation, and Technological Progress: A Test of the Schumpeterian Framework without Scale Effects," *The Canadian Journal of Economics/Revue Canadienne D'Economique* 36, no. 3 (August 2003), 566–586; Marios Zachariadis, "R&D-Induced Growth in the OECD?" *Review of Development Economics* 8, no. 3 (August 2004), 423–439. doi:10.1111/j.1467-9361.2004.00243.x.
37. Ibid., See also F. M. Scherer, *Innovation and Growth: Schumpeterian Perspective* (Cambridge, MA: The MIT Press, 1984); Daron Acemoglu and Melissa Dell, "Productivity Differences between and within Countries," *American Economic Journal: Macroeconomics* 2, no. 1 (January 2010), 169–188. doi:http://www.aeaweb.org/aej-macro/; Mohammad Ashraf, "What Explains R&D Efficiency Differences Across U.S. States," *The Journal of Economics (MVEA)* 37, no. 1 (2011), 59–75; Dirk Frantzen, "Technological Diffusion and Productivity Convergence: A Study for Manufacturing in the OECD," *Southern Economic Journal* 71, no. 2 (October 2004), 352–376; Zvi Griliches, "Productivity Puzzles and R & D: Another Nonexplanation," *The Journal of Economic Perspectives* 2, no. 4 (Autumn 1988), 9–21.
38. www.oecd.org/sti/outlook.
39. Richard T. Gretz, Joshua J. Lewer and Robert C. Scott, "R&D, Risk, and the Role of Targeted Government R&D Programs," *Journal of Economics (MVEA)* 36, no. 1 (2010), 79–104. doi:http://www.cba.uni.edu/economics/joe.htm.
40. http://www.doe.gov/articles/energy-department-launches-public-private-partnership-deploy-hydrogen-infrastructure (Accessed: May 21, 2013).
41. http://www.genome.gov/12011239 (Accessed: May 21, 2013).
42. Ibid.
43. Ashraf, "What Explains R&D Efficiency Differences Across U.S. States," 59–75.
44. Gretz, Lewer and Scott, "R&D, Risk, and the Role of Targeted Government R&D Programs," 79–104.

45. Richard T. Gretz, Jannett Highfill and Robert C. Scott, "Strategic Research and Development Policy: Societal Objectives and the Corporate Welfare Argument," *Contemporary Economic Policy* 27, no. 1 (January 2009), 28–45. doi:http://www.blackwell-synergy.com/loi/coep/.

46. Martin Falk, "What Drives Business Research and Development (R&D) Intensity Across Organisation for Economic Co-Operation and Development (OECD) Countries?" *Applied Economics* 38, no. 5 (March 2006), 533–547. doi: http://www.tandf.co.uk/journals/routledge/00036846.html.

47. Dawkins, *The Ancestor's Tale*.

48. http://www.cbsnews.com/8301-201_162-57590641/nik-wallenda-completes-tightrope-walk-across-gorge-near-grand-canyon/ (Accessed: July 22, 2013).

49. https://www.youtube.com/watch?v=3mFXHGFWR4s (Accessed: July 22, 2013).

50. http://www.opensecrets.org/lobby/ (Accessed: July 22, 2013).

51. http://www.opensecrets.org/lobby/top.php?showYear=2012&indexType=s (Accessed: July 22, 2013).

52. http://www.nytimes.com/2008/09/05/washington/05abramoff.html?_r=0 (Accessed: July 22, 2013).

53. Source: bea.gov (Accessed: May 22, 2013). These data plotted as a percentage of gross domestic product present a similar picture.

54. US Patent and Trademark Office-Patent Technology Monitoring Team (PTMT). URL: http://www.uspto.gov/web/offices/ac/ido/oeip/taf/us_stat.htm. (Accessed: May 23, 2013).

55. Data sources are as cited. I have limited the data period in figure 3.3 from 1963 to 2007 due to data availability of both variables.

56. The p value is smaller than .0001.

57. http://www.nytimes.com/2013/06/05/business/president-moves-to-curb-patent-suits.html?_r=0 (Accessed: July 20, 2013).

58. http://www.forbes.com/sites/forrester/2011/08/15/analysis-googles-acquisition-of-motorola-mobility/ (Accessed: May 25, 2013).

59. Zvi Griliches, "Patent Statistics as Economic Indicators: A Survey," *Journal of Economic Literature* 28, no. 4 (December 1990), 1661–1707; Bronwyn H. Hall, Adam B. Jaffe and Manuel Trajtenberg, *The NBER Patent Citations Data File: Lessons, Insights, and Methodological Tools*, Working Paper 8498 ed. (1050 Massachusetts Avenue Cambridge, MA 02138: National Bureau of Economic Research, 2001); W. B. Arthur, "The Structure of Invention," *Research Policy* 36, no. 2 (March 2007), 274–287. doi:http://www.elsevier.com/wps/find/journaldescription.cws_home/505598/description#description.

60. Ibid.; Helene Dernis and Dominique Guellec, *Using Patent Counts for Cross-County Comparisons of Technology Output* (OECD: Economic Analysis and Statistics Division, 2001).

61. Chien-Chiang Lee and Mei-Se Chien, "Dynamic Modelling of Energy Consumption, Capital Stock, and Real Income in G-7 Countries," *Energy Economics* 32, no. 3 (May 2010), 564–581. doi:http://www.elsevier.com/wps/find/journaldescription.cws_home/30413/description#description;Yuan Wang et al.,

"Energy Consumption and Economic Growth in China: A Multivariate Causality Test," *Energy Policy* 39, no. 7 (July 2011), 4399–4406. doi: http://www.sciencedirect.com/science/journal/03014215.

62. OECD Factbook 2012—ISSN—© 2012. Contribution of Renewables to Energy Supply. http://www.oecd.org/statistics/ (Accessed: May 27, 2013).

63. Data Source: United Nations Framework Convention on Climate Change. For definitional details see: http://unfccc.int/ghg_data/online_help/definitions/items/3817.php (Accessed: May 27, 2013).

64. United Nations Framework Convention on Climate Change (http://unfccc.int/ghg_data/ghg_data_unfccc/items/4146.php) (Accessed: May 27, 2013). See also Martin L. Weitzman, "On Modeling and Interpreting the Economics of Catastrophic Climate Change," *Review of Economics and Statistics* 91, no. 1 (February 2009), 1–19. doi: http://www.mitpressjournals.org/loi/rest., and the sources cited in it.

65. Source: United Nations Framework Convention on Climate Change (http://unfccc.int/ghg_data/ghg_data_unfccc/items/4146.php) (Accessed: May 27, 2013).

66. http://www.scientificamerican.com/article.cfm?id=fischetti-sea-level-could-rise-five-feet-new-york-city-nyc-2100 (Accessed: May 28, 2013).

67. Ibid.

68. "iPhone Maker in China is Under Fire after a Suicide," *The New York Times*, July 26, 2009. http://www.nytimes.com/2009/07/27/technology/companies/27apple.html?pagewanted=all (Accessed: May 30, 2013).

69. "one-child policy." *Encyclopædia Britannica. Encyclopædia Britannica Online Academic Edition.* Encyclopædia Britannica Inc., 2013. Web. May 30, 2013. http://0-www.britannica.com.unccdc.coast.uncwil.edu/EBchecked/topic/1710568/one-child-policy (Accessed: May 30, 2013).

70. "China's Brutal One-Child Policy," *The New York Times*, May 21, 2013. http://www.nytimes.com/2013/05/22/opinion/chinas-brutal-one-child-policy.html?src=xps (Accessed: May 30, 2013).

71. Ibid. See also "one-child policy." *Encyclopædia Britannica. Encyclopædia Britannica Online Academic Edition.* Encyclopædia Britannica Inc., 2013. Web. May 30, 2013. http://0-www.britannica.com.unccdc.coast.uncwil.edu/EBchecked/topic/1710568/one-child-policy (Accessed: May 30, 2013).

72. L. Cameron et al., "Little Emperors: Behavioral Impacts of China's One-Child Policy," *Science* 339, no. 6122 (2013), 953–957.

73. Robert J. Barro and Zavier Sala-I-Martin, *Economic Growth* (New York: McGraw-Hill, 1995); Moritz Schularick and Thomas M. Steger, "Financial Integration, Investment, and Economic Growth: Evidence from Two Eras of Financial Globalization," *Review of Economics and Statistics* 92, no. 4 (November 2010), 756–768. doi: http://www.mitpressjournals.org/loi/rest; Antonio Spilimbergo, "Growth and Trade: The North can Lose," *Journal of Economic Growth* 5, no. 2 (June 2000), 131–146. doi:10.1023/A:1009882419420.

74. Dani Rodrik, *The Globalization Paradox: Democracy and the Future of the World Economy* (New York, London: W. W. Norton & Company, 2011).

Chapter 4

1. http://occupywallst.org/ (Accessed: November 11, 2013). http://cityroom.blogs.nytimes.com/2011/09/17/wall-street-protest-begins-with-demonstrators-blocked/?ref=occupywallstreet (Accessed: November 11, 2013).
2. Edward Harris and Frank Sammartino, *Trends in the Distribution of Household Income between 1979 and 2007* (Washington, DC: Congressional Budget Office, 2011).
3. Ibid.
4. Jakob B. Madsen, "Are there Diminishing Returns to R&D?" *Economics Letters* 95, no. 2 (May 2007), 161–166. doi: 10.1016/j.econlet.2006.09.009. http://www.sciencedirect.com/science/article/pii/S0165176506003119.
5. The URL is http://stats.oecd.org.
6. The URL is www.oecd.org, *Statistics*—ISBN 92-64-05604-1—© OECD 2009.
7. The URL for patents statistics is www.oecd.org/sti/ipr-statistics.
8. J. Breitung and M. H. Pesaran, "Unit Roots and Cointegration in Panels," in *The Econometrics of Panel Data*, eds. László Mátyás and Patrick Sevestre, 3rd ed. (Heidelberg: Springer, 2008), 279–322.
9. The alternative is the so-called "heterogeneous alternative." See Breitung and Pesaran, "Unit Roots and Cointegration in Panels," (2008), 282.
10. Jack Johnston and John DiNardo, *Econometric Methods*, 4th ed. (New York: McGraw-Hill, 1997).
11. Robert J. Barro, "Inequality and Growth in a Panel of Countries," *Journal of Economic Growth* 5, no. 1 (2000), 5–32.

Chapter 5

1. "The market value of goods and services produced by labor and property in the United States, regardless of nationality." http://bea.gov/glossary/glossary.cfm?letter=G. (Accessed: June 7, 2013).
2. www.bea.gov.
3. www.bea.gov. Note that I have used the term "2005 chained dollars." This is a technical point. This method is a better way to "correct" for inflation than just evaluating goods and services in the 2005 prices. Curious reader is referred to (http://bea.gov/national/pdf/methodology/ALLchapters.pdf) for details (Accessed: June 7, 2013).
4. http://www.bea.gov/iTable/iTable.cfm?ReqID=9&step=1#reqid=9&step=3&isuri=1&903=58 (Accessed: June 6, 2013).
5. http://www.forbes.com/lists/2012/12/ceo-compensation-12_rank.html (Accessed: June 6, 2013).
6. These data are nominal terms, before taxes.

7. http://baseballplayersalaries.com/ (Accessed: June 6, 2013).
8. According to the Census Bureau's mission statement

  The Census Bureau serves as the leading sources of quality data about the nation's people and economy. We honor privacy, protect confidentiality, share our expertise globally, and conduct our work openly. We are guided on this mission by our strong and capable workforce, our readiness to innovate, and our abiding commitment to our customers. www.census.gov (Accessed: June 9, 2013)

9. http://www.census.gov/hhes/www/income/data/historical/inequality/IE-1.pdf (Accessed: June 9, 2013).
10. http://www.bea.gov/methodologies/index.htm#national_meth (Accessed: July 27, 2013).
11. The Census Bureau publishes data using these measures. See http://www.census.gov/cps/methodology/techdocs.html), for technical details on these and other measures (Accessed: June 9, 2013).
12. Data Source: Table IE-2: Measures of Individual Earnings Inequality for Full-Time Year-Round Workers by Sex (http://www.census.gov/hhes/www/income/data/historical/inequality/index.html) (Accessed: June 9, 2013).
13. See "The Changing Shape of the Nation's Income Distribution," page 8. http://www.census.gov/prod/2000pubs/p60-204.pdf (Accessed: June 10, 2013).
14. Ibid.
15. Ibid.
16. "Income, Poverty, and Health Insurance Coverage in the United States: 2011," page 9, figure 5.2. (http://www.census.gov/prod/2012pubs/p60-243.pdf) (Accessed: June 9, 2013).
17. www.oecd.org (Accessed: June 9, 2013).
18. See "The Changing Shape of the Nation's Income Distribution," page 9. http://www.census.gov/prod/2000pubs/p60-204.pdf (Accessed: June 10, 2013). See also Hans-Werner Sinn, "Social Insurance, Incentives and Risk Taking," *International Tax and Public Finance*, 3, no. 3 (1996), 258–280.
19. It can be safely said that even in North Korea the share of annual income which its ruler, Kim Jong Un, gets is not the same which a worker gets.
20. See Henry Sanborn, "Pay Differences between Men and Women," *Industrial and Labor Relations Review* 17, no. 4 (July 1964), 534–550; Francine D. Blau and Lawrence M. Kahn, "Rising Wage Inequality and the U.S. Gender Gap," *American Economic Review* 84, no. 2 (May 1994), 23–28. doi: http://www.aeaweb.org/aer/; Francine D. Blau and Lawrence M. Kahn, "Gender Differences in Pay," *Journal of Economic Perspectives* 14, no. 4 (Fall 2000), 75–99. doi: http://www.aeaweb.org/jep/; James J. Heckman, "A Partial Survey of Recent Research on the Labor Supply of Women," *American Economic Review* 68, no. 2 (May 1978), 200–207. doi: http://www.aeaweb.org/aer/; William A. Darity Jr. and Patrick L. Mason, "Evidence on Discrimination in Employment: Codes of Color, Codes of Gender," *Journal of Economic Perspectives* 12, no. 2 (Spring 1998), 63–90. doi: http://www.aeaweb.org/jep/; Doris Weichselbaumer, "Sexual

Orientation Discrimination in Hiring," *Labour Economics* 10, no. 6 (December 2003), 629–642. doi: 10.1016/S0927-5371(03)00074-5. http://www.sciencedirect.com/science/article/pii/S0927537103000745; Mohammad Ashraf, "Factors Affecting Female Employment in Male-Dominated Occupations: Evidence from the 1990 and 2000 Census Data," *Contemporary Economic Policy* 25, no. 1 (January 2007), 119–130. doi: 10.10931cep/by1007; Mohammad Ashraf, "Characteristics of Female Managers in the US Labor Market," *Applied Economics Letters* 16, no. 17 (2009), 1683–1686; Marcus Alexis, "The Economic Status of Blacks and Whites," *American Economic Review* 68, no. 2 (May 1978), 179–185. doi: http://www.aeaweb.org/aer/.

21. Joel Mokyr, "The Intellectual Origins of Modern Economic Growth," *The Journal of Economic History* 65, no. 2 (June 2005), 285–351; Elhanan Helpman, *The Mystery of Economic Growth* (Cambridge, MA: Harvard University Press, 2004).

22. *Modern History Sourcebook*, Leeds Woolen Workers Petition, 1786. (http://www.fordham.edu/halsall/mod/1786machines.asp) (Accessed: June 14, 2013).

23. See Sanborn, "Pay Differences between Men and Women", 534–550; Blau and Kahn, "Rising Wage Inequality and the U.S. Gender Gap", 23–28. doi: http://www.aeaweb.org/aer/; Blau and Kahn, "Gender Differences in Pay", 75–99. doi: http://www.aeaweb.org/jep/; Heckman, "A Partial Survey of Recent Research on the Labor Supply of Women", 200–207. doi: http://www.aeaweb.org/aer/; Darity and Mason, "Evidence on Discrimination in Employment: Codes of Color, Codes of Gender", 63–90. doi: http://www.aeaweb.org/jep/; Weichselbaumer, "Sexual Orientation Discrimination in Hiring," 629–642. doi: 10.1016/S0927-5371(03)00074-5. http://www.sciencedirect.com/science/article/pii/S0927537103000745; Ashraf, "Factors Affecting Female Employment in Male-Dominated Occupations," 119–130. doi:10.10931cep/by1007; Ashraf, "Characteristics of Female Managers in the US Labor Market," 1683–1686; Alexis, "The Economic Status of Blacks and Whites," 179–185. doi: http://www.aeaweb.org/aer/.

24. http://www.nytimes.com/library/national/race/# (Accessed: June 12, 2013).

25. http://www.nytimes.com/library/national/race/061600leduff-meat.html (Accessed: June 12, 2013).

26. "Rosa Parks." *Encyclopædia Britannica. Encyclopædia Britannica Online Academic Edition.* Encyclopædia Britannica Inc., 2013. Web. June 12 2013. http://0-www.britannica.com.uncclc.coast.uncwil.edu/EBchecked/topic/444180/Rosa-Parks.

27. http://www.jfklibrary.org/Asset-Viewer/Archives/JFKPOF-093-004.aspx (Accessed: August 29, 2013).

28. http://www.eeoc.gov/laws/statutes/epa.cfm (Accessed: August 29, 2013).

29. http://www.eeoc.gov/laws/statutes/titlevii.cfm (Accessed: August 29, 2013).

30. http://www.archives.gov/federal-register/codification/executive-orders-13.html (Accessed: August 29, 2013).

31. http://www.archives.gov/federal-register/codification/executive-order/11478.html (Accessed: August 29, 2013).

32. http://www.justice.gov/crt/about/cor/coord/titleixstat.php (Accessed: August 29, 2013).

33. http://www.justice.gov/crt/about/cor/coord/titleixstat.php#%28a%29%20 Prohibition%20against%20discrimination;%20exceptions (Accessed: August 29, 2013).

34. http://www.eeoc.gov/eeoc/history/35th/history/index.html (Accessed: August 29, 2013).

35. See Sanborn, "Pay Differences between Men and Women," 534–550; Blau and Kahn, "Rising Wage Inequality and the U.S. Gender Gap," 23–28. doi: http://www.aeaweb.org/aer/; Blau and Kahn, "Gender Differences in Pay," 75–99. doi: http://www.aeaweb.org/jep/; Heckman, "A Partial Survey of Recent Research on the Labor Supply of Women," 200–207. doi: http://www.aeaweb.org/aer/; Darity and Mason, "Evidence on Discrimination in Employment: Codes of Color, Codes of Gender," 63–90. doi: http://www.aeaweb.org/jep/; Weichselbaumer, "Sexual Orientation Discrimination in Hiring," (2003), 629–642. doi: 10.1016/S0927-5371(03)00074-5. http://www.sciencedirect.com/science/article/pii/S0927537103000745; Ashraf, "Factors Affecting Female Employment in Male-Dominated Occupations," 119–130. doi: 10.10931cep/by1007; Ashraf, "Characteristics of Female Managers in the US Labor Market," 1683–1686; Alexis, "The Economic Status of Blacks and Whites," 179–185. doi: http://www.aeaweb.org/aer/.

36. http://www.nytimes.com/2013/08/24/opinion/collins-where-credit-is-due.html?src=xps (Accessed: August 29, 2013).

37. http://www.whitehouse.gov/the-press-office/2011/03/01/white-house-releases-first-comprehensive-federal-report-status-american- (Accessed: August 29, 2013).

38. http://www.nytimes.com/2013/05/24/us/boy-scouts-to-admit-openly-gay-youths-as-members.html (Accessed: June 15, 2013).

39. http://www.documentcloud.org/documents/717750-supreme-court-ruling-on-doma-annotated.html (Accessed: August 29, 2013).

40. http://www.treasury.gov/press-center/press-releases/Pages/jl2153.aspx (Accessed: August 29, 2013).

41. http://www.ncsl.org/issues-research/human-services/same-sex-marriage-overview.aspx (Accessed: August 29, 2013).

42. See Paul Seabright, *The Company of Strangers: A Natural History of Economic Life* (Princeton, NJ: Princeton University Press, 2010), and also references cited in Quamrul Ashraf and Oded Galor, "The 'Out of Africa' Hypothesis, Human Genetic Diversity, and Comparative Economic Development," *The American Economic Review* 103, no. 1 (2013), 1–46.

43. Penny Edgell, Joseph Gerteis and Douglas Hartmann, "Atheists as 'Other': Moral Boundaries and Cultural Membership in American Society," *American Sociological Review* 71, no. 2 (2006), 211–234.

44. http://www.gallup.com/poll/26611/some-americans-reluctant-vote-mormon-72yearold-presidential-candidates.aspx (Accessed: June 12, 2013).

45. http://www.gallup.com/poll/26611/some-americans-reluctant-vote-mormon-72yearold-presidential-candidates.aspx#1 (Accessed: June 12, 2013).
46. Ibid.
47. http://data.bls.gov/pdq/SurveyOutputServlet (Accessed: June 14, 2013).
48. See Claudia Goldin and Lawrence F. Katz, *The Race between Education and Technology* (Cambridge, MA: Harvard University Press, 2008), for a detailed exposition of this point.
49. During 2012, 11.3 percent of the "Total wage and salary workers" were union members. The union membership had a wide range depending upon the industry. It also depended upon whether the employees were public sector employees (35.9 percent) or private sector employees (6.6 percent). (http://www.bls.gov/cps/cpsaat42.htm) (Accessed: June 14, 2013).
50. For more on the link between wealth and political power see Josef Falkinger and Volker Grossmann, "Institutions and Development: The Interaction between Trade Regime and Political System," *Journal of Economic Growth* 10, no. 3 (September 2005), 231–272. doi: http://www.springerlink.com/link.asp?id=102931, and the references cited in this paper.
51. http://www.nytimes.com/2011/12/08/us/blagojevich-expresses-remorse-in-courtroom-speech.html (Accessed: June 16, 2013).
52. http://www.nytimes.com/2010/11/25/us/politics/25delay.html?pagewanted=all (Accessed: June 16, 2013).
53. http://en.wikipedia.org/wiki/Category:American_politicians_convicted_of_crimes (Accessed: June 16, 2013).
54. http://bensguide.gpo.gov/6-8/government/national/president_list.html (Accessed: June 14, 2013).
55. http://www.reagan.utexas.edu/archives/reference/pressketch.html (Accessed: June 14, 2013).
56. "Margaret Thatcher." *Encyclopædia Britannica. Encyclopædia Britannica Online Academic Edition.* Encyclopædia Britannica Inc., 2013. Web. June 14, 2013. http://0-www.britannica.com.uncclc.coast.uncwil.edu/EBchecked/topic/590098/Margaret-Thatcher (Accessed: June 14, 2013). See also http://www.bbc.co.uk/history/people/margaret_thatcher (Accessed: December 8, 2013).
57. http://nber.org/cycles/cyclesmain.html (Accessed: June 14, 2013).
58. http://research.stlouisfed.org/fred2 (Accessed: June 14, 2013).
59. Traditionally, in economics literature, while there is much support for a positive correlation between *current* income and saving (e.g. Milton Friedman, *A Theory of the Consumption Function* (Princeton, NJ: Princeton University Press, 1957)), the support for a positive correlation between *lifetime* income and saving is much less so. Recent studies, however, using advanced statistical techniques and data have found this support. See, for instance, Karen E. Dynan, Jonathan Skinner and Stephen P. Zeldes, "Do the Rich Save More?" *Journal of Political Economy* 112, no. 2 (April 2004), 397–444. They find evidence of a "strong" positive correlation between "saving rate" and "lifetime income" and "weaker but still positive relationship between marginal propensity to

save"—the part of an additional dollar of income which is saved—and "lifetime income."

60. http://research.stlouisfed.org/fred2/series/GASREGW?cid=32217. Average gas price in the US on December 2, 2013.

61. Alberto Alesina and Roberto Perotti, "Income Distribution, Political Instability, and Investment," *European Economic Review* 40, no. 6 (June 1996), 1203–1228. doi: 10.1016/0014-2921(95)00030-5. http://www.sciencedirect.com/science/article/B6V64-3VW8NB4-1/2/86ba47e246e3c7d026640bc39b637c9b.

62. Torsten Persson and Guido Tabellini, "Is Inequality Harmful for Growth?" *The American Economic Review* 84, no. 3 (June 1994), 600–621.

63. Grigor Sukiassyan, "Inequality and Growth: What does the Transition Economy Data Say?" *Journal of Comparative Economics* 35, no. 1 (March 2007), 35–56. doi: 10.1016/j.jce.2006.11.002. http://www.sciencedirect.com/science/article/B6WHV-4N2DRKB-1/2/c72995bfc386f15a985e0cccb9f9f038.

64. Greif, Avner and Murat Iyigun. 2013b. "Social Organizations, Violence, and Modern Growth." *American Economic Review* 103 (3): 534–538. doi:http://www.aeaweb.org/aer/

65. Robert J. Barro, "Inequality and Growth in a Panel of Countries," *Journal of Economic Growth* 5, no. 1 (2000), 5–32.

66. Marta Bengoa and Blanca Sanchez-Robles, "Does Equality Reduce Growth? Some Empirical Evidence," *Applied Economics Letters* 12, no. 8 (June 2005), 479–483. doi: http://www.tandf.co.uk/journals/titles/13504851.asp.

67. Daron Acemoglu and Simon Johnson, "Unbundling Institutions," *Journal of Political Economy* 113, no. 5 (October 2005), 949–995. doi: http://www.journals.uchicago.edu/JPE/; Daron Acemoglu and James A. Robinson, *Why Nations Fail: The Origins of Power, Prosperity, and Poverty* (New York: Crown Publishers, 2012); Daron Acemoglu, Simon Johnson and James Robinson, "The Colonial Origins of Comparative Development: An Empirical Investigation," *American Economic Review* 91, no. 5 (2001), 1369–1401.

68. Joseph E. Stiglitz, *The Price of Inequality: How Today's Divided Society Endangers our Future* (New York: W. W. Norton and Company, Inc., 2012).

69. Adam Smith, *An Inquiry into the Nature and Causes of the Wealth of Nations*, ed. Edwin Cannan (Chicago, IL: University of Chicago Press, 2010). http://site.ebrary.com/lib/uncp/docDetail.action?docID=10381174&ppg=1.

70. John Rawls, *A Theory of Justice* (Cambridge, MA: Harvard University Press, 1973).

71. Amartya Sen, *Development as Freedom* (Westminster, MD: Alfred A. Knopf Incorporated, 1999).

72. I am sure readers have heard the phrase "Never give up." Motivational speakers and their kind—coaches, politicians, and so on—use this phrase quite frequently. Once I learned the concept of marginal cost (MC) and marginal benefit (MB), and how decision making depends upon these two, as an undergraduate student, the strangeness of this statement never left me. Of course you should give up when MC exceeds MB. Then the questions arose: why do people use this phrase

and why do people buy into this? Sitting in my armchair, I will provisionally surmise that this probably has to do with the environment in which our brains evolved—running from sabre-toothed tigers. In that environment there was no tomorrow. Giving up meant the end.

73. Shouldn't the term by "de-weeding"?

74. N. G. Mankiw, "Smart Taxes: An Open Invitation to Join the Pigou Club," *Eastern Economic Journal* 35, no. 1 (Winter 2009), 14–23. doi:10.1057/eej.2008.43; N. Gregory Mankiw, "Spreading the Wealth Around: Reflections Inspired by Joe the Plumber," *Eastern Economic Journal* 36, no. 3 (2010), 285–298.

75. Note that "marginal," "additional," "incremental" are all synonyms. So far these terms have been used to express an increase. Depending upon the situation, we may, however, need to express a decrease. That is, it may be a "decremental" change. "Marginal" represents both "incremental" as well as "decremental." This is why economists prefer to use marginal instead of "additional," "incremental," or "decremental."

76. Profit = Total Revenue − Total Cost. Where Total Revenue is Price of the product times the quantity of the product.

77. Mankiw, "Smart Taxes: An Open Invitation to Join the Pigou Club," 14–23. doi: 10.1057/eej.2008.43.

78. http://www.whitehouse.gov/the-press-office/2012/08/28/obama-administration-finalizes-historic-545-mpg-fuel-efficiency-standard (Accessed: July 28, 2013).

79. www.toyota.com (Accessed: July 29, 2013).

80. http://www.irs.gov/Businesses/Plug-In-Electric-Vehicle-Credit-%28IRC-30-and-IRC-30D%29 (Accessed: July 31, 2013).

81. http://usnews.rankingsandreviews.com/cars-trucks/best-cars-blog/2013/06/Hybrid_and_Electric_Vehicle_Owners_Could_Pay_Additional_Taxes/ (Accessed: July 31, 2013).

82. Seabright, *The Company of Strangers: A Natural History of Economic Life* (Princeton, NJ: Princeton University Press, 2010).

Chapter 6

1. James Foster et al., *A Unified Approach to Measuring Poverty and Inequality: Theory and Practice* (Washington, DC: The World Bank, 2013).

2. Ibid.

3. Adam Smith, *An Inquiry into the Nature and Causes of the Wealth of Nations*, ed. Edwin Cannan (Chicago, IL: University of Chicago Press, 1776 (2010)). http://site.ebrary.com/lib/uncp/docDetail.action?docID=10381174&ppg=1. (Part II, Book V, Chapter 2, Article 4, pp.399–400).

4. John Rawls, *A Theory of Justice* (Cambridge, MA: Harvard University Press, 1973).

5. Amartya Sen, "Poor, Relatively Speaking," *Oxford Economic Papers* 35, no. 2 (July 1983), 153–169.

6. Amartya Sen, *Development as Freedom* (Westminster, MD: Alfred A. Knopf Incorporated, 1999).

7. Sen, "Poor, Relatively Speaking," 153–169, 159.

8. Susan Jacoby, *The Age of American Unreason* (New York: Pantheon Book, 2008), details the unfortunate turn of events which led to change in meaning, and how taking pride in one's ignorance became an asset and erudition a liability in the social and political landscape in the United State.

9. Adam Smith, *An Inquiry into the Nature and Causes of the Wealth of Nations*, ed. Edwin Cannan (Chicago, IL: University of Chicago Press, 1776 (2010)). http://site.ebrary.com/lib/uncp/docDetail.action?docID=10381174&ppg=1.

10. Rawls, *A Theory of Justice* (Cambridge, MA: Harvard University Press, 1973).

11. Sen, "Poor, Relatively Speaking," 153–169; Sen, *Development as Freedom*.

12. "Notes: Income Poverty is defined as the share of people living in equivalised households with less than 50% of median equivalised household disposable income in their country.

    1. Data refer to 1994 for Greece, Turkey, United Kingdom, and to 1996 for Chile, Czech republic, France and Luxembourg. Last year of reference refers to 2009 for Hungary, Ireland, Japan, New Zealand and Turkey; 2011 for Chile. Data based on EU-SILC for 2010 are still provisional for Austria, Belgium, Czech Republic, Estonia, Finland, Greece, Iceland, Italy, Luxembourg, Poland, Portugal, Spain, Slovak Republic and Slovenia.

    2. Information on data for Israel: http://dx.doi.org/10.1787/888932315602" *Source*: OECD Income Distribution Database. (http://www.oecd.org/social/income-distribution-database.htm) (Accessed: June 22, 2013).

13. Source: OECD Website http://stats.oecd.org/Index.aspx?QueryId=47991 (Accessed: June 23, 2013).

14. http://stats.oecd.org/Index.aspx?DataSetCode=HEALTH_REAC# (Accessed: June 23, 2013).

15. Eric I. Knudsen et al., "Economic, Neurobiological, and Behavioral Perspectives on Building America's Future Workforce," *Proceedings of the National Academy of Sciences* 103, no. 27 (2006), 10155–10162.

16. http://stats.oecd.org/Index.aspx?DataSetCode=CWB (Accessed: June 22, 2013).

17. Ibid.

18. See table 6.A for detailed variable definitions and data sources.

19. Estimated Pearson correlation, using data for 30 OECD countries provided in table 6.1, between average disposable income and percent of children living in poverty is -0.417 (p-value $= 0.022$), and between average disposable income and educational deprivation is -0.52 (p-value $= 003$). I also ran regression using educational deprivation as the dependent variable and percent of children in poor homes and average disposable income as the right-hand side variables. Here are the standardized beta coefficient estimates with p-values in parentheses. Percent of children in poor homes $= 0.485$ (0.004); average disposable income $= -0.318$ (0.05); with $\bar{R}^2 = 0.42$.

20. See Eric I. Knudsen et al., "Economic, Neurobiological, and Behavioral Perspectives on Building America's Future Workforce," *Proceedings of the National Academy of Sciences* 103, no. 27 (2006), 10155–10162; Foster et al., *A Unified Approach to Measuring Poverty and Inequality: Theory and Practice* (Washington, DC: The World Bank, 2013).

21. http://stats.oecd.org/Index.aspx?DataSetCode=CWB (Accessed: June 22, 2013).

22. Ibid.

23. Pearson correlation estimate is −0.81 (p-value = 0.000). Number of countries included is 26.

24. The mean of the "overcrowding" variable is 31.95 and the standard deviation is 21.13. The maximum and minimums values are 73.96 and 10.33, respectively.

25. Pearson correlation estimate is −0.17 (p-value = 0.44). The mean of the "poor environmental conditions" is 25.22 and the standard deviation is 7.48. The maximum and minimum values are 38.71 and 10.5, respectively. Number of countries included is 24. Mexico and New Zealand data for "poor environmental conditions" are missing.

26. I ran two regression models. The first model had "poor environmental conditions" as the dependent variable, and "overcrowding" and "average disposable income" as the right-hand-side variables. The standardized beta estimates (p-values in parentheses) are "overcrowding": −0.24 (0.484), "average disposable income": −0.35 (0.309), with $\bar{R}^2 = -0.04$. The second regression model had "overcrowding" as the dependent variable and "poor environmental conditions" and "average disposable income" as the right-hand-side variables. The standardized beta estimates are (p-values in parentheses) "poor environmental conditions": −0.098 (0.484), "average disposable income": −0.793 (0.000), with $\bar{R}^2 = 0.58$.

27. http://stats.oecd.org/Index.aspx?DataSetCode=CWB (Accessed: June 22, 2013).

28. Pearson correlation estimate is 0.5 with a p-value of 0.005. There are 30 countries included in the analysis.

29. Pearson correlation estimate is −0.66 with a p-value of 0.000. There are 30 countries included in the analysis.

30. Pearson correlation estimate is −0.23 with a p-value of 0.219. There are 30 countries included in the analysis.

31. Pearson correlation estimate is −0.46 with a p-value of 0.016. There are 27 countries used in the analysis.

32. See Claudia Goldin and Lawrence F. Katz, "Long-Run Changes in the Wage Structure: Narrowing, Widening, Polarizing," *Brookings Papers on Economic Activity*, no. 2 (2007), 135–165. doi: http://www.brookings.edu/press/journals.aspx; Claudia Goldin and Lawrence F. Katz, *The Race between Education and Technology* (Cambridge, MA: Harvard University Press, 2008).

33. www.bls.gov.

34. Miles Corak, *How to Slide Down the "Great Gatsby Curve": Inequality, Life Chances, and Public Policy in the United States* (Washington, DC: Center for American Progress, December 2012).

35. http://stats.oecd.org/Index.aspx?DataSetCode=CWB (Accessed: June 22, 2013).

36. http://www.whitehouse.gov/administration/eop/cea/about/former-chairs (Accessed: November 27, 2013).

37. http://www.whitehouse.gov/sites/default/files/krueger_cap_speech_final_remarks.pdf (Accessed: June 25, 2013).

38. Michael Shermer, *The Mind of the Market: Compassionate Apes, Competitive Humans, and Other Tales from Evolutionary Economics* (New York: Henery Holt and Company, LLC, 2008).

39. http://www.nytimes.com/2013/08/31/business/cuckoos-calling-reveals-long-odds-for-new-authors.html?_r=0 (Accessed: September 1, 2013).

40. Ibid.

41. http://www.nytimes.com/2011/06/30/education/30collegeweb.html (Accessed: September 1, 2013).

42. Miles Corak, "Income Inequality, Equality of Opportunity, and Intergenerational Mobility," *Journal of Economic Perspectives* 27, no. 3 (2013), 79–102; Corak, *How to Slide Down the "Great Gatsby Curve": Inequality, Life Chances, and Public Policy in the United States* (Washington, DC: Center for American Progress, December 2012).

43. Source: U.S. Census Bureau, Current Population Survey, Annual Social and Economic Supplements. Table H-16. (www.census.gov) (Accessed: September 2, 2013).

44. Corak, "Income Inequality, Equality of Opportunity, and Intergenerational Mobility."

45. As reported in Alberto Alesina, Rafael Di Tella and Robert MacCulloch, "Inequality and Happines: Are Europeans and Americans Different?" *Journal of Public Economics* 88, no. 9–10 (2004), 2009–2042, 2011, 20. See also www.worldvaluessurvey.org (Accessed: June 26, 2013). See also, Alberto Alesina, Edward Glaeser and Bruce Sacerdote, "Why Doesn't the US have a European-Style Welfare System?" *NBER Working Papers* 8524 (2001).

46. http://stats.oecd.org/Index.aspx?DataSetCode=IDD# (Accessed: July 5, 2013).

47. Readers may also note that, for instance, before-tax Gini Coefficient estimate for the US is different from the one presented in Chapter 5, figure 5.1 (both sexes). This difference is due to estimation procedures. I have presented here before-tax and after-tax Gini Coefficient estimates from comparable estimation procedures and data sources. Refer to OECD Website for further details. http://stats.oecd.org/Index.aspx?DataSetCode=IDD#.

48. Sen, *Development as Freedom* (Westminster, MD: Alfred A. Knopf Incorporated, 1999).

49. Sudhir Anand and Martin Ravallion, "Human Development in Poor Countries: On the Role of Private Incomes and Public Services," *The Journal of Economic Perspectives* 7, no. 1 (Winter 1993), 133–150; Goldin and Katz, "Long-Run Changes in the Wage Structure: Narrowing, Widening, Polarizing." doi: http://www.brookings.edu/press/journals.aspx;

Sen, *Development as Freedom* (Westminster, MD: Alfred A. Knopf Incorporated, 1999); Hans-Werner Sinn, "Social Insurance, Incentives and Risk Taking," *International Tax and Public Finance*, 3, no. 3 (1996), 258–280; Avner Greif and Guido Tabellini, "Cultural and Institutional Bifurcation: China and Europe Compared," *American Economic Review* 100, no. 2 (May 2010), 135–140. doi: http://www.aeaweb.org/aer/; Avner Greif and Murat Iyigun, "Social Organizations, Violence, and Modern Growth," *American Economic Review* 103 (3): 534–538. doi:http://www.aeaweb.org/aer/" (2013).

50. Avner Greif and Murat Iyigun, "Social Organizations, Violence, and Modern Growth."

51. See studies cited in chapters 3, 4, and 5.

52. As I write these pages in early July 2013, Egypt is roiling in social and political unrest. Mohamed Morsi, the Egyptian president, who was elected a year ago, was removed from power by the Military and the Constitution was suspended. http://www.nytimes.com/2013/07/04/world/middleeast/egypt.html?hp (Accessed: July 6, 2013). One could hardly imagine investment in such an environment.

53. Avner Greif and Murat Iyigun, "Social Organizations, Violence, and Modern Growth"; Gary Richardson, "The Prudent Village: Risk Pooling Institutions in Medieval English Agriculture," *The Journal of Economic History* 65, no. 2 (June 2005), 386–413.

54. Elizabeth M. Caucutt, Thomas E. Cooley and Nezih Guner, "The Farm, the City, and the Emergence of Social Security," *Journal of Economic Growth* 18, no. 1 (2013), 1–32.

55. Gabriel Chodorow-Reich, Laura Feiveson, Zachary Liscow, and William Gui Woolston, "Does State Fiscal Relief during Recessions Increase Employment? Evidence from the American Recovery and Reinvestment Act," *American Economic Journal: Economic Policy* 4, no. 3 (August 2012), 118–145. doi: http://www.aeaweb.org/aej-policy/.

56. Note that deficit is a situation when government expenditure is greater than its revenue. Surplus, on the other hand, refers to a situation when government expenditure is less than government revenue. We will encounter deficit and surplus, again in Chapter 7.

57. $\left(\frac{Deficit\ (or\ Debt)}{Output} \right) \times 100.$

58. http://www.statistics.gov.uk/hub/index.html (Accessed: July 6, 2013).

59. See figure 2 on page 3 of the *Economic Review*, July 2013. http://www.ons.gov.uk/ons/dcp171766_316997.pdf (Accessed: July 6, 2013).

60. http://www.bbc.co.uk/news/business-22290407 (Accessed: July 6, 2013).

61. See, Paul Krugman, *End this Depression Now!* (New York: W.W. Norton & Company, Inc., 2012). See also John Quiggin, "Austerity Has Been Tested, and It Failed," *The Chronicles of Higher Education*, May 20, 2013. http://chronicle.com/article/Austerity-Has-Been-Tested-and/139255/?cid (Accessed: July 6, 2013).

62. http://www.oecd-ilibrary.org/economics/country-statistical-profile-spain_20752 288-table-esp (Accessed: July 6, 2013).

63. For an extensive exposition of this argument, see Paul Krugman, *End this Depression Now!* (New York: W.W. Norton & Company, Inc., 2012).

64. As Ronald Reagan, in his first inaugural address on January 20, 1981, famously ascribed government as part of the problem. http://www.reaganfoundation.org/ pdf/Inaugural_Address_012081.pdf (Accessed: July 6, 2013).

65. See, for instance, Chodorow-Reich et al., "Does State Fiscal Relief during Recessions Increase Employment? Evidence from the American Recovery and Reinvestment Act."; Krugman, *End this Depression Now!* (New York: W.W. Norton & Company, Inc., 2012), among others.

66. http://www.nber.org/cycles/jan08bcdc_memo.html (Accessed: August 4, 2013).

67. Susanto Basu and John G. Fernald, "What Do We Know (And Not Know) about Potential Output?" *Federal Reserve Bank of St. Louis Review* 91, no. 4 (2009), 187–213.

68. http://www.cbo.gov/sites/default/files/cbofiles/ftpdocs/30xx/doc3020/potential output.pdf (Accessed: October 11, 2013).

69. Alan J. Auerbach and Yuriy Gorodnichenko, "Measuring the Output Responses to Fiscal Policy," *American Economic Journal: Economic Policy* 4, no. 2 (May 2012), 1–27. doi: http://www.aeaweb.org/aej-policy/; Krugman, *End this Depression Now!* (New York: W.W. Norton & Company, Inc., 2012); Michael Woodford, "Simple Analytics of the Government Expenditure Multiplier," *American Economic Journal: Macroeconomics* 3, no. 1 (January 2011), 1–35. doi: http://www.aeaweb.org/aej-macro/.

70. Ibid.

71. "Statement on Longer-Run Goals and Monetary Policy Strategy (As amended effective on January 29, 2013)". http://federalreserve.gov/monetarypolicy/files/ FOMC_LongerRunGoals.pdf (Accessed: August 4, 2013).

72. Martin Feldstein, *Effects of Taxation on Economic Behavior* (Cambridge, MA: National Bureau of Economic Research, Working Paper No. 13745, January 2008).

73. Alan J. Auerbach and Laurence J. Kotlikoff, *Dynamic Fiscal Policy* (New York: Cambridge University Press, 1987).

74. Alan J. Auerbach, "The Bush Tax Cut and National Saving," *National Tax Journal* 55, no. 3 (September 2002), 387–407. doi: http://ntj.tax.org.

75. Larry M. Bartels, "A Tale of Two Tax Cuts, a Wage Squeeze, and a Tax Credit," *National Tax Journal* 59, no. 3 (September 2006), 403–423. doi: http://ntj. tax.org.

76. Lester C. Thurow, "The Income Distribution as a Pure Public Good," *Quarterly Journal of Economics* 85, no. 2 (May 1971), 327–336. doi: http://www. mitpressjournals.org/loi/qjec.

77. Alesina, Di Tella and MacCulloch, "Inequality and Happines: Are Europeans and Americans Different?"

Chapter 7

1. Deficit: Government Expenditure > Government Revenue; Surplus: Government Revenue > Government Expenditure.

2. The CBO notes that "The data in this file supplements information in CBO's March 2013 report *The Effects of Automatic Stabilizers on the Federal Budget as of 2013*, www.cbo.gov/publication/43977. That report is itself a supplement to CBO's February 2013 report *The Budget and Economic Outlook: Fiscal Years 2013 to 2023*, www.cbo.gov/publication/43907." (Accessed: September 29, 2013). Data from 2013 to 2018 are estimates.

3. To be more precise, monetary base which is the sum of currency and bank reserves. See the Federal Reserve Website (http://federalreserve.gov/monetarypolicy/default.htm) for details.

4. http://research.stlouisfed.org/fred2/categories/82 (Accessed: October 2, 2013). On October 01, 2013, the interest rate on five-year inflation-indexed constant maturity bond was −0.35.

5. "Social expenditure is the provision by public (and private) institutions of benefits to, and financial contributions targeted at, households and individuals in order to provide support during circumstances which adversely affect their welfare, provided that the provision of the benefits and financial contributions constitutes neither a direct payment for a particular good or service nor an individual contract or transfer. Such benefits can be cash transfers, or can be the direct ('in-kind') provision of goods and services." http://stats.oecd.org/glossary/detail.asp?ID=2485 (Accessed: September 26, 2013). Note that the data presented above are total public expenditure. These do not include private expenditure.

6. Data for Turkey for the year 2000 are also unavailable. I used average of the proceeding and preceding years' social expenditure, which is 7.8 percent. The percent of GDP dedicated to social expenditure during 1995 was 5.6 percent and during 2005 it was 9.9 percent. I made the choice to include Turkey in the figure because data for the rest of years were available.

7. The mean squared error of "Between Groups" is 71.51, and the mean squared error of "Within Groups" is 32.81, where years 1980, 1985, 1990, 1995, 2000, and 2005 are the "Groups." This gives an F-stat of 2.18, with a p-value of 0.06.

8. Note that in figure 1.1, years were on the horizontal axis, and countries were represented by differences in the line styles (solid versus various "broken" patterns), whereas in figure 7.2, in order to plot data for a larger group of countries, I have depicted countries on the horizontal axis. The years are represented by the differences in the line styles (solid versus various "broken" patterns). One may read the data in figure 1.1 by moving horizontally, from left to right. In figure 7.2, to ascertain how expenditures have changed over time, one may read data vertically, from bottom to top.

9. The difference in the number of countries selected in figure 7.2 versus 7.3 is due to the availability of comparable data. Data are not available for all countries for all years.

10. http://timeline.stlouisfed.org/index.cfm?p=timeline (Accessed: December 8, 2013).

11. http://stats.oecd.org/Index.aspx?DataSetCode=SOCX_AGG (Accessed: September 26, 2013).

12. Ibid.

13. http://stats.oecd.org/Index.aspx?QueryId=48234 (Accessed: September 26, 2013). Data for 2013 and 2014 are forecasts.

14. Ibid.

15. Alberto Alesina and Roberto Perotti, "Income Distribution, Political Instability, and Investment," *European Economic Review* 40, no. 6 (June 1996), 1203–1228. doi: 10.1016/0014-2921(95)00030-5. http://www.sciencedirect.com/science/article/B6V64-3VW8NB4-1/2/86ba47e246e3c7d026640bc39b637c9b; Robert J. Barro, "Inequality and Growth in a Panel of Countries," *Journal of Economic Growth* 5, no. 1 (2000), 5–32; Joseph E. Stiglitz, *The Price of Inequality: How Today's Divided Society Endangers our Future* (New York: W. W. Norton and Company, Inc., 2012).

16. "The law was enacted in two parts: The Patient Protection and Affordable Care Act was signed into law on March 23, 2010 and was amended by the Health Care and Education Reconciliation Act on March 30, 2010. The name 'Affordable Care Act' is used to refer to the final, amended version of the law." https://www.healthcare.gov/glossary/affordable-care-act/ (Accessed: September 4, 2013).

17. Casey B. Mulligan, *Average Marginal Labor Income Tax Rates Under the Affordable Care Act* (Cambridge, MA: The National Bureau of Economic Research, Working Paper No. 19365, August 2013).

18. http://www.nytimes.com/2013/10/18/us/politics/government-reopens.html?_r=0 (Accessed: October 20, 2013).

19. Martin Feldstein, *Effects of Taxation on Economic Behavior* (Cambridge, MA: National Bureau of Economic Research, Working Paper No. 13745, January 2008).

20. Emmanuel Saez, "Using Elasticities to Derive Optimal Income Tax Rates," *Review of Economic Studies* 68, no. 1 (January 2001), 205–229. doi: http://www.blackwellpublishing.com/journal.asp?ref=0034-6527; N. G. Mankiw, Matthew Weinzierl and Danny Yagan, "Optimal Taxation in Theory and Practice," *Journal of Economic Perspectives* 23, no. 4 (Fall 2009), 147–174. doi: http://www.aeaweb.org/jep/; James A. Mirrlees, "An Exploration in the Theory of Optimum Income Taxation," *Review of Economic Studies* 38, no. 114 (April 1971), 175–208. doi: http://www.blackwellpublishing.com/journal.asp?ref=0034-6527.

21. Mathematically it is defined as the percentage change in one variable, say, X, to 1 percent change in variable, say, Y. It may be represented as: $\in_{XY} = \%\Delta X / \%\Delta Y$. The symbol "$\Delta$" represents change. The absolute value of $\in_{XY}$ is between zero and infinity. The value of zero means that X is not affected at all by any change in Y, and the value of infinity means

that even an extremely small change in Y leads to an infinitely large change in X.

22. N. G. Mankiw, "Smart Taxes: An Open Invitation to Join the Pigou Club," *Eastern Economic Journal* 35, no. 1 (Winter 2009), 14–23. doi: 10.1057/eej.2008.43.

23. More precisely, according to the Classical Theory of Asset Price, the price of an asset is the present value of the asset's expected income over the life of the asset. In the case of a share of stock, the income is the share of profit, and in the case of a bond, the income is the interest payments. In the case of real estate, the price reflects the present value of the expected services provided by the asset.

24. Thomas L. Hungerford, *Taxes and the Economy: An Economic Analysis of Top Tax Rates since 1945* (Washington, DC: Congressional Research Service, 2012).

25. http://www.bls.gov/bls/productivity.htm (Accessed: October 14, 2013).

26. Thomas L. Hungerford, *Taxes and the Economy: An Economic Analysis of Top Tax Rates since 1945* (Washington, DC: Congressional Research Service, 2012).

27. Ibid.

28. Ibid.

29. http://www.youtube.com/watch?v=WmW19uoyuO8 (Accessed: October 26, 2013).

30. http://www.youtube.com/watch?v=tFEyBKssP6Q (Accessed: October 26, 2013).

31. Austan Goolsbee, "What Happens when You Tax the Rich? Evidence from Executive Compensation," *Journal of Political Economy* 108, no. 2 (2000), 352–378.

32. Some executives may have the option to get compensation in the form of company shares (stocks). In this case, the executives are given certain shares of the company. The executives then have the "option," (not the obligation) to sell the stock when they deem appropriate, within a given time period. This is referred to as "exercising the stock option."

33. See, among his other writings, for instance, Amartya Sen, *Development as Freedom* (Westminster, MD: Alfred A. Knopf Incorporated, 1999).

34. Alberto Alesina, Rafael Di Tella and Robert MacCulloch, "Inequality and Happines: Are Europeans and Americans Different?" *Journal of Public Economics* 88, no. 9–10 (2004), 2009–2042.

35. Lester C. Thurow, "The Income Distribution as a Pure Public Good," *Quarterly Journal of Economics* 85, no. 2 (May 1971), 327–336. doi: http://www.mitpressjournals.org/loi/qjec.

36. http://www.huffingtonpost.com/2012/03/20/paul-ryan-welfare-reform_n_1368277.html (Accessed: November 2, 2013).

37. I find it rather curious that NFL has a non-profit status, and apparently I am not alone. http://www.theatlantic.com/magazine/archive/2013/10/how-the-nfl-fleeces-taxpayers/309448/ (Accessed: November 3, 2013).

38. http://www.urban.org/UploadedPDF/412923-The-Nonprofit-Sector-in-Brief.pdf (Accessed: November 3, 2013).

39. "Reporting public charities include only organizations that both reported (filed IRS Forms 990) and had $25,000 or more in gross receipts. Organizations that had their tax-exempt status revoked for failing to file a financial return for three consecutive years are not included in the 2011 figure. Foreign organizations, government-associated organizations, and organizations without state identifiers were also excluded. All amounts are in current dollars and are not adjusted for inflation." Note on table 7.1 of the report.

40. Just by way of comparison, real GDP grew by about 18.7 percent from 2001 to 2011. (www.bea.gov). It would be interesting to find out, in detail, reasons behind the increase in non-profit sector's revenue and assets of 35 percent over the same period. What role, if any, changes in tax policies and the Great Recession of 2007–2009 played any role in this increase? What role, if any, changing social mores played?

41. http://www.irs.gov/Charities-&-Non-Profits/Charitable-Organizations/Exemption-Requirements-Section-501%28c%29%283%29-Organizations (Accessed: November 3, 2013).

42. http://www.irs.gov/Charities-&-Non-Profits/Charitable-Organizations/Exempt-Purposes-Internal-Revenue-Code-Section-501%28c%29%283%29 (Accessed: November 3, 2013).

43. http://www.nytimes.com/2012/12/16/business/the-charitable-deduction-and-why-it-needs-to-stay.html?src=xps (Accessed: August 18, 2013).

Chapter 8

1. www.pewforum.org. For detailed data sources and definitions, see http://www.globalreligiousfutures.org/explorer/about-GRF-data (Accessed: August 21, 2013).

2. http://www.globalreligiousfutures.org/religions/unaffiliated (Accessed: August 22, 2013).

3. Ibid.

4. Ibid.

5. http://www.fns.usda.gov/snap/rules/Legislation/pdfs/PL_104-193.pdf (Accessed: August 10, 2013).

6. http://georgewbush-whitehouse.archives.gov/government/fbci/president-initiative.html (Accessed: August 10, 2013).

7. Richard M. Clerkin and Kirsten A. Gronbjerg, "The Capacities and Challenges of Faith-Based Human Service Organizations," *Public Administration Review* 67, no. 1 (January 2007), 115–126. doi: http://www.blackwellpublishing.com/journal.asp?ref=0033-3352.

8. http://www.whitehouse.gov/the_press_office/ObamaAnnouncesWhiteHouseOfficeofFaith-basedandNeighborhoodPartnerships/ (Accessed: August 10, 2013).

9. http://www.state.gov/secretary/remarks/2013/08/212781.htm   (Accessed: August 10, 2013).

10. Anna A. Amirkhanyan, Hyun Joon Kim and Kristina T. Lambright, "Faith-Based Assumptions about Performance: Does Church Affiliation Matter for Service Quality and Access?" *Nonprofit and Voluntary Sector Quarterly* 38, no. 3 (June 2009), 490–521. doi: http://nvs.sagepub.com/archive/.

11. http://transcripts.cnn.com/TRANSCRIPTS/0002/28/se.01.html   (Accessed: August 11, 2013).

12. http://www.washingtonpost.com/wp-dyn/content/article/2006/05/13/AR2006051300647.html (Accessed: August 11, 2013).

13. http://www.liberty.edu/index.cfm?PID=6921 (Accessed: August 11, 2013).

14. http://www.washingtonpost.com/wp-dyn/content/article/2006/05/13/AR2006051300647_2.html (Accessed: August 11, 2013).

15. http://transcripts.cnn.com/TRANSCRIPTS/0808/17/se.01.html   (Accessed: August 11, 2013).

16. http://www.youtube.com/watch?v=gAVHeRKQUAo (Accessed: August 11, 2013).

17. http://www.politico.com/news/stories/0512/76109.html; http://www.nytimes.com/2011/06/19/us/politics/19marriage.html?pagewanted=all; http://www.cnn.com/2013/03/22/politics/court-same-sex-obama (Accessed: August 11, 2013).

18. http://www.cnn.com/2013/03/22/politics/court-same-sex-obama   (Accessed: August 11, 2013).

19. https://www.au.org (Accessed: August 13, 2013).

20. Robert Wright, *The Evolution of God* (New York: Little, Brown, 2009).

21. http://www.julianjaynes.org/pdf/dennett_jaynes-software-archeology.pdf (Accessed: August 13, 2013).

22. "Faith-Based and Community Initiative: Improvements in Monitoring Grantees and Measuring Performance Could Enhance Accountability (GAO-06-616, June 19, 2006)" http://www.gao.gov/products/GAO-06-616 (Accessed: August 15, 2013).

23. Amirkhanyan, Kim and Lambright, "Faith-Based Assumptions about Performance: Does Church Affiliation Matter for Service Quality and Access?"

24. Laura A. Reese, "A Matter of Faith: Urban Congregations and Economic Development," *Economic Development Quarterly* 18, no. 1 (February 2004), 50–66. doi: http://edq.sagepub.com/archive/.

25. "Faith-Based and Community Initiative: Improvements in Monitoring Grantees and Measuring Performance Could Enhance Accountability (GAO-06-616, June 19, 2006)" http://www.gao.gov/products/GAO-06-616 (Accessed: August 15, 2013).

26. Richard M. Clerkin and Kirsten A. Gronbjerg, "The Capacities and Challenges of Faith-Based Human Service Organizations," *Public Administration Review* 67, no. 1 (January 2007), 115–126. doi: http://www.blackwellpublishing.com/journal.asp?ref=0033-3352.

27. Clerkin and Gronbjerg, "The Capacities and Challenges of Faith-Based Human Service Organizations."

28. Bruni, Frank, "The Church's Errant Shepherds" http://www.nytimes.com/2013/07/07/opinion/sunday/bruni-the-churchs-errant-shepherds.html?ref=frankbruni (Accessed: August 18, 2013).

29. "Yeshiva University High School Former Students File $380 Million Sex Abuse Lawsuit" http://www.nydailynews.com/new-york/yeshiva-university-high-school-students-file-380-million-sex-abuse-lawsuit-article-1.1393327 (Accessed: August 18, 2013); Frank Bruni, "The Faithful's Failings," http://www.nytimes.com/2013/07/23/opinion/bruni-the-faithfuls-failing.html (Accessed: August 18, 2013).

30. "Dolan Sought to Protect Church Assets, Files Show" http://www.nytimes.com/2013/07/02/us/dolan-sought-vatican-permission-to-shield-assets.html?pagewanted=all (Accessed: August 18, 2013).

31. "The Great Catholic Cover-Up" http://www.slate.com/articles/news_and_politics/fighting_words/2010/03/the_great_catholic_coverup.html (Accessed: August 18, 2013).

32. http://www.npr.org/2011/11/08/142111804/penn-state-abuse-scandal-a-guide-and-timeline (Accessed: August 25, 2013).

33. Max Blumenthal, *Republican Gamorrah: Inside the Movement that Shattered the Party* (New York: National Books, 2009).

34. http://topics.nytimes.com/top/reference/timestopics/people/a/lance_armstrong/index.html?8qa (Accessed: August 18, 2013).

35. http://topics.nytimes.com/top/reference/timestopics/people/j/marion_jones/index.html (Accessed: August 18, 2013).

36. http://www.baseballssteroidera.com/bse-list-steroid-hgh-users-baseball.html (Accessed: August 18, 2013).

37. In order to locate the Biblical and the Koranic verses related to human rights, I used Project Reason (http://www.project-reason.org), co-founded by Sam Harris and Annaka Harris. I double-checked the verses reported in the Project Reason by going to the texts of the Bible and the Koran. For Biblical texts, I used the website biblegateway.com (http://www.biblegateway.com). For the Koranic verses I used the translation by M. A. S. Abdel Haleem, *Qur'An* (Oxford, GBR: Oxford University Press, UK, 2005). http://site.ebrary.com/lib/uncp/docDetail.action?docID=10271441&ppg=1.

38. http://www.biblegateway.com/passage/?search=Genesis%2022&version=NIV (Accessed: August 20, 2013).

39. *Genesis* 22.11–13 (http://www.biblegateway.com/passage/?search=Genesis%2022&version=NIV) (Accessed: August 20, 2013.)

40. Haleem, M. A. S. Abdel (Translated by). *Qur'an* (Oxford, GBR: Oxford University Press, UK, 2005), 287. http://site.ebrary.com/lib/uncp/Doc?id=10271441&ppg=332. Copyright © 2005. Oxford University Press, UK. All rights reserved. (Accessed: September 9, 2013).

41. See, for instance, Reza Aslan, *No god but God: The Origins, Evolution, and Future of Islam* (New York: Random House, Inc., 2005).
42. http://www.vatican.va/holy_father/paul_vi/encyclicals/documents/hf_p-vi_enc_25071968_humanae-vitae_en.html (Accessed: September 8, 2013).
43. "hajj." *Encyclopædia Britannica*. *Encyclopædia Britannica Online Academic Edition*. Encyclopædia Britannica Inc., 2013. Web. August 20, 2013. http://www.britannica.com/EBchecked/topic/252050/hajj. See also Reza Aslan, *No god but God: The Origins, Evolution, and Future of Islam* (New York: Random House, Inc., 2005).
44. http://pediatrics.aappublications.org/content/early/2012/08/22/peds.2012-1990.abstract (Accessed: August 20, 2013).
45. http://www.biblegateway.com/quicksearch/?quicksearch=circumcision&qs_version=NIV (Accessed: August 20, 2013).
46. http://www.amednews.com/article/20120903/health/309039955/4/ (Accessed: August 20, 2013).
47. http://www.nytimes.com/2013/08/22/nyregion/hasidic-jews-turn-up-pressure-on-city-to-accommodate-their-traditions.html?pagewanted=1&src=xps (Accessed: September 3, 2013).
48. http://www.huffingtonpost.com/2013/05/30/metzitzah-bpeh-blood-sucking-jewish-circumcision-ritual-debated-by-nyc-mayoral-candidates-video_n_3360526.html (Accessed: September 3, 2013).
49. http://pediatrics.aappublications.org/content/early/2012/08/22/peds.2012-1990.abstract (Accessed: August 20, 2013).
50. Ibid.
51. http://www.intactamerica.org/ (Accessed: August 20, 2013).
52. http://www.slate.com/blogs/atlas_obscura/2013/08/29/see_the_cathedral_of_human_sacrifices_in_belize_s_cave_of_the_crystal_maiden.html (Accessed: September 4, 2013).
53. Richard Dawkins, *The God Delusion* (New York: Houghton Mifflin Company, 2006).
54. Christopher Hitchens, *God is Not Great: How Religion Poisons Everything* (New York: Hachette Book Group USA, 2007).
55. http://galileo.rice.edu/chr/inquisition.html (Accessed: August 25, 2013).
56. http://www.nytimes.com/books/99/04/18/specials/rushdie-khomeini.html (Accessed: August 25, 2013); "Assassins of the Mind" http://www.vanityfair.com/politics/features/2009/02/hitchens200902 (Accessed: August 18, 2013).
57. http://topics.nytimes.com/top/reference/timestopics/subjects/s/sept_11_2001/index.html?s=oldest& (Accessed: August 25, 2013).
58. http://www.nytimes.com/2008/03/20/books/20cartoon.html?ref=danishcartoon controversy (Accessed: August 18, 2013).
59. http://www.washingtonpost.com/world/asia_pacific/christian-girl-accused-of-blasphemy-in-pakistan-is-released-on-bail/2012/09/08/2616744c-f9cb-11e1-a945-6cd36411d000_story.html (Accessed: August 25, 2013).

60. http://www.theguardian.com/world/2012/aug/19/pakistan-christian-tensions-quran-burning-allegations (Accessed: August 25, 2013).
61. http://thelede.blogs.nytimes.com/2012/10/09/pakistani-activist-14-shot-by-taliban/ (Accessed: August 25, 2013).
62. http://thelede.blogs.nytimes.com/2013/07/12/video-of-malala-yousafzai-at-u-n-calling-on-world-leaders-to-provide-education-to-every-child/ (Accessed: August 25, 2013).
63. http://www.nytimes.com/2013/08/25/world/asia/battling-superstition-indian-paid-with-his-life.html?pagewanted=1&hp (Accessed: August 25, 2013).
64. http://www.tonyrobbins.com/events/unleash-the-power-within/ (Accessed: August 25, 2013).
65. http://www.tonyrobbins.com/events/ (Accessed: August 25, 2013).
66. http://www.tonyrobbins.com/events/platinum-partnership/ (Accessed: August 25, 2013).
67. http://www.npr.org/blogs/thetwo-way/2013/08/25/215454970/new-york-a-g-sues-donald-trump-over-unlicensed-university (Accessed: August 27, 2013).
68. http://www.nytimes.com/2013/08/27/opinion/inside-donald-trumps-university.html?src=xps (Accessed: September 3, 2013).
69. "The law was enacted in two parts: The Patient Protection and Affordable Care Act was signed into law on March 23, 2010, and was amended by the Health Care and Education Reconciliation Act on March 30, 2010. The name 'Affordable Care Act' is used to refer to the final, amended version of the law." https://www.healthcare.gov/glossary/affordable-care-act/ (Accessed: September 4, 2013).
70. These practices may sound unduly harsh, cunning, and even deceitful to the lay observer. Numerous economists who have worked in this area, however, have argued that this is an instance of a "market failure," a situation where markets fail to allocate resources in an efficient manner. Perhaps the most prolific author is Professor Uwe E. Reinhardt of Princeton University. His very readable blog posts appear regularly in *The New York Times*. http://economix.blogs.nytimes.com/author/uwe-e-reinhardt/ (Accessed: September 5, 2013). Markets are, by design, not equipped to provide certain goods and services, and healthcare happens to be one of them.
71. https://www.healthcare.gov/how-does-the-health-care-law-protect-me/#part=8 (Accessed: September 5, 2013).
72. https://www.healthcare.gov/what-are-my-preventive-care-benefits/#part=2 (Accessed: September 5, 2013).
73. http://www.nytimes.com/2012/02/17/health/religious-groups-equate-some-contraceptives-with-abortion.html (Accessed: September 8, 2013).
74. Ibid.
75. http://www.nytimes.com/2012/02/17/us/politics/birth-control-coverage-rule-debated-at-house-hearing.html (Accessed: September 8, 2013).

76. http://www.nytimes.com/2012/05/22/us/catholic-groups-file-suits-on-contraceptive-coverage.html (Accessed: September 5, 2013).

77. "Dolan Sought to Protect Church Assets, Files Show" http://www.nytimes.com/2013/07/02/us/dolan-sought-vatican-permission-to-shield-assets.html?pagewanted=all (Accessed: August 18, 2013).

78. http://www.nytimes.com/2012/04/19/us/vatican-reprimands-us-nuns-group.html (Accessed: September 5, 2013).

79. Ibid.

80. Michael Steele, chairman of the Republican National Committee at the time, had to apologize for making unflattering remarks about Mr. Limbaugh. He called Rush Limbaugh an "entertainer" and whose radio show is "incendiary." http://www.nbcnews.com/id/29478402/ns/politics-more_politics/t/gop-chief-apologizes-limbaugh-remarks/#.Uij2PHeDmSo (Accessed: September 5, 2013).

81. http://www.nytimes.com/2012/03/05/business/media/limbaugh-advertisers-flee-show-amid-storm.html (Accessed: September 5, 2013).

82. http://www.time.com/time/person-of-the-year/2012/ (Accessed: November 27, 2012).

83. http://www.latimes.com/news/politics/la-pn-sandra-fluke-gop-20120905,0,7008930.story (Accessed: November 27, 2012).

84. http://www.biblegateway.com/passage/?search=Leviticus%2018&version=KJV (Accessed: September 8, 2013).

85. See 1 Kings 14:24; 1 Kings 15:12; 1 Kings 22:46. http://www.project-reason.org/scripture_project/Annotations:homosexuality::The_Bible (Accessed: September 8, 2013).

86. http://www.biblegateway.com/passage/?search=1%20Corinthians%206&version=KJV (Accessed: September 8, 2013).

87. http://www.biblegateway.com/passage/?search=Deuteronomy%2022:5&version=KJV (Accessed: September 8, 2013).

88. Haleem, M. A. S. Abdel (Translated by). *Qur'an* (Oxford, GBR: Oxford University Press, UK, 2005), 100. http://site.ebrary.com/lib/uncp/Doc?id=10271441&ppg=145. Copyright © 2005. Oxford University Press, UK. All rights reserved. (Accessed: September 8, 2013).

89. Haleem, M. A. S. Abdel (Translated by). *Qur'an* (Oxford, GBR: Oxford University Press, UK, 2005), 236. http://site.ebrary.com/lib/uncp/Doc?id=10271441&ppg=281. Copyright © 2005. Oxford University Press, UK. All rights reserved. (Accessed: September 8, 2013).

90. Haleem, M. A. S. Abdel (Translated by). *Qur'an* (Oxford, GBR: Oxford University Press, UK, 2005), 242. http://site.ebrary.com/lib/uncp/Doc?id=10271441&ppg=287. Copyright © 2005. Oxford University Press, UK. All rights reserved. (Accessed: September 8, 2013).

91. Haleem, M. A. S. Abdel (Translated by). *Qur'an* (Oxford, GBR: Oxford University Press, UK, 2005), 254. http://site.ebrary.com/lib/uncp/Doc?id=10271441&ppg=299. Copyright © 2005. Oxford University Press, UK. All rights reserved. (Accessed: September 8, 2013).

92. http://nymag.com/news/frank-rich/gay-marriage-2012-3/ (Accessed: September 9, 2013).
93. http://www.senate.gov/legislative/LIS/roll_call_lists/roll_call_vote_cfm.cfm? congress=104&session=2&vote=00280 (Accessed: September 10, 2013).
94. www.senate.gov/legislative/LIS/roll_call_lists/roll_call_vote_cfm.cfm?congress= 104&session=2&vote=00280 (Accessed: September 10, 2013).
95. http://www.supremecourt.gov/opinions/12pdf/12-307_6j37.pdf (Accessed: September 19, 2013).
96. http://www.nytimes.com/2013/05/19/nyregion/killing-in-greenwich-village-looks-like-hate-crime-police-say.html (Accessed: September 9, 2013).
97. http://www.nytimes.com/2008/11/15/us/politics/15marriage.html?emc=eta1& _r=0 (Accessed: September 11, 2013).
98. http://www.nationaljournal.com/politics/african-americans-the-last-democratic-holdouts-on-gay-marriage-20130501 (Accessed: September 11, 2013).
99. http://www.bbcfnc.org/seniorpastor.php (Accessed: September 8, 2013).
100. http://www.fayobserver.com/articles/2012/05/02/1174936?sac=fo.home (Accessed: September 9, 2013).
101. http://www.youtube.com/watch?v=5qh0gVFfqrc (Accessed: September 8, 2013).
102. http://www.fayobserver.com/articles/2012/05/02/1174936?sac=fo.home (Accessed: September 9, 2013).
103. http://www.prbcnc.com/Pastor (Accessed: September 9, 2013).
104. http://thinkprogress.org/lgbt/2012/05/21/487707/north-carolina-electric-pen/ (Accessed: September 9, 2013).
105. http://content.time.com/time/magazine/article/0,9171,2147719,00.html (Accessed: September 10, 2013).
106. http://www.nytimes.com/2013/07/30/world/europe/pope-francis-gay-priests. html (Accessed: September 10, 2013).
107. http://content.time.com/time/magazine/article/0,9171,2148640,00.html (Accessed: September 10, 2013).
108. http://content.time.com/time/magazine/article/0,9171,2148640-1,00.html (Accessed: September 10, 2013).
109. http://www.secularhumanism.org/index.php?section=fi&page=cragun_32_4 (Accessed: September 19, 2013). I am grateful to Dr. Lewis Hershey for referring me to this study.
110. For a great and quick reference for various contradictions in religious texts— the Bible, the Koran, and the Book of Mormon—and various interpretations, please see http://www.project-reason.org. For various interpretations of the Koranic verses, see Aslan, *No god but God: The Origins, Evolution, and Future of Islam* (New York: Random House, Inc., 2005). See also, Hitchens, *God is Not Great: How Religion Poisons Everything* (New York: Hachette Book Group USA, 2007); Wright, *The Evolution of God* (New York: Little, Brown, 2009); Dawkins, *The God Delusion* (New York: Houghton Mifflin Company, 2006).
111. Aslan, *No god but God: The Origins, Evolution, and Future of Islam* (New York: Random House, Inc., 2005).

112. Aslan does not consider "apologist" a derogatory term. In fact he is proud of being called one. In the prologue of his book, *No god but God*, he writes, "An apology is a defense, and there is no higher calling than to defend one's faith . . . "

Chapter 9

1. Amartya Sen, *Development as Freedom* (Westminster, MD: Alfred A. Knopf Incorporated, 1999).

Bibliography

Acemoglu, Daron and Melissa Dell. 2010. "Productivity Differences between and within Countries." *American Economic Journal: Macroeconomics* 2 (1): 169–188. doi: http://www.aeaweb.org/aej-macro/; http://search.ebscohost.com/login.aspx?direct=true&db=eoh&AN=1075734&site=ehost-live; http://www.aeaweb.org/aej-macro/.

Acemoglu, Daron and Simon Johnson. 2005. "Unbundling Institutions." *Journal of Political Economy* 113 (5): 949–995. doi: http://www.journals.uchicago.edu/JPE/; http://search.ebscohost.com/login.aspx?direct=true&db=eoh&AN=0823806&site=ehost-live; http://www.journals.uchicago.edu/JPE/.

Acemoglu, Daron, Simon Johnson, and James Robinson. 2001. "The Colonial Origins of Comparative Development: An Empirical Investigation." *American Economic Review* 91 (5): 1369–1401.

Acemoglu, Daron and James A. Robinson. 2012. *Why Nations Fail: The Origins of Power, Prosperity, and Poverty*. New York: Crown Publishers.

Adema, Willem, Pauline Fron, and Maxime Ladaique. 2011. *Is the European Welfare State Really More Expensive?* Organisation for Economic Co-operation and Development. doi:10.1787/5kg2d2d4pbf0-en.

Adema, W. and M. Ladaique. 2009. *How Expensive is the Welfare State?: Gross and Net Indicators in the OECD Social Expenditure Database (SOCX)*. Paris, France: OECD Publishing.

Aghion, Philippe and Peter Howitt. 1998. *Endogenous Growth Theory*. Cambridge, MA: The MIT Press.

Alesina, Alberto, Edward Glaeser, and Bruce Sacerdote. 2001. "Why Doesn't the US have a European-Style Welfare System?" *NBER Working Papers* 8524.

Alesina, Alberto and Roberto Perotti. 1996. "Income Distribution, Political Instability, and Investment." *European Economic Review* 40 (6): 1203–1228. doi: 10.1016/0014-2921(95)00030-5.

Alesina, Alberto, Rafael Di Tella, and Robert MacCulloch. 2004. "Inequality and Happines: Are Europeans and Americans Different?" *Journal of Public Economics* 88 (9–10): 2009–2042.

Alexis, Marcus. 1978. "The Economic Status of Blacks and Whites." *American Economic Review* 68 (2): 179–185. doi: http://www.aeaweb.org/aer/; http://0-search.ebscohost.com.uncclc.coast.uncwil.edu:80/login.aspx?direct=true&db=eoh&AN=0101799&site=ehost-live; http://www.aeaweb.org/aer/.

Alfo, M., G. Trovato, and R. J. Waldmann. 2008. "Testing for Country Heterogeneity in Growth Models using a Finite Mixture Approach." *Journal of Applied Econometrics* (23): 487–514.

Amirkhanyan, Anna A., Hyun Joon Kim, and Kristina T. Lambright. 2009. "Faith-Based Assumptions about Performance: Does Church Affiliation Matter for Service Quality and Access?" *Nonprofit and Voluntary Sector Quarterly* 38 (3): 490–521. doi: http://nvs.sagepub.com/archive/; http://0-search.ebscohost.com.uncclc.coast. uncwil.edu:80/login.aspx?direct=true&db=eoh&AN=1049082&site=ehost-live; http://nvs.sagepub.com/archive/.

Anand, Sudhir and Martin Ravallion. 1993. "Human Development in Poor Countries: On the Role of Private Incomes and Public Services." *The Journal of Economic Perspectives* 7 (1): 133–150. http://www.jstor.org/stable/2138325.

Arrow, Kenneth J. 1962. "The Economic Implications of Learning by Doing." *The Review of Economic Studies* 29 (3): 155–173. http://www.jstor.org/stable/ 2295952.

Arthur, W. B. 2007. "The Structure of Invention." *Research Policy* 36 (2): 274–287. doi:http://www.elsevier.com/wps/find/journaldescription.cws_home/ 505598/description#description; http://0-search.ebscohost.com.uncclc.coast. uncwil.edu:80/login.aspx?direct=true&db=eoh&AN=0898206&site=ehost-live; http://dx.doi.org/10.1016/j.respol.2006.11.005; http://www.elsevier.com/wps/ find/journaldescription.cws_home/505598/description#description.

Ashraf, Mohammad. 2007. "Factors Affecting Female Employment in Male-Dominated Occupations: Evidence from the 1990 and 2000 Census Data." *Contemporary Economic Policy* 25 (1): 119–130. doi: 10.10931cep/by1007. http:// search.ebscohost.com/login.aspx?direct=true&db=bth&AN=25910836&site= ehost-live

———.2009. "Characteristics of Female Managers in the US Labor Market." *Applied Economics Letters* 16 (17): 1683–1686.

———. 2011. "What Explains R&D Efficiency Differences Across U.S. States." *The Journal of Economics (MVEA)* 37 (1): 59–75.

Ashraf, Quamrul and Oded Galor. 2013. "The "Out of Africa" Hypothesis, Human Genetic Diversity, and Comparative Economic Development." *The American Economic Review* 103 (1): 1–46.

Ashraf, Mohammad and Khan A. Mohabbat. 2010. "Output Convergence and the Role of Research and Development." *Annals of Economics and Finance* 11 (1): 35–71.

Aslan, Reza. 2005. *No god but God: The Origins, Evolution, and Future of Islam.* New York, NY: Random House, Inc.

Auerbach, Alan J. 2002. "The Bush Tax Cut and National Saving." *National Tax Journal* 55 (3): 387–407. doi: http://ntj.tax.org; http://0-search.ebscohost.com. uncclc.coast.uncwil.edu:80/login.aspx?direct=true&db=eoh&AN=0633331&site= ehost-live; http://ntj.tax.org.

Auerbach, Alan J. and Yuriy Gorodnichenko. 2012. "Measuring the Output Responses to Fiscal Policy." *American Economic Journal: Economic Policy* 4 (2): 1–27. doi: http://www.aeaweb.org/aej-policy/; http://0-search.ebscohost.com.

uncclc.coast.uncwil.edu:80/login.aspx?direct=true&db=eoh&AN=1292449&site=
ehost-live; http://www.aeaweb.org/aej-policy/.

Auerbach, Alan J. and Laurence J. Kotlikoff. 1987. *Dynamic Fiscal Policy*. New York:
Cambridge University Press.

Barro, Robert J. 2000. "Inequality and Growth in a Panel of Countries." *Journal of
Economic Growth* 5 (1): 5–32.

Barro, Robert J. and Zavier Sala-I-Martin. 1995. *Economic Growth*. New York:
McGraw-Hill.

Bartels, Larry M. 2006. "A Tale of Two Tax Cuts, a Wage Squeeze, and a Tax Credit."
National Tax Journal 59 (3): 403–423. doi: http://ntj.tax.org; http://0-search.
ebscohost.com.uncclc.coast.uncwil.edu:80/login.aspx?direct=true&db=eoh&AN=
0887228&site=ehost-live; http://ntj.tax.org.

Basu, Susanto and John G. Fernald. 2009. "What Do We Know (and Not Know)
about Potential Output?" *Federal Reserve Bank of St. Louis Review* 91 (4): 187–213.

Bengoa, Marta and Blanca Sanchez-Robles. 2005. "Does Equality Reduce Growth?
Some Empirical Evidence." *Applied Economics Letters* 12 (8): 479–483. doi: http://
www.tandf.co.uk/journals/titles/13504851.asp; http://0-search.ebscohost.com.
uncclc.coast.uncwil.edu:80/login.aspx?direct=true&db=eoh&AN=0807333&site=
ehost-live; http://www.tandf.co.uk/journals/titles/13504851.asp.

Blau, Francine D. and Lawrence M. Kahn. 1994. "Rising Wage Inequality and the
U.S. Gender Gap." *American Economic Review* 84 (2): 23–28. doi: http://www.
aeaweb.org/aer/; http://0-search.ebscohost.com.uncclc.coast.uncwil.edu:80/login.
aspx?direct=true&db=eoh&AN=0329431&site=ehost-live; http://www.aeaweb.
org/aer/.

———. 2000. "Gender Differences in Pay." *Journal of Economic Perspectives* 14
(4): 75–99. doi: http://www.aeaweb.org/jep/; http://0-search.ebscohost.com.
uncclc.coast.uncwil.edu:80/login.aspx?direct=true&db=eoh&AN=0557253&site=
ehost-live; http://www.aeaweb.org/jep/.

Blumenthal, Max. 2009. *Republican Gamorrah: Inside the Movement that Shattered the
Party*. New York: National Books.

Breitung, J. and M. H. Pesaran. 2008. "Unit Roots and Cointegration in Panels."
In *The Econometrics of Panel Data*, edited by László Mátyás and Patrick Sevestre.
3rd ed., 279–322. Heidelberg: Springer.

Cameron, L., N. Erkal, L. Gangadharan, and X. Meng. 2013. "Little Emperors:
Behavioral Impacts of China's One-Child Policy." *Science* 339 (6122): 953–957.

Caucutt, Elizabeth M., Thomas E. Cooley, and Nezih Guner. 2013. "The Farm, the
City, and the Emergence of Social Security." *Journal of Economic Growth* 18 (1):
1–32.

Chodorow-Reich, Gabriel, Laura Feiveson, Zachary Liscow, and William Gui
Woolston. 2012. "Does State Fiscal Relief during Recessions Increase Employment? Evidence from the American Recovery and Reinvestment Act." *American
Economic Journal: Economic Policy* 4 (3): 118–145. doi: http://www.aeaweb.org/
aej-policy/; http://0-search.ebscohost.com.uncclc.coast.uncwil.edu:80/login.aspx?
direct=true&db=eoh&AN=1303738&site=ehost-live; http://www.aeaweb.org/aej-
policy/.

Clerkin, Richard M. and Kirsten A. Gronbjerg. 2007. "The Capacities and Challenges of Faith-Based Human Service Organizations." *Public Administration Review* 67 (1): 115–126. doi: http://www.blackwellpublishing.com/journal. asp?ref=0033-3352; http://0-search.ebscohost.com.uncclc.coast.uncwil.edu:80/ login.aspx?direct=true&db=eoh&AN=0903684&site=ehost-live; http://www. blackwellpublishing.com/journal.asp?ref=0033-3352.

Coe, David T. and Elhanan Helpman. 1995. "International R&D Spillovers." *European Economic Review* 39 (5): 859–887. doi: 10.1016/0014-2921(94) 00100-E.

Corak, Miles. December 2012. *How to Slide Down the "Great Gatsby Curve": Inequality, Life Chances, and Public Policy in the United States.* Washington, DC: Center for American Progress.

——. 2013. "Income Inequality, Equality of Opportunity, and Intergenerational Mobility." *Journal of Economic Perspectives* 27 (3): 79–102.

Darity, William A., Jr. and Patrick L. Mason. 1998. "Evidence on Discrimination in Employment: Codes of Color, Codes of Gender." *Journal of Economic Perspectives* 12 (2): 63–90. doi: http://www.aeaweb.org/ jep/; http://0-search.ebscohost.com.uncclc.coast.uncwil.edu:80/login.aspx?direct= true&db=eoh&AN=0470751&site=ehost-live; http://www.aeaweb.org/jep/.

Dawkins, Richard. 2004. *The Ancestor's Tale: A Pilgrimage to the Dawn of Evolution.* New York: Houghton Mifflin Company.

——. 2006. *The God Delusion.* New York: Houghton Mifflin Company.

Dernis, Helene and Dominique Guellec. 2001. *Using Patent Counts for Cross-County Comparisons of Technology Output* OECD. Economic Analysis and Statistics Division.

Dynan, Karen E., Jonathan Skinner, and Stephen P. Zeldes. 2004. "Do the Rich Save More?" *Journal of Political Economy* 112 (2): 397–444. http://0-search. ebscohost.com.uncclc.coast.uncwil.edu:80/login.aspx?direct=true&db=bth&AN= 12856437&site=ehost-live.

Edgell, Penny, Joseph Gerteis, and Douglas Hartmann. 2006. "Atheists as 'Other': Moral Boundaries and Cultural Membership in American Society." *American Sociological Review* 71 (2): 211–234.

Falk, Martin. 2006. "What Drives Business Research and Development (R&D) Intensity across Organisation for Economic Co-Operation and Development (OECD) Countries?" *Applied Economics* 38 (5): 533–547. doi: http://www.tandf. co.uk/journals/routledge/00036846.html; http://search.ebscohost.com/login.aspx? direct=true&db=eoh&AN=0851648&site=ehost-live; http://www.tandf.co.uk/ journals/routledge/00036846.html.

Falkinger, Josef and Volker Grossmann. 2005. "Institutions and Development: The Interaction between Trade Regime and Political System." *Journal of Economic Growth* 10 (3): 231–272. doi: http://www.springerlink.com/link.asp?id=102931; http://search.ebscohost.com/login.aspx?direct=true&db=eoh&AN=0819306& site=ehost-live; http://dx.doi.org/10.1007/s10887-005-3534-4; http://www. springerlink.com/link.asp?id=102931.

Feldstein, Martin. January 2008. *Effects of Taxation on Economic Behavior*. Cambridge, MA: National Bureau of Economic Research, Working Paper No. 13745.

Foster, James, Suman Seth, Michael Lokshin, and Zurab Sajaia. 2013. *A Unified Approach to Measuring Poverty and Inequality: Theory and Practice*. Washington, DC: The World Bank.

Frantzen, Dirk. 2004. "Technological Diffusion and Productivity Convergence: A Study for Manufacturing in the OECD." *Southern Economic Journal* 71 (2): 352–376. http://www.jstor.org/stable/4135296.

Friedman, Milton. 1991. *The Island of Stone Money*. E-91-3 ed. Stanford, CA: Stanford University, The Hoover Institution.

Goldin, Claudia and Lawrence F. Katz. 2007. "Long-Run Changes in the Wage Structure: Narrowing, Widening, Polarizing." *Brookings Papers on Economic Activity* Fall (2): 135–165. doi: http://www.brookings.edu/press/journals.aspx; http://0-search.ebscohost.com.uncclc.coast.uncwil.edu:80/login.aspx?direct=true&db=eoh&AN=0961382&site=ehost-live; http://www.brookings.edu/press/journals.aspx.

———. 2008. *The Race between Education and Technology*. Cambridge, MA: Harvard University Press.

Goolsbee, Austan. 2000. "What Happens when You Tax the Rich? Evidence from Executive Compensation." *Journal of Political Economy* 108 (2): 352–378.

Greif, Avner and Guido Tabellini. 2010. "Cultural and Institutional Bifurcation: China and Europe Compared." *American Economic Review* 100 (2): 135–140. doi: http://www.aeaweb.org/aer/; http://0-search.ebscohost.com.uncclc.coast.uncwil.edu:80/login.aspx?direct=true&db=eoh&AN=1098718&site=ehost-live; http://dx.doi.org/10.1257/aer.100.2.135; http://www.aeaweb.org/aer/.

Greif, Avner and Murat Iyigun. 2013. "Social Organizations, Violence, and Modern Growth." *American Economic Review* 103 (3): 534–538. doi:http://www.aeaweb.org/aer/

Gretz, Richard T., Jannett Highfill, and Robert C. Scott. 2009. "Strategic Research and Development Policy: Societal Objectives and the Corporate Welfare Argument." *Contemporary Economic Policy* 27 (1): 28–45. doi: http://www.blackwell-synergy.com/loi/coep/; http://search.ebscohost.com/login.aspx?direct=true&db=eoh&AN=1023679&site=ehost-live; http://www.blackwell-synergy.com/loi/coep/.

Gretz, Richard T., Joshua J. Lewer, and Robert C. Scott. 2010. "R&D, Risk, and the Role of Targeted Government R&D Programs." *Journal of Economics (MVEA)* 36 (1): 79–104. doi: http://www.cba.uni.edu/economics/joe.htm; http://search.ebscohost.com/login.aspx?direct=true&db=eoh&AN=1133377&site=ehost-live; http://www.cba.uni.edu/economics/joe.htm.

Griliches, Zvi. 1988. "Productivity Puzzles and R & D: Another Nonexplanation." *The Journal of Economic Perspectives* 2 (4): 9–21. http://www.jstor.org/stable/1942775.

———.1990. "Patent Statistics as Economic Indicators: A Survey." *Journal of Economic Literature* 28 (4): 1661–1707. http://www.jstor.org/stable/2727442.

Hall, Bronwyn H., Adam B. Jaffe, and Manuel Trajtenberg. 2001. *The NBER Patent Citations Data File: Lessons, Insights, and Methodological Tools*. Working Paper 8498 ed. 1050 Massachusetts Avenue Cambridge, MA 02138: National Bureau of Economic Research.

Harris, Edward and Frank Sammartino. 2011. *Trends in the Distribution of Household Income between 1979 and 2007*. Washington, DC: Congressional Budget Office.

Heckman, James J. 1978. "A Partial Survey of Recent Research on the Labor Supply of Women." *American Economic Review* 68 (2): 200–207. doi: http://www.aeaweb. org/aer/; http://0-search.ebscohost.com.uncclc.coast.uncwil.edu:80/login.aspx? direct=true&db=eoh&AN=0101844&site=ehost-live; http://www.aeaweb.org/ aer/.

Helpman, Elhanan. 2004. *The Mystery of Economic Growth*. Cambridge, MA: Harvard University Press.

Hitchens, Christopher. 2007. *God is Not Great: How Religion Poisons Everything*. New York: Hachette Book Group USA.

Hungerford, Thomas L. 2012. *Taxes and the Economy: An Economic Analysis of Top Tax Rates since 1945*. Washington, DC: Congressional Research Service.

Islam, Nazrul. 2003. "What have We Learnt from the Convergence Debate?" *Journal of Economic Surveys* 17 (3): 309–362. doi: http://www.blackwellpublishing.com/ journal.asp?ref=0950-0804; http://www.blackwellpublishing.com/journal.asp?ref= 0950-0804; http://search.ebscohost.com/login.aspx?direct=true&db=eoh&AN= 0663517&site=ehost-live.

Jacoby, Susan. 2008. *The Age of American Unreason*. New York: Pantheon Book.

Johnston, Jack and John DiNardo. 1997. *Econometric Methods*. 4th ed. New York: McGraw-Hill.

Knudsen, Eric I., James J. Heckman, Judy L. Cameron, and Jack P. Shonkoff. 2006. "Economic, Neurobiological, and Behavioral Perspectives on Building America's Future Workforce." *Proceedings of the National Academy of Sciences* 103 (27): 10155–10162.

Krugman, Paul. 2012. *End this Depression Now!* New York: W.W. Norton & Company, Inc.

Lee, Chien-Chiang and Mei-Se Chien. 2010. "Dynamic Modelling of Energy Consumption, Capital Stock, and Real Income in G-7 Countries." *Energy Economics* 32 (3): 564–581. doi: http://www.elsevier.com/wps/find/journaldescription.cws_ home/30413/description#description; http://search.ebscohost.com/login.aspx? direct=true&db=eoh&AN=1106836&site=ehost-live; http://dx.doi.org/10.1016/ j.eneco.2009.08.022; http://www.elsevier.com/wps/find/journaldescription.cws_ home/30413/description#description.

Lewis, Michael. 2011. *The Big Short: Inside the Doomsday Machine*. New York: W. W. Norton and Company, Inc.

Maddison, Angus. 2008. "Shares of the Rich and the Rest in the World Economy: Income Divergence between Nations, 1820–2030." *Asian Economic Policy Review* 3 (1): 67–82. doi: http://www3.interscience.wiley.com/journal/118501086/home; http://0-search.ebscohost.com.uncclc.coast.uncwil.edu:80/login.aspx?direct=

true&db=eoh&AN=0991437&site=ehost-live; http://www3.interscience.wiley.com/journal/118501086/home.

Madsen, Jakob B. 2007. "Are there Diminishing Returns to R&D?" *Economics Letters* 95 (2): 161–166. doi: 10.1016/j.econlet.2006.09.009.

Madsen, Jakob, James Ang, and Rajabrata Banerjee. 2010. "Four Centuries of British Economic Growth: The Roles of Technology and Population." *Journal of Economic Growth* 15 (4): 263–290. doi: 10.1007/s10887-010-9057-7. http://0-search.ebscohost.com.uncclc.coast.uncwil.edu:80/login.aspx?direct=true&db=bth&AN=55592246&site=ehost-live.

Mankiw, N. Gregory. 2009. "Smart Taxes: An Open Invitation to Join the Pigou Club." *Eastern Economic Journal* 35 (1): 14–23. doi: 10.1057/eej.2008.43. http://0-search.ebscohost.com.uncclc.coast.uncwil.edu:80/login.aspx?direct=true&db=bth&AN=35908360&site=ehost-live.

———. 2010. "Spreading the Wealth Around: Reflections Inspired by Joe the Plumber." *Eastern Economic Journal* 36 (3): 285–298.

Mankiw, N. G., Matthew Weinzierl, and Danny Yagan. 2009. "Optimal Taxation in Theory and Practice." *Journal of Economic Perspectives* 23 (4): 147–174. doi: http://www.aeaweb.org/jep/. http://0-search.ebscohost.com.uncclc.coast.uncwil.edu:80/login.aspx?direct=true&db=eoh&AN=1070271&site=ehost-live; http://dx.doi.org/10.1257/jep.23.4.147; http://www.aeaweb.org/jep/.

Marshall Alfred, *Principles of Economics* (1920). (Book IV, Chapter IX, p.25). Macmillan and Co. Ltd, Library of Economics and Liberty. Retrieved May 18, 2013 from the World Wide Web: http://www.econlib.org/library/Marshall/marP.html.

Mirrlees, James A. 1971. "An Exploration in the Theory of Optimum Income Taxation." *Review of Economic Studies* 38 (114): 175–208. doi: http://www.blackwellpublishing.com/journal.asp?ref=0034-6527; http://0-search.ebscohost.com.uncclc.coast.uncwil.edu:80/login.aspx?direct=true&db=eoh&AN=0061221&site=ehost-live; http://www.blackwellpublishing.com/journal.asp?ref=0034-6527.

Mokyr, Joel. 2005. "The Intellectual Origins of Modern Economic Growth." *The Journal of Economic History* 65 (2): 285–351. http://www.jstor.org/stable/3875064.

Moser, Petra. 2013. "Patents and Innovation: Evidence from Economic History." *Journal of Economic Perspectives* 27 (1): 23–44.

Mulligan, Casey B. August 2013. *Average Marginal Labor Income Tax Rates under the Affordable Care Act*. Cambridge, MA: The National Bureau of Economic Research, Working Paper No. 19365.

Persson, Torsten and Guido Tabellini. 1994. "Is Inequality Harmful for Growth?" *The American Economic Review* 84 (3): 600–621. http://www.jstor.org/stable/2118070.

Qur'An. 2005. Oxford, GBR: Oxford University Press, UK.

Radford, R. A. 1945. "The Economic Organisation of a P.O.W. Camp." *Economica* 12 (48): 189–201. http://www.jstor.org/stable/2550133.

Rawls, John. 1973. *A Theory of Justice*. Cambridge, MA: Harvard University Press.

Reese, Laura A. 2004. "A Matter of Faith: Urban Congregations and Economic Development." *Economic Development Quarterly* 18 (1): 50–66. doi: http://edq.

sagepub.com/archive/; http://0-search.ebscohost.com.uncclc.coast.uncwil.edu: 80/login.aspx?direct=true&db=eoh&AN=0735708&site=ehost-live; http://edq. sagepub.com/archive/.

Reinhart, Carmen M. and Kenneth Rogogg. 2009. *This Time is Different: Eight Centuries of Financial Folly.* Princeton, NJ: Princeton University Press.

Richardson, Gary. 2005. "The Prudent Village: Risk Pooling Institutions in Medieval English Agriculture." *The Journal of Economic History* 65 (2): 386–413. http:// www.jstor.org/stable/3875066.

Rodrik, Dani. 2011. *The Globalization Paradox: Democracy and the Future of the World Economy.* New York, London: W. W. Norton & Company.

Romer, Paul M. 1987. "Growth Based on Increasing Returns due to Specialization." *The American Economic Review* 77 (2, Papers and Proceedings of the Ninety-Ninth Annual Meeting of the American Economic Association): 56–62. http://www.jstor. org/stable/1805429.

Saez, Emmanuel. 2001. "Using Elasticities to Derive Optimal Income Tax Rates." *Review of Economic Studies* 68 (1): 205–229. doi: http://www.blackwellpublishing. com/journal.asp?ref=0034-6527; http://0-search.ebscohost.com.uncclc.coast. uncwil.edu:80/login.aspx?direct=true&db=eoh&AN=0565839&site=ehost-live; http://www.blackwellpublishing.com/journal.asp?ref=0034-6527.

Sanborn, Henry. 1964. "Pay Differences between Men and Women." *Industrial and Labor Relations Review* 17 (4): 534–550. http://www.jstor.org/stable/2520614.

Scherer, F. M. 1984. *Innovation and Growth: Schumpeterian Perspective.* Cambridge, MA: The MIT Press.

Schularick, Moritz and Thomas M. Steger. 2010. "Financial Integration, Investment, and Economic Growth: Evidence from Two Eras of Financial Globalization." *Review of Economics and Statistics* 92 (4): 756–768. doi: http://www. mitpressjournals.org/loi/rest; http://0-search.ebscohost.com.uncclc.coast.uncwil. edu:80/login.aspx?direct=true&db=eoh&AN=1149468&site=ehost-live; http:// www.mitpressjournals.org/loi/rest.

Seabright, Paul. 2010. *The Company of Strangers: A Natural History of Economic Life.* Princeton, NJ: Princeton University Press.

Sen, Amartya. 1983. "Poor, Relatively Speaking." *Oxford Economic Papers* 35 (2): 153–169. http://www.jstor.org/stable/2662642.

———. 1999. *Development as Freedom.* Westminster, MD: Alfred A. Knopf Incorporated.

Shermer, Michael. 2008. *The Mind of the Market: Compassonate Apes, Competitive Humans, and Other Tales from Evolutionary Economics.* New York: Henery Holt and Company, LLC.

Sinn, Hans-Werner. 1996. "Social Insurance, Incentives and Risk Taking." *International Tax and Public Finance* 3 (3): 258–280.

Smith, Adam. 1776 (2010). *An Inquiry into the Nature and Causes of the Wealth of Nations,* edited by Edwin Cannan. Chicago, IL: University of Chicago Press.

Solow, Robert M. 1956. "A Contribution to the Theory of Economic Growth." *The Quarterly Journal of Economics* 70 (1): 65–94. http://www.jstor.org/stable/1884513.

Spilimbergo, Antonio. 2000. "Growth and Trade: The North can Lose." *Journal of Economic Growth* 5 (2): 131–146. doi: 10.1023/A:1009882419420; http://0-search.ebscohost.com.uncclc.coast.uncwil.edu:80/login.aspx?direct=true&db=bth&AN=49892305&site=ehost-live.

Stiglitz, Joseph E. 2012. *The Price of Inequality: How Today's Divided Society Endangers our Future*. New York: W. W. Norton and Company, Inc.

Stiglitz, Joseph E., Amartya Sen, and Jean-Paul Fitoussi. 2010. *Mismeasuring our Lives: Why GDP Doesn't Add Up*. New York: The New Press.

Stritt, Steven B. 2008. "Estimating the Value of the Social Services Provided by Faith-Based Organizations in the United States." *Nonprofit and Voluntary Sector Quarterly* 37 (4): 730–742. doi: http://nvs.sagepub.com/archive/; http://0-search.ebscohost.com.uncclc.coast.uncwil.edu:80/login.aspx?direct=true&db=eoh&AN=1012514&site=ehost-live; http://nvs.sagepub.com/archive/.

Sukiassyan, Grigor. 2007. "Inequality and Growth: What does the Transition Economy Data Say?" *Journal of Comparative Economics* 35 (1): 35–56. doi: 10.1016/j.jce.2006.11.002.

Thurow, Lester C. 1971. "The Income Distribution as a Pure Public Good." *Quarterly Journal of Economics* 85 (2): 327–336. doi: http://www.mitpressjournals.org/loi/qjec; http://www.nclive.org/cgi-bin/nclsm?url=%22http://search.ebscohost.com/login.aspx?direct=true&db=eoh&AN=0061155&site=ehost-live%22; http://www.mitpressjournals.org/loi/qjec.

Trofimov, Yaroslav. 2008. "Shrinking Dollar Meets its Match in Dolphin Teeth; Solomon Islands Prize Commodity Over Cash; Closing in for the Kill." *The Wall Street Journal*: A.1–A.1.

Truman, Edwin M. 2010. *The International Monetary System and Global Imbalances*. Washington: The Peterson Institute of International Economics.

Wang, Yuan, Yichen Wang, Jing Zhou, Xiaodong Zhu, and Genfa Lu. 2011. "Energy Consumption and Economic Growth in China: A Multivariate Causality Test." *Energy Policy* 39 (7): 4399–4406. doi: http://www.sciencedirect.com/science/journal/03014215; http://search.ebscohost.com/login.aspx?direct=true&db=eoh&AN=1248716&site=ehost-live; http://dx.doi.org/10.1016/j.enpol.2011.04.063; http://www.sciencedirect.com/science/journal/03014215.

Weichselbaumer, Doris. 2003. "Sexual Orientation Discrimination in Hiring." *Labour Economics* 10 (6): 629–642. doi: 10.1016/S0927-5371(03)00074-5.

Weitzman, Martin L. 2009. "On Modeling and Interpreting the Economics of Catastrophic Climate Change." *Review of Economics and Statistics* 91 (1): 1–19. doi: http://www.mitpressjournals.org/loi/rest; http://0-search.ebscohost.com.uncclc.coast.uncwil.edu:80/login.aspx?direct=true&db=eoh&AN=1021160&site=ehost-live; http://www.mitpressjournals.org/loi/rest.

Woodford, Michael. 2011. "Simple Analytics of the Government Expenditure Multiplier." *American Economic Journal: Macroeconomics* 3 (1): 1–35. doi: http://www.aeaweb.org/aej-macro/; http://0-search.ebscohost.com.uncclc.coast.uncwil.edu:80/login.aspx?direct=true&db=eoh&AN=1143234&site=ehost-live; http://www.aeaweb.org/aej-macro/.

Wright, Robert. 2009. *The Evolution of God*. New York: Little, Brown.

Zachariadis, Marios. 2003. "R&D, Innovation, and Technological Progress: A Test of the Schumpeterian Framework without Scale Effects." *The Canadian Journal of Economics/Revue Canadienne D'Economique* 36 (3): 566–586. http://www.jstor.org/stable/3131874.

———. 2004. "R&D-Induced Growth in the OECD?" *Review of Development Economics* 8 (3): 423–439. doi: 10.1111/j.1467-9361.2004.00243.x. http://search.ebscohost.com/login.aspx?direct=true&db=bth&AN=14032710&site=ehost-live.

Zook, George F. 1947. "The President's Commission on Higher Education." *Bulletin of the American Association of University Professors* 33 (1): 10–28. http://www.jstor.org/stable/40221180.

Index

240 • Index

Printed in the United States of America